T0186331

Multilevel Modeling of Secure Systems in QoP-ML

Multilevel Modeling of Secure Systems in QoP-ML

Bogdan Księżopolski

CRC Press
Taylor & Francis Group
Boca Raton   London   New York

CRC Press is an imprint of the
Taylor & Francis Group, an **informa** business
AN AUERBACH BOOK

Printed and bound in Great Britain by
TJ International Ltd, Padstow, Cornwall

To my wife Beata and my son Mateusz

Contents

List of Figures

List of Tables

Listings

Chapter 1

Introduction to multilevel modeling of secure systems

CONTENTS

Today, security aspects are becoming more and more important in the engineering and security fields. Profuse conditions are essential in building a secure system. It is indispensable to analyze security from the system design phase through the stages of implementation and testing till the final stage of security policy achievement, because each stage includes a broad organizational perspective. Growing complexity of existing systems challenges an analysis of today's security development process. Then strong abstraction mechanisms can be an effective way to deal with analyzing complex systems. Important connections in real world systems and processes can be highlighted, using a model which is an abstract representation. It can be also applied in more complex systems development. Formal framework of the model enables making predictions about the system being modeled. Predictions can be accepted or rejected, later disclosing the truths concerning the abstracted problem. Therefore security modeling language became the subject of research and experiments because security is a basic requirement of IT systems. It requires analysis, specification and implementation by means of proper abstractions. Thus the whole process is formalized using security modeling languages exploiting systematic approaches, definitions and tools.

The aim of a model-driven development system is to create models based on general purpose modeling languages. This approach is known as model driven security (MDS). It is a specialization of the model driven architecture where models are an essential part of the system definition. MDS designers determine the security objectives including security requirements. Useful infrastructure from the modeled abstractions is automatically generated by proper tools. However, there is some limitation in the secure system development based on the model driven security design cycle, namely that the specification of security requirements is not supported by well known general purpose modeling language. Moreover, security objectives are not properly captured by the available system design tools as regards various security aspects.

1.1 Model driven security

To address those problems several approaches have been introduced. Presented solutions being derived from model driven security approaches are the general purpose modeling languages transformed and extended by modeling primitives, generation rules, stereotypes, and tagged values into language dialects in order to integrate security into the development cycle. Among them one can enumerate PL/SQL, SecureUML and UMLsec. Contrary to SecureUML and UMLsec being extensions of the existing general purpose modeling languages, QoP-ML [42] as a dedicated, specialized solution sheds another light on the security modeling problem. Presenting a high level of abstraction, having the possibility of maintaining processes and communication steps consistently, QoP-ML provides a flexible approach for modeling complex systems and performance of multilevel security analysis. Additionally, in QoP-ML the security economics analysis which is named adaptable security in literature [43, 48] can be performed. Since both SecureUML and UMLsec speak for an example of model driven security, in light of the presented development methodologies,

QoP-ML excellently fits into a design known as Model-Driven Engineering. Model-Driven Engineering (simply known as MDE) is meant to focus on the creation and utilization of the abstract representations of the knowledge that governs a particular domain, rather than on computing, algorithmic, or implementation concepts. Model-Driven Engineering is a broader concept than Model-Driven Architecture (MDA), or Model-Driven Security (MDS). MDE adds multiple modeling dimensions and the notion of a software engineering process. The various dimensions and their intersections with a Domain-Specific Language (DSL) form a powerful framework, capable of describing engineering and maintenance processes by defining the order in which models should be produced and how they are transformed into each other. Being a consistent theoretical framework, MDE specifies a set of key characteristics which an engineering model must possess, namely *abstraction, understandability, accuracy*, and *predictiveness* as well as *inexpensiveness*. In addition to the enumerated features, major MDE concepts, like *system, model*, and *model-driven* approach form a minimal set of requirements for a development environment to be MDE. Analyzing the quality of protection modeling language one is able to easily indicate all of the concepts mentioned, which leads to the conclusion that QoP-ML can be considered as the MDE approach, serving as a domain-specific language capable of expressing security models in a formalized, consistent, and logical manner.

Models prepared with QoP-ML supply factual representation of the modeled systems, thereby providing the *accuracy*, while the possibility of creating a simplified, formal view of reality (QoP-ML models), fulfills the *abstraction* requirement. QoP-ML provides predefined abstractions to directly represent concepts from the security domain. Consequently, security experts themselves can understand, validate, and modify QoP-ML with no effort, which assures possession of the *understandability* characteristic. *Predictiveness* is achieved with the Automate Quality of Protection Analysis Tool (Chapter 8), which provides the ability to analyze a prepared model in a formalized way. While transformation of the security model prepared with SecureUML or UMLsec usually results in an executable application [61], in QoP-ML, the performance analysis of the modeled system is the final product. QoP-ML's evaluation can be seen in the context of the quality of protection, time, or energy consumption. The *inexpensiveness* feature is shown by the fact that it is no doubt *significantly cheaper* to model a network containing thousands of hosts than to physically construct a huge infrastructure. In MDE, as well as in the QoP-ML, the model is an artifact that plays a major role. QoP-ML, as the example of the MDA superset, treats the model as the primary source for documenting, analyzing, designing, constructing, deploying and maintaining a preexisting system.

1.2 Quality of protection models

As can be found in the literature, the security adaptable models are used as the Quality of Protection (QoP) ones. In this section, related work in this field is presented. The attempt to extend the security layers in a few Quality of Service (QoS) architectures are made by S. Lindskog and E. Jonsson. However, the methods are confined to the data confidentiality and based on different configurations of the cryptographic modules. The QoP mechanisms which determine security levels depending on security parameters are described by C.S. Ong et al. in [67]. The security parameters are: key length, block length, and the contents of encrypted blocks of data. An adaptable protocol focusing on the authentication was proposed by P. Schneck and K. Schwan [80]. Based on it, the version of the authentication protocol can be modified which, in turn, changes the parameters of the asymmetric and symmetric ciphers. The QoP models based on the vulnerability analysis represented by the attack trees were created by Y. Sun and A. Kumar [83] where special metrics of security describe the leaves of the trees. They are applied to describe individual characteristics of the attack. The mechanisms for adaptable security with the possible use in all security services were worked out by B. Ksiezopolski and Z. Kotulski in [43]. The quality of protection in this model consists in the risk level of the analyzed processes. The quality of protection analysis for the IP multimedia systems (IMS) is performed by A. Lua et al. [57] using Queening Networks and Stochastic Petri Nets. In turn, the adversary-driven state-based system security evaluation, which is the method for determining the system security strength, is made by E. LeMay et al. [52]. The performance analysis of security aspects in the UML models is described by D. C. Petriu et al. in the paper [69]. They make use of the UML model of a system designed by the UMLsec extension of the UML modeling language as an input [36]. The UML model annotated with the standard UML Profile was used for schedulability, and performance and time analysis.

Different languages providing the methods for modeling security in cryptographic protocols can be found in the literature. They are based on the BAN logic [19] Communicating Sequential Processes [33] or PI, SPI, API calculus [11, 10, 65]. The most commonly applied in the formal analysis is the BAN logic put forward by Burrows, Abadi and Needham. Its advantages are its clear concept, simplicity, and it is easy to understand and use. Moreover, it is effective in finding secure vulnerability which is difficult to detect in the protocol. The description of communication patterns of concurrent systems components interacting through message passing is obtained using CSP [33], which is a process algebra. By means of it, the security protocols (cryptographic protocols) defining a sequence of messages between two or more participants can be modeled. The goal (e.g., authentication between participants, secrecy of a message, etc.) can be achieved by applying cryptographic mechanisms such as encryption, decryption and hashing, even if the underlying medium is insecure. Processes, parallel composition of processes, synchronous communication between the processes through channels, creation of fresh channels, and replication of processes can be represented using the PI calculus [65] which is a model of computation. Cryptographic primitives are added to the PI calculus and an equivalence-based specification of security properties is introduced using the SPI [11], whereas cryptographic primitives modeling with functions and equation theories is introduced by means of the API [10]. The UMLsec [36] created by J. Jürjens extends UML for secure system development which enables expression of security-relevant information within diagrams in a system specification. Using it, it is possible to design the system with associated constraints referring to system security and providing criteria for a security evaluation of the system [38].

The languages discussed above refer to formal methods of modeling and analyzing cryptographic protocols. With respect to the Quality of Protection analysis, all of them (except UMLsec [36]) have two limitations. The first one includes the types of the functions to be modeled, as it is possible to model only cryptographic primitives and cryptographic algorithms. However, as mentioned above, the full QoP analysis must take into account all security factors affecting the overall system security. The second limitation refers to the fact that these languages do not provide the structure for evaluation of the performance of the security factors.

Quality of Protection Modeling Language (QoP-ML) is the one which can be used for making an abstraction of cryptographic protocols putting emphasis on the details concerning quality of protection. The aim of using it is representation of the series of steps described as a cryptographic protocol. As mentioned earlier, not only primary cryptographic operations or basic communication steps can be taken into consideration, but this must also be a multilevel analysis. This is the QoP-ML which introduces the multilevel protocol analysis where every single operation defined by the QoP-ML is described by the security metrics whose task is to evaluate the operation's impact on the overall system security. It is possible to set the protection level for all analyzed systems only when the security impact is defined for all the actions in the protocol. By performing the multilevel analysis of the security systems and extending the description of the environment state it enables balancing security against the efficiency of the system. Moreover, the required quality of protection (QoP) is determined and some security measures are adjusted to these requirements, which promotes efficient system performance. In this case the Automatic Quality of Protection Analysis Tool (AQoPA) can be applied to accomplish profound analyses to evaluate the impact of each single operation within the prepared security model as part of the overall system security. Other approaches were also examined which proved successful in evaluating the time, energy and quality of protection of the analysed IT environments.

In Table 1.1 the Quality of Protection approaches are presented with the existing methodologies. These approaches can be characterized by the following main attributes.

- **Quantitative Assessment [QA]** which refers to the quantitative assessment of the estimated quality of protection of the system.

- **Executability [E]** which specifies the possibility of the implementation of an automated tool able to perform the QoP evaluation.

- **Consistency [Con]** which is the ability to model the system while maintaining its states and communication steps consistency.

- **Performance evaluation [PE]** which enables the possibility of performance evaluation of the analyzed system.

- **Energy evaluation [EE]** which enables the possibility of energy efficiency evaluation of the analyzed system.

Table 1.1: The characterization of the QoP models.

	QA	E	Con	EE	H	Com	PE	F	G
Agarwal A.K. et al. [13]	✓	-	-	-	✓	✓	✓	-	-
Ksiezopolski B. et al. [43]	✓	✓	-	-	✓	✓	-	-	-
LeMay E. et al. [52]	-	✓	✓	-	-	-	-	-	-
Lindskog S. et al. [54]	✓	-	✓	-	-	-	✓	-	-
Luo A. et al. [57]	✓	-	-	-	✓	✓	✓	-	-
Ong C.S. et al. [67]	✓	-	-	-	-	-	-	-	-
Petriu D. C. et al. [69]	-	✓	—	-	-	✓	✓	-	-
Schneck P. et al. [80]	✓	-	✓	-	-	-	✓	-	-
Sun Y. et al. [83]	✓	-	-	-	-	-	-	-	-
QoP-ML approach	✓	✓	✓	✓	✓	✓	✓	✓	✓

- **Holistic [H]** which deals with evaluation of all security attributes.

- **Completeness [Com]** – provides possibility of the representation of all security mechanisms. This attribute is provided for all models.

- **Financial evaluation [F]** which enables the possibility of financial analysis.

- **Green Computing [G]** – which refers to environmental impact analysis (carbon dioxide emission).

It is worth noting that only QoP-ML can be used for finding the trade-off between the security (QA) and the performance (PE) with the energy efficiency evaluation (EE), financial analysis (F) and environmental impact (G) of the system modeled in a formal way including the communication steps consistency (Com). Using this method it is possible to evaluate all security attributes (H) and to abstract all security mechanisms protecting the system (C). Moreover, this approach is supported by the tool (E) which is needed for the complex system analysis.

1.3   Multi-level analysis scheme

To perform a detailed, profound analysis of security systems, focusing on every aspect of the examined environment, many different components need to be taken into consideration. To facilitate this complex process in an interrelated IT system, implement and utilize the analysis scheme below. A well-organized, consistent solution, the proposed QoP-ML approach allows for a precise, specific analysis of the systems studied, focusing on every significant detail, and making the analysis process multilevel. In the following sections all the proposed analysis stages are presented.

Step 1: Model Creation To organize and examine existing alternatives accurately, a modeling process should be appointed. The quality of the outcome relies upon the correctness and accuracy of the modeling solution. Being a representation of reality, models capture in a finite number of parameters the way a part of the world reacts. As reality abstractions, models do not behave exactly as reality, but should – within the boundaries set – provide a reliable estimation of the outputs. They help us refine our understanding of how to choose the most suitable security mechanisms, adjusting the choice according to what seems to be the best option in a given situation. Model creation, being the very first stage in the analysis process, aims at creating a model of the chosen IT environment with the use of the Quality of Protection modeling language. To begin the whole analysis process, it is reasonable to first map the reality using the framework provided and then perform the actual analysis, taking into account all the crucial details. QoP-ML as a dedicated, specialized solution, uses qualitative models that help highlight important connections in real world systems and processes, and recommend the solution to a given problem. This step is described in Chapter 2.

Step 2: Security Metrics Definition Because the Security Metrics Definition phase consists of security metrics gathering and configuration, it can be automated by the Crypto Metrics Tool [64] (Chapter 8). To be able to make a *good* decision, one needs to have relevant and accurate information, on which to base choices among alternatives. Right decisions impose a requirement for input parameters to be as solid and adequate as possible. Obtaining robust, repeatable security metrics, one should rely on the results gathered by the Crypto Metrics Tool, since the framework was designed to use statistics to ensure the most reliable measurements. A robust method proposed in [64], and discussed further in the Chapter 7, involves characterizing a system based upon its statistical parameters such as mean, mode, variance or coefficients. It is particularly significant in helping identify patterns and underlying relationships between data sets together with eliminating possible data irregularities. The approach examined and discussed in [64] guarantees that obtained results are accurate and free of random errors. The proposed tool yields the results in a form that is appropriate for the automatic tool AQoPA – the Automated Quality of Protection Analysis tool for cryptographic protocols modeled in QoP-ML. The Crypto Metrics Tool can be downloaded from the webpage of the QoP-ML project [7].

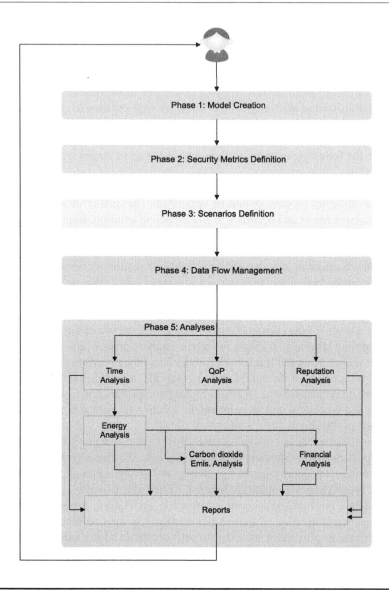

Figure 1.1: Multilevel analysis scheme.

Step 3: Scenarios Definition Scenarios represent different versions of the evaluated model. They are also known as versions, in which one can assess the quality of protection of the modeled environment, using miscellaneous security mechanisms and applying them to the same model.

Step 4: Data Flow Management In any e-business solution, it is integral to manage every piece of data. To provide high quality services and drive a successful business, a company must have complete, accurate, combined data available in a timely manner. It is relevant to think about data flow as it pertains to every functional requirement — what kind of data with what kind of system within what time frame — in order to maintain efficiency and control throughout every process. To meet the given requirements the Data Flow Management analysis process is proposed. The introductory phase uses data flow management to help reduce the security risks, preventing security vulnerabilities at the same time. The main goal of this stage is to indicate the most suitable mechanisms to optimize the data flow and make data available as quickly and consistently as possible. This step is discussed in Chapter 5.

Step 5: Multilevel Analysis Since QoP-ML provides the possibility of multilevel analysis, this process can be performed in six connected substeps. One can enumerate six types of analysis: Time analysis, energy analysis, QoP analysis, the finance estimation, carbon dioxide emissions evaluation and reputation systems evaluation.

The outline of the underlying concepts of each of the proposed analysis phases is presented below. As shown in Figure 1.1, the time analysis is the analysis on which the three remaining analyses are based.

The Time Analysis The aim of the time analysis is to estimate the time used by all the security operations performed during the execution of the cryptographic protocol. Based on the results, one can choose the security solution which best meets the time criteria. The time analysis helps to determine the mechanisms that are the most time efficient among the proposed security operations. The basis of this type of analysis is presented in Chapter 2.

The QoP Analysis Another crucial aspect of the multi-level analysis is the assessment of the security quality (commonly referred to as the quality of protection). Such analysis is based on the evaluation of the impact of security mechanisms on system performance. Estimation of quality of protection (QoP) is a challenging task: the approach used should be flexible enough to allow for evaluation of the quality of protection of different versions of the cryptographic protocols (security policies) in an economical manner. In Chapter 3 the model and framework which permits one to assess the quality of protection of previously predefined security mechanisms, as well as for security configurations not directly defined is introduced. A proposed solution, being an automated approach, lets one define all possible scenarios for all IT processes. This can be very complex and in many cases is not feasible with other existing frameworks.

The Energy Usage Analysis Besides the time analysis, the power consumption analysis process can be realized, in order to evaluate the energy consumption of the system modeled. To obtain the total amount of the energy consumed by the security operations, the time analysis module must be included in the performance analysis process, since it tracks the time of the operations and communication steps. The energy consumption is calculated as the sum of energy consumed by simple operations (security operations, arithmetic operations, and others too numerous to mention) that use the CPU, and communication operations (listening, receiving and sending). This module is presented in Chapter 4.

The Financial and Economic Analyses The reason for the introduction to the multilevel analysis scheme is the crucial role of the finances in IT. There is a high demand for a standardized method for measuring the total cash outlay of the physical infrastructure of data centers or other IT architectures. Designing IT budgets, identifying IT budgets items, developing appropriate pricing strategies, implementing and operating financial management enables companies to get more purchasing power out of their budgets and preserve cash for operational issues. One of the essential parts of the enterprise economic policy is the effective management of the utilized power, which is also covered in our pleasantly new analysis scheme. In large IT environments, consisting of tens — if not hundreds — of thousands of working machines, electricity is the factor which generates one of the biggest expenditures. This module is discussed in Chapter 5.

The Carbon Dioxide Emissions Analysis Nowadays, designing and deploying effective IT environments is a challenging task. Green computing is no longer just a boardroom discussion, but a reality for many companies. The recent growth of data centers requires more energy-efficient server design. However, these days saving some money on energy bills is one thing, but reducing the CO_2 is a much more admirable goal. Since data centers are a large fraction of the IT, there is a high demand for lowering emissions of CO_2 (and in turn, bills) by reducing power consumption. Green computing includes the implementation of best practices, such as energy efficiency central processing units (CPUs), peripherals and servers. In addition, green technology aims to reduce resource consumption and improve the disposal of electronic waste. Reducing emissions of CO_2 is significant, in particular when it comes to the large data centers. Besides servers, data centers also use storage and network components, which, as well produce huge amounts of carbon dioxide. Estimating the amount of the CO_2 emissions, it is important to note that its total quantity depends on miscellaneous factors, such as the size of the data center (number of all its working components), server load (which translates into the utilized kilowatt-hours) and the type of resource utilized to generate electricity. Hence, machines which consume a great deal of power, cause a negative environmental impact. As stated before, reduction of the energy usage from green computing techniques translates into lower emissions of carbon dioxide, stemming from a reduction in the resources used in power plants. The details are described in Chapter 5.

Reputation Systems Analysis The main aim of the reputation systems analysis is possibility of analyzing reputation systems from a technical and information security perspective. The reputation values of the agents are calculated according to defined algorithms which are abstracted as the process in the operating system which is realized by means of the host. This host is defined as the part of whole IT architecture by means of which distributed communities can be abstracted. In this infrastructure one can abstract different types of the adversaries which are performing attacks for reputation systems and one can analyze the defined reputation algorithms and the performance of IT architecture which realize the reputation systems. In the other side, one can model the defense mechanisms and analyse the impact for the reputation system and the IT architecture performance. The reputation module is introduced in Chapter 6.

1.4 Model-based multi-level decision support system

Nowadays the companies working in complex IT environments face the need for comprehensive and dynamic systems to cope with the security requirements [31], [40], [20]. Not all the questions can be solved by security planning, so it is necessary to discuss a model for security management. One method is the use of the decision support system which can support decision-making activities. Such a system is interactive, computerized, and software-based, and it helps gather information from raw data. documents, personal knowledge and business models, in order to identify problems, solve them, and make decisions.

Various types of decision support systems are reported in the literature [12]. Some of them are model-driven DSS [70], data-driven DSS, communication-driven DSS, document-driven DSS and knowledge-driven DSS [74]. The most complex of all existing types of decision support system is the model-driven decision support one. It is based on statistical, financial, optimization or simulation models using the input parameters and the data provided by users to facilitate the decision making process for stakeholders. As for data-driven DSS, the most significant part is the data itself. When a large amount of accurate, well organized data stored in databases or in data warehouses is available, the task of the system is to look for specific information and to report the obtained data to users. Network and communication technologies can be used for the communication-driven decision support systems as a result of rapid development of the interconnected network environments. Collaboration and communication can be facilitated by such tools as group-ware, video conferencing and computer based bulletin boards. Its main focus is managing, retrieving and manipulating unstructured information in the form of various electronic formats. To obtain a solution of a given problem, one can use a knowledge-based decision support system based on expert systems and artificial intelligence. Thus knowledge-based DSS helps a decision-maker when specialized knowledge is required by simulating reasoning, explaining the logic behind its conclusion. However, simplification of authorization management and review is a main objective of the security-driven data flow management.

Detailed and precise examination of input parameters and comprehensive analysis of all possibilities result in good decisions. To solve a problem, it should be formulated by means of standardized methodologies and all relevant information should be collected. As the decision making action is a reproducible process, a more comprehensive view should be taken into account. The decision cycle includes four phases: *problem definition* (a decision situation dealing with a difficulty or with an opportunity), *model construction* (for a description of the real-world problem using

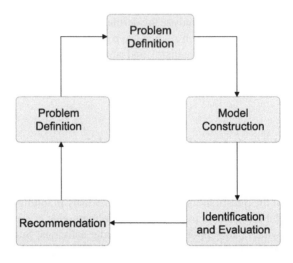

Figure 1.2: Basic flow in the decision making process.

specialized tools), *identification and evaluation* (the identification and evaluation of possible solutions) and *recommendation* and *implementation* (examination, comparison and choice of potential solutions) (Figure 1.2).

Different solutions of a given problem can be considered and evaluated. Such a decision support system enables defining distinct scenarios and examining the obtained results. The scenarios, also referred to as versions, are possible sets of input parameters and characteristics of the modeled environment which allow analysis of consequences of decision alternatives from past experience in a context being described. The decision-making cycle is useful in proper security management. Properly designed, specialized, dedicated support systems allow defining and modeling various scenarios differing in utilized security mechanisms and assessing their quality. The above advantages are evident as far as security based data flow management is concerned.

Based on the multi-level analysis scheme, the foundations of the new decision support system can be introduced. The decision support system (DSS) constitutes a framework for supporting decision making based on modeling problems and using quantitative models for solution analysis. This system is interactive, programmed and computer based, helping decision makers use assets and resources for identification and solution of problems, completing the decision process and making a decision.

Applying analyses as the base, it was possible to design a decision support system. As a multi-level, model-driven method, DSS enables description, examination and analyses of complex IT environments. What's more, using abstract models, DSS is used to determine difference between distinct operations. Figure 1.3 presents the general concept of this system.

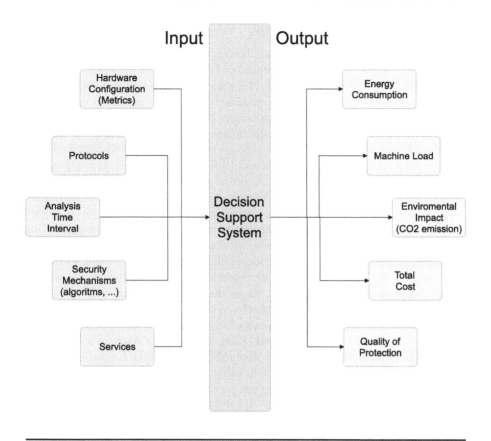

Figure 1.3: Hypothetical, multilevel decision support system.

Besides the above, this approach applies some general attributes like: *adaptability and flexibility, high level of interactivity, ease of use, efficiency and effectiveness, extensibility, ease of development* and *complete control by decision-makers*.

To be applied as a specialized solution for secure systems, the decision support system as an input takes characteristics of the environment traffic which are the number of established connections, available services, protocol with configuration details as well as other security mechanisms which can be applied in the environment under construction. These are encryption, decryption, hashing algorithms and others. Besides the above, hardware metrics must be provided to obtain proper configuration of the most effective parameters for a given machine. As complex IT environments are very dynamic, the approximate time of analysis should be determined (a month, a year, with, for instance, one hour intervals, when the traffic characteristic can change and the whole analysis process can be repeated). The system is directed toward efficient management of incoming connections based on physical resources, system load, Qop level, financial costs, CO_2 emissions and the amount of consumed power.

1.5   Structure of the book

To make ideas consistent and logical, the rest of the book is organized as follows. The second chapter presents the overview of QoP-ML where the syntax and semantics are presented. In this chapter the TLS protocols are presented as the case study. The methodology of the quality of protection evaluation of the security modules used is presented in Chapter 3. In the third chapter the QoP evaluation of the modeled in chapter 2 TLS protocol is presented. In the next chapter, the structures for advanced communication modeling and energy analysis is presented. Such advanced modeling is important for wireless sensors networks (WSN). In this chapter the analysis of the authentication protocols for WSN architecture is presented. The financial, economic and CO_2 emission analysis phase is presented in Chapter 5. For a demonstration of the proposed approach, the role-based access control was chosen as the example of security-based data flow management in a cloud computing architecture. In Chapter 6, the reputation analysis module is described, in which the defense mechanisms which protect transactions where modeled and an analysis of the impact of security mechanisms used for the average reputation system is evaluated. The methodology for generation of security metrics are discussed in Chapter 7; The generation of robust security metrics of cryptographic primitives is presented. The analysis of complex systems is impossible without tool support. In Chapter 8 the architecture of three tools is presented: the Automated Quality of Protection Analysis tool (AQoPA), the Security Mechanisms Evaluation Tool (SMETool) and the Crypto-Metrics Tool (CMTool). Chapter 9 presents the functionality and unsuitability assessment of QoP-ML. In this chapter the QoP-ML was compared with the PL/SQL, SecureUML and UMLsec approaches by means of the SEQUAL framework. In the last chapter, the Appendix materials are presented which include: the QoP-ML syntax in BNF, all the QoP-ML algorithms, the model for QoP evaluation of the TLS protocols and the validation algorithms for robust security metrics generation.

Chapter 2

Basis of QoP-ML

CONTENTS

The high level of abstraction of the structures applied in the Quality of Protection Modeling Language (QoP-ML) makes it possible to concentrate on the multilevel analysis. The components of the QoP-ML are processes, functions, message channels, variables and QoP metrics. Global objects grouped into the main process representing the single computer (host) are processes. Within a process functions, message channels and variables can be declared globally or locally. Behavior is specified by the process; a single operation or a group of operations is represented by functions, the environment in which the process is executed is defined by global variables and channels. The functions and channels are defined by the QoP metrics from their influence on the quality of protection.

At the beginning it is worth presenting the goals of Quality of Protection Modeling Language which are as follows.

■ Modeling the IT systems and as a part of it the cryptographic protocols maintaining consistency of processes and communications steps.

■ Abstraction of all security operations/mechanisms executed during the process of cryptographic protocols.

■ Modeling of the operations dealing with all security attributes/properties.

■ Introduction of the evaluation of quality of protection with respect to the security operations/mechanisms which are being modeled.

■ Making the scalable analysis possible in the situation when different versions of the same protocol can be defined.

■ Making the analysis of temporal properties of the cryptographic protocol steps possible.

In this section the basis of the Quality of Protection Modeling Language is presented. The full QoP modeling language syntax is presented in Appendix A. The first version of the QoP-ML can be found in [42].

2.1 Data types

An infinite set of variables is assumed to be used for description of communication channels, processes and functions. The information about the system or the specific process is stored by means of variables. Because the QoP-ML is an abstract modeling language, no special data types, sizes and value ranges exist. Thus there is no need to declare variables before their use.

The variables declared inside the high hierarchy process (host) are in the global scope which refers to all processes defined inside the host.

2.2 Functions

The functions modifying the states of the variables and passing the objects by communication channels change the system behavior. The function is declared in Listing 2.1.

```
1 fun new_pk(sk)[Confidentiality:bitlength,algorithm; Time:alg]
```

Listing 2.1: Function definition.

The function named new_pk(sk) is preceded by the phrase fun. When the name of the function is defined, its arguments must be set, which should describe two types of factors. The execution of the function requires the functional parameters to be written in round brackets. The system quality of protection is affected by the additional parameters written in square brackets. Moreover, there are unrestricted names of arguments.

As shown in Listing 2.1, generation of a public key is defined by the function new_pk. There are six set parameters: sk – the id of the secret key from which the public key will be generated (functional parameter); Confidentiality – the name of the security attribute which describes the qop parameters defined after colon (qop parameter); bitlength – the bit length of the public key (qop parameter); algorithm – the algorithm name (qop parameter); Time – the name of the next attribute which describes the qop parameters defined after the colon (qop parameter) and alg – the algorithm name (qop parameter).

2.3 Equational rules

In the quality of protection protocol analysis, equational rules are of significant importance. For a specific protocol they are composed of a set of equations ensuring the equality of cryptographic primitives and other security functions. Modeling of the asymmetric cryptography is presented in Listing 2.2.

```
1 eq dec(enc(message,pk(SKid)),SKid) = message;
```

Listing 2.2: Equational rules definition.

Here, the message represents the plaintext, SKid is a secret key of the site id and Pkid is a public key for the same site. The enc symbol defines the encryption operation and the dec symbol defines the decryption operation.

2.4 Process types

The main objects in the QoP-ML are processes which are created by grouping the objects describing the system behavior (functions, message passing). They are declared in Listing 2.3.

```
1 process Start(ch1, ch2)
2 {
3   key_alice = key_2048();
4
5   subprocess Next(ch2)
6     {
7         key_bob = key_1024();
8     }
9 }
```

Listing 2.3: Process types definition.

The process named Start can communicate with another one using two channels ch1 and ch2. It is necessary to define them now (communication channels will be discussed later). Curly brackets enclose the body of the declarations. The process Start covers two simultaneous operations, the declaration of a variable key_alice and assigning the value which will be returned by the function key_2048 to it. The semicolon separates the statements inside the declaration body.

Subprocesses (subprocess operator) can be defined inside the processes (process operator). The subprocesses can be defined only inside the processes already defined. Such a process can communicate with another one by means of channel ch2. Curly brackets enclose the body of the declarations. One operation, the declaration of a variable key_bob and assigning the value which will be returned by the function key_1024 to it, constitutes the subprocess Next. The semicolon separates the statements inside the declaration body.

However, a single computer executes and maintains the processes in the real system. The sets of processes are grouped in the higher hierarchy process named host in the QoP-ML. This process is defined in Listing 2.4.

```
1 host Start(fifo)(ch1,ch2)
2 {
3   process A(ch1)
4   {
5     key_alice = key_2048();
6   }
7   process B(ch2)
8   {
9     key_bob = key_1024();
10  }
11 }
```

Listing 2.4: Process types definition – Host.

The process A and the process B are grouped into the higher hierarchy of process defined by the operator host and the unique name A. There are two parameters characterizing the host operator, of which the first one is related to the CPU scheduler algorithm which will set the process queue. It could be fifo or round robin where the quantum of time is the single operation. Inside the process the operations are executed one by one including those defined in the subprocesses (subprocess operator). The other parameter is related to the channels available for the processes grouped into the host process. The star in the second round brackets indicates that all channels are available. The sign that no channels are available is when the second bracket is empty.

Here the discussion of the scope of the variables inside the processes is of significant importance. All variables in the high hierarchy process (host) have a global scope for all processes grouped by them. Generally, it is not possible to use the variables inside the host process for another high hierarchy process. Such an operation can take place only when the communication channels send the variable.

2.5 Message passing

Channels are used for modeling the communication between processes. All data independent of type can be passed through the channels, which must be declared before passing the data through them. The declaration of channels is presented in Listing 2.5.

```
1 channel ch1 (10);
```

Listing 2.5: Message passing definition.

The channel ch1 which can store 10 messages (buffer size) is thus declared. A star in round brackets indicates that message passing by this channel is limitless (the buffer is not set). When channels are characterized by the same parameters, they can be declared in one statement (Listing 2.6).

```
1 channel ch2,ch3 (*);
```

Listing 2.6: Multiple channel definition.

The channels are applied for sending or receiving the data. Sending the data is modeled in Listing 2.7.

```
1 out(ch1:M1);
```

Listing 2.7: Multiple message sending.

The value of the expressions M1 is sent through the channel ch1. The data are received by the process in which the statement is modeled in Listing 2.8.

```
1 in ( ch1 : X );
```

Listing 2.8: Message listing definition.

The values of the expression M1 can be assigned to the variable X. The message is passed through the channels in the FIFO order.

2.5.1 Synchronous communication

The communication is considered to be asynchronous for channels declared with a non-zero buffer size. The communication is considered to be synchronous in a case where the buffer size is equal to zero. In such a case the data will be transmitted through the synchronous channel by the sender only when the receiver is listening on the channel. In a case where the size of the buffer channel is at least 1, the message can be sent through the channel without the process of listening. When the listening process is executed, the message will be transmitted to the receiver.

2.6 Control operators

Two types of construction, condition statement and repetition control, control the objects describing the system behavior.

2.6.1 Condition statement

When the `if` statement evaluating the expression is `true`, then the statement is executed. This is exemplified in Listing 2.9.

```
1 if  (A==B)
2 {
3    out ( ch1 : M1 );
4 }
5 else
6 {
7    out ( ch1 : M3 );
8 }
```

Listing 2.9: If statement definition.

The messages M1 will be sent through the channel ch1 if the A==B conditional expression is true. If the condition expression is `false`, then the `else` statement is executed.

2.6.2   Repetition

The iterative loop is provided by the `while` structure (Listing 2.10).

```
1  while(A==B)
2  {
3    out(ch1:M1);
4  };
```

Listing 2.10: While loop definition.

Here, if the expression (A==B) is true, the messages M1 will be sent through the channel ch1. The while operator is followed by the conditional expression.

2.6.3   Other structures

Two types of structure controlling loop flows, `break` and `continue` can be used in the QoP-ML (Listing 2.11). The `break` operator runs away from the nearest outer loop, whereas the program execution is switched to the test condition by the continue in the `while` loop. It is meaningless to use the `break` and `continue` operators inside the loops.

```
1  while(A==B)
2  {
3      if (A==Z)
4      {
5        break;
6      }
7
8      if (A==T)
9      {
10        out(ch1:M1);
11        continue;
12      }
13      out(ch1:M1);
14  };
15  out(ch2:M5);
```

Listing 2.11: Another structure definition.

The `while` condition can be checked (while (A==B)). If the expression (A==Z) is true, the `while` loop can be stopped. Then the out(ch2:M5) expression will proceed. It is also possible that when the expression (A==T) is true, the out (ch1:M1) is executed. Then the `continue` statement follows, so the loop will stop.

The `stop` operator is another operator useful in the protocol modeling. It will stop further execution of the modeled protocol which points to protocol failure and return of an error. The `end` operator can also stop the protocol. Using it points to successful execution of the protocol and no return of errors (Listing 2.12).

```
1  while(A==B)
2  {
3    if (A==Z)
4    {
5      stop;
6    }
7    out(ch1:M1);
8  };
```

Listing 2.12: Stop and end operator definition.

The example shows that further execution will be canceled and the error will return if the expression (A==Z) is true.

More operators can be used in the QoP-ML. The `true/false` operator indicates that an expression is `true` or `false`. The operator # preceding an expression in the process indicates execution of this expression in the past (before running the given process). Using the # operator, it is possible to define the variables to be used by the processes but that are not to be taken into account during the quality of protection analysis.

In the QoP-ML one can use other operators which are the same as in the language C [76]. They are: &&, | |, <, >, <=, >=, +, -, *, /, ==, !=.

2.7 Security metrics

The proposed QoP-ML can model the system behavior formally described by the cryptographic protocol. Its main aim is abstraction of the quality of protection of a particular version of the analyzed cryptographic protocol. The functions represent the influence of the system protection. In the process of function declaration it is possible to define the quality of protection parameters and describe the details about this function; the flow of the protocol is not affected by these factors. However, they are essential for the quality of protection analysis during which the function qop parameters combine with another structure of QoP-ML called security metrics. In this structure it is possible to abstract the functions' time performance, their effect on the security attributes needed for the cryptographic protocol or other essential factors in the process of qop analysis.

The operator `metrics` starts the security metrics and the curly brackets close the body of the metrics. Five operators defining the metrics are as follows:

1. `conf` – defining the hardware and software host configuration;

2. `data` – defining the security metrics which can be measured and depend only on the host configuration[9];

3. `data+` – defining the security metrics which can be measured but depend on the randomness factors which can not be clearly defined by host configuration[9];

4. `data*` – defining the security metrics which can not be measured but can be modeled [9];

5. set – defining the set of security metrics for the processes grouped into the high hierarchy process named host.

The next part of this section will include the exemplary declaration of this structure (Listing 2.13) which will be described later.

```
 1  metrics
 2  {
 3    conf(host1)
 4    {
 5      CPU = Intel Core 2 1.83 GHz;
 6      CryptoLibrary = Crypto++5.6.0;
 7      OS = Windows Vista in 32-bit;
 8    }
 9
10    conf(host2)
11    {
12      CPU = AMD Opteron 8354 2.2 GHz;
13      CryptoLibrary = Crypto++5.6.0;
14      OS = Linux 64-bit;
15    }
16
17    data(host1)
18    {
19      primhead [function][bit_length][algorithm][time:exact(ms)];
20      primitive[aenc][2048][RSA][0.16];
21      #
22      primhead [function][bit_length][algorithm][mode][time:block(←↵
            ms,B)];
23      primitive[enc][256][AES][CBC][1:21.7:1];
24      primitive[dec][256][AES][CBC][1:21.7:1];
25      decryption
26    }
27
28    data(host2)
29    {
30      primhead [function][bit_length][algorithm][time:exact(ms)];
31      primitive[aenc][2048][RSA][0.08];
32      #
33      primhead [function][bit_length][algorithm][mode][time:block(←↵
            ms,B)];
34      primitive[enc][256][AES][CBC][1:18.5:1];
35      primitive[dec][256][AES][CBC][1:18.5:1];
36    }
37
38    data+(host1.1)
39    {
40      primhead [function][bit_length][algorithm][time:exact(ms)];
41      primitive[pk_gen][2048][RSA][10];
42    }
43  }
```

Listing 2.13: Security metrics definition.

Here two types of host configuration (conf()) are defined. The first one is denoted as host1 and the second one as host2. Both hosts were declared using the three parameters: the processor type (CPU), Crypto Library, and Operating System (OS). The analysis requirements are set for the number of parameters and the description detail.

Then the security metrics to be measured and dependent only on the host configuration were defined (data()). One argument automatically linking the data with the earlier defined name of the host configuring is required by the data operator. Here the security metrics were defined for host1 (data(host1)) and host2 (data(host2)). The two operators contained in the body of the data() structure are: primhead and primitive. They define security metrics for security algorithms or mechanisms. The parameters for security mechanisms description are defined by the primhead operator. The example for data(host1) shows the following parameters: the unique (for the data(host1) structure) number of the primitive ([nr]), the bit length of the algorithm ([bit length]), the algorithm name ([algorithm]), the type of operation ([operation]) and the execution time of this operation ([time]). Then the primitive operator determines details about the security mechanisms defined earlier. As follows from the example, the execution time for the 2048 key bit RSA encryption is defined by the primitive, indexed as 1 ([1]).

The official benchmarks [http://www.cryptopp.com/] provide the execution time for the cryptographic algorithm implemented in Crypto++ library. Many benchmarks for the cryptographic primitives, which can be used as security metrics, can be found in the literature [84]. Another primitive was defined using the same data (host1) structure; however, one more parameter had to be used for its description. Thus a new set of parameters is defined using the new primhead operator. The sign # separates these two types of parameters. The second primitive (primitive [2]) which defines the execution time of 256 key bit AES encryption/decryption in the CBC mode of operation is declared. For host 2 (data(host2)) similar security metrics were defined.

At this stage, security metrics which can be measured are defined but they depend on the random factors. The operator data+(host1.1) defined this structure. One argument linking the data with the host configuration named host1 belongs to this operator. The version of the data is indicated by (.1) after the colon. Actually, it must be set as the security metrics depending on the randomness factors can be different for the hosts characterized by the same parameters which are defined by the conf structure. The application of the primhead and primitive operators used inside the body of the data+() structure is the same as in the data() structure.

2.8   Process instantiation

The operator process describing its behavior is not automatically executed. The first executed process in the QoP-ML is called init.

The operator version can be used in the init process. This operator uses one argument, which refers to the specification of the protocol version and executes it. The structure named version defines the specification which initializes global variables and other processes. It is possible to define the version structure as in Listing 2.14.

```
1  version v1
2  {
3
4    set host A(host1.1);
5    set host B(host1.1);
6    set host C(host1.1);
7    set host D(host2);
8
9    run host A(*)
10     {
11       run A1(A1A,A1B)
12       run A2() -> run A3(*)
13     }
14
15   run host B(*)
16     {
17       run B1(*)
18     }
19
20   run host C(*)
21     {
22       run C1(*)
23       run C2()
24     }
25
26   run host D(*)
27     {
28   run B1(*)
29     }
30
31 }
```

Listing 2.14: Process instantiation definition – Long example.

Run is the main operator in the version structure executing the process. It takes the name of any type process executing it. However, normal processes proceed only inside the high hierarchy process host(run host A).

Round brackets are other parameters used in the run operator. Here the subprocess to be executed as the child of the parent process can be selected. If all child processes are to be run in the main process then a star (*) has to be written in the round bracket. Empty brackets indicate no child process to be run.

After termination, a running process disappears but not before termination of all child processes. Termination of the process takes place after reaching the end of the process body, or is done by the operators: stop or end (the operators will be discussed in a following part).

An arrow (->), which is another operator, indicates the instruction written after the operator can be executed on the condition that the process preceding the operator in terminated without an error.

Finally, it is necessary to link the defined security metrics with the high hierarchy system processes declared by the host operator. The high hierarchy processes together with their child processes are executed on one computer. They are linked using the set() operator. As shown here the four processes host A, host B, host C, and host B link the defined metrics. One more parameter is required by the set() operator and this is the host configuration declared by the conf structure in the security metrics. As follows from the example, there are host1.1 for the host A, host B and host C processes and host2 for the host D process. Other defined security metrics can be pointed out after the declaration of the name of the host configuration. In the example (set host A(host1.1)), the version of the security metrics being defined is indicated after the colon.

When security metrics are linked with the host high hierarchy processes, concrete primitives defined in metrics should be linked with specific security functions applied in the modeling of the system behavior. It is necessary to define the quality of protection parameters written in square brackets for the declaration function in the QoP-ML. These factors are related to the primitives defined in security metrics.

2.9   QoP-ML base algorithms

The concrete version of the protocol is executed by the init process. The QoP-ML processing algorithms are used for simulation of the protocol flow estimated in the QoP-ML. The pseudocode of these algorithms is given in the appendix. Some of them are: init, main, check protocol state, execute operation, next operation, communication, link, qop evaluation (time analysis), final qop evaluation (time analysis), loop next operation and communication next operation.

Algorithm **init** is used for reading all the definitions of hosts and setting the initial state of the protocol's execution algorithm. Algorithm **main**, the main one calls other algorithms to check the state of the protocol, process the current operation and move pointer to the next operation. The task of **check protocol state** is to check the state of the protocol (whether it is finished) and that of the process as well as the host of the operation selected for execution. It is possible for the current process or host to be finished and the pointer is then moved to the next operation in the unfinished process by the algorithm. An algorithm **execute operation** executes a currently selected operation depending on its type. Two other algorithm are called and the pointer is moved to the next operation (algorithm **next operation**) and the next step of protocol execution is run (algorithm **main**) when QoP is executed and evaluated. Algorithm **next operation** moves the pointer to the next operation to be executed in the next step of the protocol execution process, including the type of task scheduling algorithm (round robin, fifo). Algorithm **communication** is responsible for validating the channel in a currently selected operation and linking it with the related communication operation. Algorithm **link** carries out the process of linking communication operations. Algorithm **qop evaluation** carries out the process of qop evaluation of the currently selected operation. In this case, the security attribute being evaluated is availability. Algorithm **final qop evaluation** calculates the total execution time of the protocol. Algorithm **loop next operation** moves the pointer to the next operation to be executed when the currently selected operation is any type of loop operation. If the currently selected operation is a type of communication operation, the pointer is moved to the next one by algorithm **communication next operation**.

The concrete version of the protocol is executed by the init process. The QoP-ML processing algorithms are used for simulation of the protocol flow estimated in the QoP-ML. The pseudocode of these algorithms is given in the Appendix. Some of them are: init (algorithm A.1), main (algorithm A.2), check protocol state (algorithm A.3), execute operation (algorithm A.4), next operation (algorithm A.5), communication (algorithm A.6), link (algorithm A.7), qop evaluation (availability) (algorithm A.8), final qop evaluation (availability) (algorithm A.9), loop next operation (algorithm A.10) and communication next operation (algorithm A.11).

Algorithm A.1 is used for reading all the definitions of the hosts and setting the initial state of protocol's execution algorithm. Algorithm A.2, the main one, calls other algorithms to check the state of the protocol, process the current operation, and move the pointer to the next operation. The task of A.3 is to check the state of the protocol (whether it is finished) and that of the process as well as the host of the operation selected for execution. It is possible for the current process or host to be finished and then the pointer is moved to the next operation in the unfinished process by the algorithm. Algorithm A.4 executes the currently selected operation depending on its type. Two other algorithms are called and the pointer is moved to the next operation (algorithm A.5) and the next step of protocol execution is run (algorithm A.2) when the QoP is executed and evaluated. Algorithm A.5 moves the pointer to the next operation to be executed in the next step of the protocol execution process including the type of tasks scheduling algorithm (round robin, fifo). Algorithm A.6 is responsible for validating the channel in the currently selected operation and linking it with the related communication operation. Algorithm A.7 carries out the process of linking communication operations. Algorithm A.8 carries out the process of qop evaluation of the currently selected operation. In this case, the security attribute being evaluated is availability. Algorithm A.9 calculates the total execution time of the protocol. Algorithm A.10 moves the pointer to the next operation to be executed when the currently selected operation is any type of loop operation. If the currently selected operation is a type of communication operation, the pointer is moved to the next one by algorithm A.11.

2.10 Experimental validation of the QoP-ML

For validation of the QoP-ML approach the different protocols were experimentally tested. In the [42] the protocol runtime estimated in the QoP-ML compared to the runtime of an actual Needham–Schroeder protocol implementation was tested. Comparing the results of the protocol runtime estimated in the QoP-ML to runtime of an actual Needham–Schroeder protocol implementation, one can conclude that the protocol runtime estimated in the QoP-ML is in the range specified by the standard deviation. This result confirms the correctness of the modeling based on the QoP-ML approach.

The second protocol which was experimentally validated was the TLS protocol [45]. In this test the runtime estimated in the QoP-ML and runtime of an actual TLS protocol implementation were compared and one can conclude that the protocol runtime estimated in the QoP-ML is in the range specified by the standard deviation.

The next set of protocols which was modeled in QoP-ML and their actual implementation was experimentally validated as were multihop node authentication protocols for Wireless Sensor Networks [60]. As with the previous protocols, the runtime of the WSN protocols estimated in the QoP-ML and runtime of an actual implementation were compared and the protocol runtime estimated in the QoP-ML was in the range specified by the standard deviation.

2.11 Case study: TLS handshake protocol with secure data transmission

The object of this section is the case study of QoP modeling of a TLS cryptographic protocol [8]. Five steps are employed to accomplish the flow of the TLS Handshake protocol. Figure 2.1 presents the scheme.

Notation for Figure 2.1:
PK_X - the public key of the X;
ID_{SX} - the id of the session X;
SK_X - the secret key of the X;
V_{TLS} - the version of TLS protocol;
$V_{TLS}(SET)$ - the established version of TLS protocol;
Cip_X - the available cipher suite for the session X;
Com_X - the compression method for the session X;
CA - the certificate authority;
$PK_X(cert) = (PK_X, ID_X, T)_{SK_{CA}}$ - the certificate of the X;
T - the timestamp;
ID_X - the id of the site X;
N_X - the nonce of the X.

Figure 2.1 presents the standard version of the TLS protocol which is fully analyzed and described in [8, 68]. It is briefly described according to the notation in Figure 2.1, in the next section.

Step 1:
The message containing the following attributes: TLS Protocol version (V_{TLS}), session id (ID_{S1}), a list of available cipher suites (Cip_1), a compression method (Com_1) and random values(N_1) is sent to the Client Hello by a Client.

Step 2:
The response of the server is a ServerHello establishing the version of TLS Protocol ($V_{TLS}(SET)$), cipher suite ($Cip_1(SET)$) as well as compression method

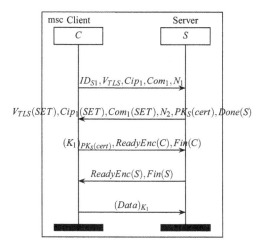

Figure 2.1: The protocol flow of the TLS handshake protocol.

$(Com_1(SET))$. Also random values (N_2) within ServerHello and the Certificate message including its certificate $(PK_S(cert))$ are sent. Finally, the ServerHelloDone message $(Done(S))$ is sent, signalling the accomplishment of this phase by the server.

Step 3:
Then the ClientKeyExchange message, which can have different contents depending on the selected cipher, is sent by the client. In the version being analyzed the symmetric session key (K_1) encrypted by the received certificate of the server S $(PK_S(cert))$ is sent by the client. In turn a ChangeCipherSpec message is sent $(ReadyEnc(C))$ to signal the server that the encryption has begun to be used by the client. In the end, the Finished message is sent by the client $(Fin(C))$.

Step 4:
As a response, the ChangeCipherSpec $(ReadyEnc(S))$ and the Finished message $(Fin(S))$ are sent by the server.

Step 5:
When the handshake is complete, encrypted Application Data $((Data)_{K_1})$ can by exchanged by the server and client.

In the example presented we chose six versions of the TLS protocol which are presented in Table 2.1. These cipher suites are described in detail in the TLS specification [8].

The fourth, fifth, and sixth versions are modified according to those versions presented in the TLS specification. In the fourth version we analyze the case when the new cryptographic module, according to the defined ones, will be possible. This

Table 2.1: The analyzed versions of TLS protocol.

version	the cipher suite
1	TLS_RSA_WITH_RC4_128_MD5
2	TLS_RSA_WITH_3DES_EDE_CBC_SHA
3	TLS_RSA_WITH_AES_256_CBC_SHA
4	TLS_RSA_WITH_RC4_128_newSHA512
5	TLS_RSA_WITH_AES_256_SHA + COM(bin)
6	TLS_RSA_WITH_AES_256_SHA + COM(txt)

module is the implementation of HMAC-SHA512 [66]. The fifth version is the same as the third one except that compression is enabled. For all five protocol versions the binary file is transmitted. The sixth version is the same as the fifth one except that the text file is transmitted, which matters in case of the fact that compression is enabled. These six versions are analyzed as 6 cases which represent 6 different realizations of TLS protocol.

2.11.1   Protocol modeling

Five steps: protocol modeling, security metrics definition, precess instantiation, QoP-ML processing and QoP evaluation are used in the QoP analysis process (Figure 2.2). They are described during modeling of the TLS protocol in the next section.

The first step includes modeling of all the operations needed in the TLS Handshake protocol. They are presented in the protocol flow scheme (Figure 2.1). Many aspects should be included in the complete QoP analysis of cryptographic protocols. They are: the use of any security mechanism (not only a cryptographic operation), key management operations, security policy management, legal compliance, implementation of the protocol and cryptographic algorithms, communication process, data storage and other factors which influence the system security. This example presents one level analysis with a cryptographic operation considered. Different security attributes can be addressed by the QoP analysis and each of them can be treated based on the dedicated algorithms. QoP-ML [42] is introduced, the algorithm referring to the available security attribute [35] (Time analysis) according to which the TLS Handshake protocol will be analyzed. These algorithms are presented in the Appendix A.2

The four operations: function defining, equation defining, channel defining and the protocol flow description are included in the protocol modeling step.

2.11.1.1   Functions

The functions referring to the cryptographic operations required in the protocol are defined for modeling of TLS. They are discussed below (Listing 2.15) and their description is presented in Table 2.2.

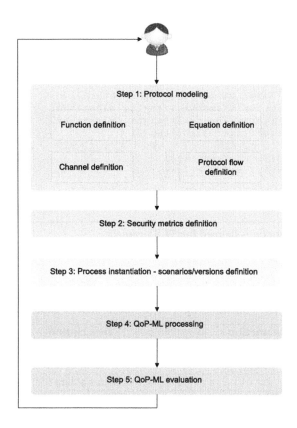

Figure 2.2: The scheme of QoP analysis.

```
 1  functions {
 2
 3      fun id();
 4      fun idh();
 5      fun data()[Time:size];
 6      fun Vlist();
 7      fun Clist();
 8      fun Comlist();
 9
10      fun set(X);
11      fun info(X);
12
13      fun ReadyEncClient();
14      fun FinClient();
15      fun ReadyEncServer();
16      fun FinServer();
17      fun Done();
18
```

```
19    fun cert(pk,id,t,ca)[Time: bitlength, algorithm];
20    fun sk(id)[Time: bitlength, algorithm];
21    fun pk(sk)[Time: bitlength, algorithm];
22    fun nonce() [Time: bitlength, algorithm];
23
24    fun skey()[Time: bitlength, algorithm];
25    fun enc(data,key)[Time: bitlength, algorithm];
26    fun dec(data,key)[Time: bitlength, algorithm];
27    fun hmac(data)[Time: algorithm];
28
29 fun com(data)[Time: algorithm];
30 fun decom(data)[Time: algorithm];
31
32 }
```

Listing 2.15: Functions defined for TLS protocol.

Table 2.2: QoP-ML's functions for TLS protocol model – Description.

Function	Description
id()	creates id of a session
idh()	creates id of a host
date()	creates a data file
Vlist()	TLS versions list
Clist()	creating ciphers list
Comlist()	creating compression method list
set(X)	setup the X parameter
info(X)	creating information message about X
ReadyEncClient()	client ready for encrypted transmission
FinClient()	client create FIN flag
ReadyEncServer()	server ready for encrypted transmission
FinServer()	server create FIN flag
Done()	creating Done flag
cert(pk,id,t,ca)	generate certificate
sk(id)	generate secret key for id
pk(sk)	generate public key for secret key
nonce()	generate new nounce
skey()	generate symmetric key
enc(data,key	encrypt the data
dec(data,key)	decrypt the data
hmac(data)	hmac generation
com(data)	data compression function
decom(data)	data decompression function

Table 2.3: QoP-ML's equation for TLS protocol model – Description.

Equation	Description
`adec(aenc(data,pk(SKid)),SKid) = data`	asymmetric encryption/decryption
`dec(enc(data,K),K) = data`	symmetric encryption/decryption
`decom(com(data)) = data`	data compression/decompression

2.11.1.2   Equations

After defining the functions one can describe the relationship between them (Listing 2.16). The description of this equation is presented in Table 2.3.

```
1 eq adec(aenc(data,pk(SKid)),SKid) = data;
2 eq dec(enc(data,K),K) = data;
3 eq decom(com(data)) = data;
```

Listing 2.16: Equations defined for TLS protocol.

2.11.1.3   Channels

Two synchronous channels are defined in the example presented (Listing 2.17).

```
1 channels {
2   channel ch1, ch2 (0);
3 }
```

Listing 2.17: Channels defined for TLS protocol.

2.11.1.4   Protocol flow

Abstracting the protocol flow is the last and the most important operation in modeling. Six versions of the TLS protocol are analyzed in the case study presented here. In order to do this, it is necessary to abstract them in one protocol flow. The parameters characteristic of a specific version of a TLS Handshake protocol can be specified while defining the protocol instantiation. This section will describe in detail the hierarchy processes.

host Client (Listing 2.18)

The `rr` algorithm defining the quantum of time in QoP-ML as the single operation schedules the processes inside the process - `host Client`. This process accepts all communication channels (`*`).

```
 1 host Client(rr)(*) {
 2
 3    process handC(ch1, ch2) {
 4     ID1 = id();
 5     V1 = Vlist();
 6     C1 = Clist();
 7     Com1 = Comlist();
 8     N1 = nonce()[256, Linux_PRNG];
 9     M1 = (ID1, V1, C1, Com1, N1);
10     out(ch1:M1);
11
12     in(ch2:Y);
13     PKS = Y[4];
14     K1=skey()[256, Linux_PRNG];
15     K1E=aenc(K1,PKS)[2048,RSA];
16     ReadyEC=info(ReadyEncClient());
17     FinC=info(FinClient());
18     M3=(K1E,ReadyEC,FinC);
19     out(ch1:M3);
20
21     in(ch2:Q);
22
23             subprocess c1(*) {
24               D1=data()[file1];
25               D1E=enc(D1,K1)[128,RC4,stream];
26               D1MAC=hmac(D1E)[MD5];
27               M5=(D1E,D1MAC);
28               out(ch1:M5);
29                                           }
30
31             subprocess c2(*) {
32               D1=data()[file1];
33               D1E=enc(D1,K1)[56, 3DES, CBC];
34               D1MAC=hmac(D1E)[SHA1];
35               M5=(D1E,D1MAC);
36               out(ch1:M5);
37                                           }
38
39             subprocess c3(*) {
40               D1=data()[file1];
41               D1E=enc(D1,K1)[256, AES, CBC];
42               D1MAC=hmac(D1E)[SHA1];
43               M5=(D1E,D1MAC);
44               out(ch1:M5);
45                                           }
46
47             subprocess c4(*) {
48               D1=data()[file1];
49               D1E=enc(D1,K1)[256, AES, CBC];
50               D1MAC=hmac(D1E)[SHA512];
51               M5=(D1E,D1MAC);
52               out(ch1:M5);
53                                           }
54
55             subprocess c5(*) {
56               D1=data()[file1];
```

```
57        D1Com=com(D1)[bin,DEFLATE];
58        D1ComE=enc(D1Com,K1)[256, AES, CBC];
59        D1MAC=hmac(D1ComE)[SHA1];
60        M5=(D1ComE,D1MAC);
61        out(ch1:M5);
62                                    }
63
64          subprocess c6(*) {
65        D1=data()[file2];
66        D1Com=com(D1)[txt,DEFLATE];
67        D1ComE=enc(D1Com,K1)[256, AES, CBC];
68        D1MAC=hmac(D1ComE)[SHA1];
69        M5=(D1ComE,D1MAC);
70        out(ch1:M5);
71                                    }
72
73                }
74          }
```

Listing 2.18: Model for the client in TLS protocol.

handC

Process handC can communicate with other processes by the channels ch1 and ch2. In the first operation the id of the session is created and is assigned to the variable ID1. In the second operation the client creates the list of supported versions of TLS protocol and this information is assigned to the variable V1. In the third operation the list of supported ciphers is created and assigned to the variable C1. In the fourth operation the list of supported compression methods is created and assigned to the variable Com1. The next operation creates nonce and this nonce is assigned with the variable N1. Additionally, the qop parameters are defined (according to the defined function description), there is the bits length - 256 and the algorithm used in the Linux Ubuntu System named - Linux_PRNG. In the next operation the message M1 is created and it will contain the following data: ID1, V1, C1, Com1, N1. In the next step the message M1 is sent by the channel ch1 and after that, listening on the channel ch2 starts.

The message which will be received by the channel ch2 is assigned to the variable Y[4], which is a tuple of data. The fifth element from the tuple assigned to the variable Y is assigned to the Server certificate PKS. Next, the session key (symmetric key) is created (function - skey) and assigns it to the variable K1. After this the session key K1 is encrypted by the Server certificate PKScert and assigned to the variable K1E. In the next step, two information messages are created, the first that Client is ready for encrypted communication (ReadyEC) and the second that this phase of TLS protocol is finished (FinC). Finally, the message M3 is created and is sent by the channel ch1.

After this, listening on the channel ch2 starts and one of the subprocesses (c1, c2, c3, c4, c5 or c6) can be run. These subprocesses can not be run simultaneously and which one will be executed is defined during the process instantiation. The first four subprocesses contain the same operations but they differ in the type of ciphers used for cryptographic operations and they refer to these presented in the Table

2.1. The subprocesses c5 and c6 differ from the previous ones in only one operation - the compression (function - com). As the output of these subprocesses, the message M5 is created and sent through the channel ch1.

subprocess c1
Subprocess c1 can communicate with other processes by any channel (*). In the first operation the the data file is created and is assigned to the variable D1. After this the data D1 are encrypted (function - enc) by the symmetric algorithm RC4 with the 128-bit key K1 and the result of this operation is assigned with the variable D1E. In the third operation the message authentication code is created (function - hmac) from the encrypted data and the result of this operation is assigned with the variable D1MAC. To this function qop parameters are defined which describe the type of MAC algorithm; in this subprocess it wil be MD5. Next the message M5 is created and is sent by the channel ch1.

subprocess c2
As we described above, this subprocess is the same as subprocess c1, with one difference, that the type of cryptographic algorithms are changed. In this case the 3DES cipher is used with 56-key for one DES and CBC mode, as the hmac function the SHA1 hash function is defined.

subprocess c3
In this case the AES cipher is used with 256-key and CBC mode, as the hmac function the SHA1 hash function is defined.

subprocess c4
In this case the AES cipher is used with 256-key CBC mode, as the hmac function the SHA512 hash function is defined.

subprocess c5
In this subprocess there is one difference from the first four versions. In this subprocess the data D1 is compressed com before encryption enc. For the compression the DEFLATE algorithm is used. In this version the data are binary and this fact is indicated in the qop parameters for the compression function ([bin,DEFLATE]). In this case the AES cipher is used with 256-key for one DES and CBC mode. As the hmac function the SHA1 hash function is defined.

subprocess c6
In this subprocess there is one difference from the subprocess c5. In this subprocess the data D1 are not binary but textual. This fact is indicated in the qop parameters for the compression function ([txt,DEFLATE]). In this case the AES cipher is used with 256-key for one DES and CBC mode. As the hmac function the SHA1 hash function is defined.

subprocess Cv2
Subprocess Cv2 can communicate with other processes by any channels (*). As we described above, this subprocess is the same as the subprocess Cv1 but with one difference. There is no compression (function - com) of sending data D1.

host Server (Listing 2.19)

The processes are scheduled by the `rr` algorithm where the quantum of time is defined in QoP-ML as the single operation. All communication channels are accepted by this process (*). First the operations which are executed before the main process host Server starts are defined (# operator). There are: ServerID - the id of the session, CA - the if of CA; T1 - the time stamp of certificate; SKS - the secret key for S; PKS - the public key for the secret key SKS; PKScert - the certificate of the public key PKS for the owner ServerID; T1 - the date of certificate PKScert generation; trusted by the Certificate Authority CA.

```
 1  host Server(rr)(*) {
 2
 3    #ServerID = id();
 4    #CA = idh();
 5    # T1=date();
 6    #SKS=sk(ServerID)[2048, RSA];
 7    #PKS=pk(SKS)[2048, RSA];
 8    #PKScert=cert(PKS,ServerID,T1,CA)[2048, RSA];
 9
10    process handS(ch1, ch2) {
11
12            in(ch1:X);
13            V1ok=set(X[1]);
14            C1ok=set(X[2]);
15            Com1ok=set(X[3]);
16            N2=nonce()[256, Linux_PRNG];
17            DoneS=info(Done());
18            M2=(V1ok,C1ok,Com1ok,N2,PKS,DoneS);
19            out(ch2:M2);
20
21
22            in(ch1:Y);
23            ReadyES=info(ReadyEncServer());
24            FinS=info(FinServer());
25            M4=(ReadyES, FinS);
26            out(ch2:M4);
27
28            in(ch1:Z);
29            K1E=Y[0];
30            D1E=Z[0];
31            D1MAC=Z[1];
32
33            subprocess s1(*) {
34            K1=adec(K1E,SKS)[2048,RSA];
35            D1EVerif=hmac(D1E)[MD5];
36            if (D1EVerif == D1MAC) {
37                D1=dec(D1E,K1)[128, RC4, stream];
38            } else {
39                stop;
40                    }
41                            }
42
```

```
43      subprocess s2(*) {
44      K1=adec(K1E,SKS)[2048,RSA];
45      D1EVerif=hmac(D1E)[SHA1];
46      if (D1EVerif == D1MAC) {
47          D1=dec(D1E,K1)[56, 3DES, CBC];
48        } else {
49          stop;
50            }
51                    }
52
53    subprocess s3(*) {
54        K1=adec(K1E,SKS)[2048,RSA];
55        D1EVerif=hmac(D1E)[SHA1];
56        if (D1EVerif == D1MAC) {
57            D1=dec(D1E,K1)[256, AES, CBC];
58    } else {
59    stop;
60            }
61                }
62
63      subprocess s4(*) {
64      K1=adec(K1E,SKS)[2048,RSA];
65      D1EVerif=hmac(D1E)[SHA512];
66      if (D1EVerif == D1MAC) {
67          D1=dec(D1E,K1)[256, AES, CBC];
68      } else {
69        stop;
70            }
71                }
72
73      subprocess s5(*) {
74      K1=adec(K1E,SKS)[2048,RSA];
75      D1EVerif=hmac(D1ComE)[SHA1];
76      if (D1EVerif == D1MAC) {
77          D1Com=dec(D1ComE,K1)[256, AES, CBC]
78          D1=decom(D1Com)[bin,DEFLATE];
79        } else {
80          stop;
81            }
82                    }
83
84    subprocess s6(*) {
85      K1=adec(K1E,SKS)[2048,RSA];
86      D1EVerif=hmac(D1ComE)[SHA1];
87      if (D1EVerif == D1MAC) {
88          D1Com=dec(D1ComE,K1)[256, AES, CBC];
89          D1=decom(D1Com)[txt,DEFLATE];
90        } else {
91          stop;
92                }
93            }
94
95                }
```

Listing 2.19: Model for the server in TLS protocol.

process handS

The process handS can communicate with other processes by the channels ch1 and ch2. In the first operation the process starts listening on the channel ch1 and the received message will be assigned to the variable X. The content of the received message X is a tuple of data and at this moment the Server will set up the following parameters for the TLS session: the version of the TLS protocol V1ok, available ciphers C1ok, available compression methods Com1ok. The next operation creates nonce and this nonce is assigned with the variable N2. As in the process handC, qop parameters are defined. After this, the information about finishing this phase of the TLS handshake is created (DoneS). Finally, the message M2 is created and sent by the channel ch2.

In the next step, listening on the channel ch1 starts. When the the data is received on the channel ch1 the message will be assigned to the variable Y. After this, the server creates the information that it is ready for the encrypted communication (ReadyES) and that this phase of the TLS protocol is finished (FinS). In the next step, the message M4 is created and sent by the channel ch2. In the next step, the server starts listening on the channel ch1. When the the data is received on the channel ch1 the message will be assigned to the variable Z. To the first data in the tuple Y is assigned variable K1E which is encrypted by the client session key. To the first data in the tuple Z is assigned variable D1E which is encrypted data sent by the client. The second data in the tuple Z is the MAC value of the data D1 and this value is assigne to the variable D1MAC. After this, one of the subprocesses (s1, s2, s3, s4, s5 or s6) can be run. These subprocesses can not be run simultaneously and which one will be executed is defined during the process instantiation. The first four subprocesses contain the same operations but they differ in the type of ciphers used for cryptographic operations and they refer to these presented in the Table 2.1. The subprocesses s5 and s6 differ from the previous ones in only one operation - the decompression (function - decom).

subprocess s1

Subprocess s1 can communicate with other processes using any channel (*). In the first operation the encrypted session key K1E is decrypted by the secret key of the Server SKS (function - dec). As in any function which is taken into account during the qop evaluation, the qop parameters are defined; in this case there is the name of the asymmetric algorithm, and the bit length of the key. In the next step, the message authentication code is created D1EVerif from the input data D1E. After this the created MAC D1EVerif and the received MAC D1MAC are compared. After the positive verification the received encrypted data D1E are decrypted by the symmetric algorithm RC4 with the key K1 and the protocol is finished with success end. In the case of negative verification of the MAC value of the D1E, the protocol will be stopped with error stop.

subprocess s2

This subprocess is the same as subprocess s1 with one difference – that the type of cryptographic algorithms is changed. In this case the 3DES cipher is used with the

56-key for one DES and CBC mode. As the `hmac` function the `SHA1` hash function is defined.

subprocess s3
In this case the `AES` cipher is used with the 256-key and CBC mode. As the `hmac` function the `SHA1` hash function is defined.

subprocess s4
In this case the `AES` cipher is used with the 256-key CBC mode. As the `hmac` function the `SHA512` hash function is defined.

subprocess s5
In this subprocess there is one difference according to the first four versions. In this subprocess the data `D1Com` is decompressed `decom` after encryption `enc`. For the compression the `DEFLATE` algorithm is used. In this version, the data are binary (`[bin,DEFLATE]`). In this case the `AES` cipher is used with the 256-key for one DES and CBC mode. As the `hmac` function the `SHA1` hash function is defined.

subprocess s6
In this subprocess there is one difference according to the subprocess s5. In this subprocess the data `D1Com` are not binary but textual. This fact is indicated in the qop parameters for the compression function (`[txt,DEFLATE]`). In this case the `AES` cipher is used with the 256-key for one DES and CBC mode. As the `hmac` function the `SHA1` hash function is defined.

2.11.2 Security metrics definition

In modeling the protocol, the security metrics must be defined by the designer for all functions connected with each security attribute to be tested. Here the time analysis (availability) of six different configurations of the TLS Handshake protocol is tested. Thus metrics are needed for all functions affecting the execution time (availability). The execution times of the operations used in the TLS protocol that may be configured (i.e., compression, encryption) have been checked.

A lot of security metrics might be obtained from the benchmark present in both official hardware specifications and literature [84]. However, some of them may depend on the hardware on which protocol is executed [9]. Thus those metrics should be computed on hosts on which the protocol will be executed. Commonly applied software for metrics computation has been used do that. In the case study presented, the new methodology of generating security metrics for cryptographic primitives was used. The methodology is described in Chapter 7. Based on this methodology, the Crypto Metrics Tool (CMTool) was implemented (Chapter 8) and this tool was used for generating security metrics required for cryptographic primitives.

For compression and decompression the *gzip/gunzip* is used. It contains the *zlib* library processing implementation of the compression algorithm based on *deflate*. It is known as the standard reference implementation used in a huge amount of software. The software discussed in [42] was prepared for the function generating the nonce and asymmetric keys. The security metrics defined for the TLS Handshake protocol are presented in Listing 2.20.

```
1  metrics {
2
3  conf (host1) {
4      CPU =  Intel(R) Xeon(R) CPU X5675 @ 3.07GHz processor;
5      OS = Linux Ubuntu 12.04.4 LTS 3.2.0-58-generic 64 bit OS ;
6      Lib =  OpenSSL 1.0.1 14 Mar 2012;
7  }
8  data(host1) {
9      primhead [function] [bit_length] [algorithm] [time: exact (ms)];
10     primitive [aenc] [2048] [RSA] [0.049];
11     primitive [adec] [2048] [RSA] [1.611];
12     #
13     primhead [function] [bit_length] [algorithm] [mode] [time: exact (←
           mspB)] [Size: ratio];
14     primitive [enc] [256] [AES] [CBC] [0.0000059:1] [1:1];
15     primitive [dec] [256] [AES] [CBC] [0.0000059:1] [1:1];
16     primitive [enc] [128] [RC4] [stream] [0.0000011:1] [1:1];
17     primitive [dec] [128] [RC4] [stream] [0.0000011:1] [1:1];
18     primitive [enc] [56] [3DES] [CBC] [0.0000367:1] [1:1];
19     primitive [dec] [56] [3DES] [CBC] [0.0000367:1] [1:1];
20     #
21     primhead [function] [algorithm] [time: exact (mspB)] [Size: exact (b←
           )];
22     primitive [hmac] [SHA1] [0.000002735:1] [160];
23     primitive [hmac] [SHA512] [0.000005078:1] [512];
24     primitive [hmac] [MD5] [0.000002422:1] [128];
25     #
26     primhead [function] [file] [size: exact (B)];
27     primitive [data] [file1] [1224065679];
28     primitive [data] [file2] [1224065679];
29  }
30  data+(host1.1) {
31     primhead [function] [bit_length] [algorithm] [time: exact (ms)];
32     primitive [nonce] [256] [LinuxPRNG] [0.0025];
33     #
34     primhead [function] [data_type] [algorithm] [time: exact (ms)] [←
           Size: ratio];
35     primitive [com] [bin] [DEFLATE] [31150] [1:0.9];
36     primitive [decom] [bin] [DEFLATE] [6506] [1:1.1];
37     primitive [com] [txt] [DEFLATE] [31150] [1:0.3];
38     primitive [decom] [txt] [DEFLATE] [6506] [1:3.33];
39  }
40  }
```

Listing 2.20: Security metrics for the TLS protocol.

For the case study presented the security metrics were generated for the following environment: Linux Ubuntu 12.04.4 LTS 3.2.0-58-generic 64 bit OS; Intel(R)

Xeon(R) CPU X5675 @ 3.07GHz processor and OpenSSL 1.0.1 14 Mar 2012. This configuration is defined as host1.

Two types of data are defined for our case; the first one which defines the security metrics which can be measured and depend only on the host configuration data, and the second one which defines the security metrics which can be measured but depend on random factors which cannot be clearly defined by the host configuration.

data

In the case of asymmetric cryptography the **RSA** algorithm is used. In the case study analyzed the **RSA** encryption and decryption is performed for only one block of data, thus the execution time is defined as the exact time of this operation in ms (time:exact(ms)).

The execution time for symmetric cryptography depends on the amount of input data and is represented as the millisecond per byte (time:exact(mspB)). After defining the execution time of cryptographic primitives the additional parameters must be defined [Size:ratio]. The first one defines the id of the argument for the specific function (functional parameter) for which this function will be executed and the second one defines the size of the output data after the execution of this function (1 - the same size after the operation). For the symmetric cryptography the value of this additional parameter will be always equal [1:1].

The execution time for hmac functions is represented as the millisecond per byte (time:exact(mspB)). In this case the size of the output data is represented as the constant value in bits [Size:exact(b)].

After this, the function which generates the data is defined. Two types of data are defined; the first one is a binary file (file1 – it could be iso file of Linux MEPHIS – 1.14GB) and the second one is the textural data of the same size (file2).

data+

As the data which depends on the randomness factor the pseudo-number bit generator is defined as nonce. In this situation the concrete execution time for 256-length data are defined [time:exact(ms)].

The last security metrics refers to the compression/decompression operation. In this case it is difficult to represent the execution time as the function of the input data, thus the execution time is defined for the concrete size of data ([time:exact(ms)]) which can be generated by data function (1.14GB). The DEFLATE algorithm is defined for two types of input data: binary [bin] and textual [txt]. The execution time of this function is the same but the size of output data after compression/decompression is different. For binary data the compression ratio is equal to **0.9** but for textual it is equal to **0.3**.

2.11.3 *Process instantiation*

The versions of the modeled protocol can be defined during the process instantiation (Listing 2.21). Here six versions of the TLS protocol are set2.1. For all analyzed versions, the Client and Server in the TLS protocol have the same parameters which refer to CPU, openssl library and operating system (host1.1). For all versions, two high hierarchy processes: host Client and host Server are executed. For the first version (case1_RSA_RC4128_MD5), the process handC is executed (function - run) with the subprocess c1 inside the process host Client, whereas the handS is executed with the subprocess s1 inside the process host Server. For all six analyzed versions of TLS protocol the same scheme of process execution is preserved. The difference is that different subprocesses are executed inside the handC and the handS process. For example, for the version 2 case2_RSA_3DES56_SHA1 the c2 and s2 subrocess are executed, etc.

```
1
2  versions {
3
4  version case1_RSA_RC4128_MD5 {
5
6      set host Client(host1.1);
7      set host Server(host1.1);
8
9        run host Client(*) {
10       run handC(c1)
11     }
12
13       run host Server(*){
14       run handS(s1)
15     }
16    }
17
18 version case2_RSA_3DES56_SHA1 {
19
20     set host Client(host1.1);
21     set host Server(host1.1);
22
23       run host Client(*) {
24       run handC(c2)
25     }
26
27       run host Server(*){
28       run handS(s2)
29     }
30    }
31
32 version case3_RSA_AES256_SHA1 {
33     set host Client(host1.1);
34     set host Server(host1.1);
35
36       run host Client(*) {
37       run handC(c3)
38     }
39
40       run host Server(*){
41       run handS(s3)
42     }
43
44 }
```

```
45
46 version case4_RSA_AES256_SHA512 {
47
48     set host Client(host1.1);
49     set host Server(host1.1);
50
51       run host Client(*) {
52       run handC(c4)
53     }
54
55       run host Server(*){
56       run handS(s4)
57     }
58   }
59
60 version case5_RSA_AES256_SHA1_COM {
61
62     set host Client(host1.1);
63     set host Server(host1.1);
64
65       run host Client(*) {
66       run handC(c5)
67     }
68
69       run host Server(*){
70       run handS(s5)
71     }
72   }
73
74 version case6_RSA_AES256_SHA1_COM_txt {
75
76     set host Client(host1.1);
77     set host Server(host1.1);
78
79       run host Client(*) {
80       run handC(c6)
81     }
82
83       run host Server(*){
84       run handS(s6)
85     }
86   }
87
88 }
```

Listing 2.21: Protocol instantiation for the TLS protocol.

2.11.4 QoP-ML processing and QoP evaluation

QoP-ML processing and QoP evaluation are the final steps in the QoP analysis process to investigate the influence of the security mechanisms to ensure security attributes. This case study is focused on the availability (time analysis) of the

Table 2.4: The TLS protocol – QoP-ML estimation.

Version	Description	T_{Total} [ms] - QoP-ML estimation
1	RSA, RC4128, MD5	8623.98
2	RSA, 3DES56, SHA1	96543.72
3	RSA, AES256, SHA1	21141.27
4	RSA, AES256, SHA512	26877.25
5	RSA, AES256, SHA1, COM-bin	56683.31
6	RSA, AES256, SHA1, COM-txt	43999.54

cryptographic protocol. Based on the QoP base algorithms presented in Appendix A.2 and in the article [42], the QoP-ML processing of this security attribute should be prepared. However, accomplishment of this security attribute is a complex task as it is related to configuration of the whole teleinformatic infrastructure in which the protocol can be accomplished. Here the QoP evaluation focused on one level of security aspect is related to the cryptographic algorithm. The total execution time (T_{Total}) of the six analyzed versions of the TLS protocol is calculated and is presented in Table 2.4.

For the first version of the protocol, the execution time is $T_{Total} = 8.62\ s$. This case is the most efficient one but the **RC4** and **MD5** algorithms are less secure than those used in the analyzed cases.

In the second case, the **RC4** algorithm was replaced by the **3DES** and **MD5** by the **SHA1**. The execution time of this version is $T_{Total} = 96.54\ s$. The efficiency of the second case is an order of magnitude less than in the first case. It worth noticing that the cryptographic ciphers used in this version are much more secure than in the first one.

In the third version the **AES** algorithm is used with the 256-bit key and **SHA1** hmac function. In this case the performance is much better than in the second one and the execution time is $T_{Total} = 21.14\ s$. The security of the **AES** algorithm is better than in **3DES**; the reason for that could be the length of the key (AES-256, 3DES-112).

In the fourth version the hmac function was replaced from the **SHA1** to the **SHA512**. The execution time in this case is $T_{Total} = 26.88\ s$ so the execution time in the fourth case is 36% longer than in the third case. The security of the fourth version is better than the third version because the length of the **MAC** value (**SHA512**) is more than triple the third version **SHA1**. The improvement in security does not refer to all security attributes but only to the **integrity** security attribute so when this security attribute is not the crucial one, the third protocol version might be better than the fourth one.

The fifth and the sixth versions of the TLS protocol are the ones which use data compression. In these cases the same ciphers are used; the **AES** with the 256-bit key for symmetric encryption/decryption and **SHA1** as a hmac algorithm. In the fifth version the compression was made for binary data and the execution time is $T_{Total} =$

56.68 *s*. In the sixth version the textual data are compressed and the execution time is $T_{Total} = 44$ *s*. The difference in execution time for the fifth and sixth versions depends on the compression ratio; for the binary data it is only 10% but for textual data the ratio amount is about 70% for the algorithm *Deflate*. Compression is used for reduction of the data size which will result in a decrease in the execution time used for creation and transmission of the message authentication code.

Chapter 3

Quality of protection evaluation of security mechanisms

CONTENTS

Carrying out a quality of protection evaluation of security mechanisms for various versions of the cryptographic protocols (security policies) is one of the most challenging issues in the QoP models. Different formulas assessing the effect of security mechanisms on QoP are presented in the approaches [13, 43, 57, 69]. However, their significant limitation is that only the versions directly defined and described in detail previously can be evaluated by these models. Earlier predefined configurations of security mechanisms for the IT processes are regarded to be directly defined scenarios. However, it is very complex, and not always possible to define all scenarios for all IT processes. A scenario not defined can cause an evaluation of the security mechanisms of the specific IT process to not take place. The QoP evaluation of security mechanisms can be done as the part of either the risk analysis process or the decision support system in which appropriate configuration mechanisms are defined in an adaptable way. Thus due to the lack of QoP evaluation of security mechanisms the action relevent to the situation would not be performed by the risk analysis process or decision support system. This advantage is of particular importance in the realtime systems. In this chapter, the model of QoP evaluation of security mechanisms is presented and the evaluation can be made for not directly defined configurations of security mechanisms. The basis of the model can be found in [47]. Moreover, the Security Mechanisms Evaluation Tool (SMETool) is implemented to support the method presented and can be applied by either a researcher or security engineers. The SMETool can be downloaded from the web page of the Quality of Protection Modeling Language Project [7].

The model is aimed at creating a method for evaluating the quality of security protection of the IT system under consideration. This can be accomplished by evaluating a set of security attributes understood as various aspects of a given protection system. The evaluation process starts with a system which can be described by the set of facts which represent all its elements. From a set of facts using knowledge base, knowledge representation mechanisms and an expert system like forward chaining mechanisms, it is possible to obtain a more general description of a given system to evaluate the quality of protection of the system under consideration. It is also assumed that the model utilizes the inference mechanisms which are an insignificant modified version of an expert system like forward chaining mechanisms.

The model presented has the following goals.

1. Possibility of applying the QoP evaluation of security mechanisms for not directly defined scenarios.

2. Possibility of evaluation quality of protection of all security mechanisms.

3. All security attributes can be analyzed.

4. Application for any QoP models.

3.1 Facts and rules

It is assumed that the system behavior modeled in one of the QoP models can be represented by a set of propositions called facts:

$$F = \{f_1, f_2, f_3, \ldots f_n\};$$
where:
$f_1 \ldots f_n$ - the facts describing a system.

Any security mechanism can be defined by means of the facts. There is assumed a set of operators OP=$\{\neg, \sim, \vee, \wedge, \Rightarrow, \rightarrow\}$;
where:

■ $\neg$ is a classical (strong) negation;

■ $\sim$ is a negation as failure;

■ $\vee$ is a disjunction;

■ $\wedge$ is a conjunction;

■ $\Rightarrow$ is a defeasible implication;

■ $\rightarrow$ is a strict implication.

Definition 3.1 Literals
Facts (negated in a strict way or non negated) are literals. The set of all literals is $L = \{l_1, l_2, \ldots, l_m\}$.

For example if $F = \{f_1, f_2\}$ is a set of facts then $L = \{f_1, f_2, \neg f_1, \neg f_2\}$ is a set of literals.

Definition 3.2 Case
A case is a model of an evaluated system represented by a set of literals $C = \{l_a, l_b, \ldots, l_s, l_z, \ldots\}$, which may be also expressed by a set of positive or negated facts: $C = \{f_a, f_b, \ldots, \neg f_s, \neg f_z, \ldots\}$.

Definition 3.3 Security Attribute
Security attribute is defined as the one describing the system behavior for information security requirements.

As an example, it is possible to enumerate the following security attributes [35, 51, 43] integrity, confidentiality, authentication, availability or anonymity. The Security Attributes (*SA*) set is composed of an unlimited but finite number of security attributes. The evaluation result of each of them is expressed by a positive integer number. It represents the estimation of its security attribute which may have a positive or negative character. Greater value of the security attribute evaluation may indicate a better (for positive) or worse (for negative) evaluation.

Definition 3.4 Rule

A rule is a formula in the form:
Conditions → *Conclusion*;
where:

■ *Conditions* refers to a list of rule conditions.
List of conditions is in the form: wl_a ***func*** wl_b ***func*** … wl_d, where ***func*** is one of the operators from the set=$\{\vee, \wedge\}$, and $\{wl_a, wl_b, \ldots, wl_d\}$ are the facts (non-negated or negated by failure). Only one kind of operator should be used in one rule.

■ *Conclusion* is a rule conclusion in the form: *Conclusion* $= (lx \wedge ly \wedge \ldots)$, where: $(lx \wedge ly \wedge \ldots) \in L$.

A negation as failure can negate conditions and a classical negation can negate conclusions. A classical negation must not be used in the antecedent part of the rule. However, a negation as failure must not be used in the consequent part of the rule. *RF* denotes of the set of rules.

The relations between various facts are represented by rules as existence of chosen feature causes existence (or not) of other features in real life systems. Rules also enable pointing out which facts are exclusive in the sense that existence of one of them results in non-existence of others. This fact is significant because it enables preservation of the model consistency.

3.2 Evaluation rules

Facts and evaluation rules are the basis for assessment of the security attributes of a given computer system.

Definition 3.5 Evaluation rule

Evaluation rules are formulas in the form:
Conditions $\Rightarrow Inf^V (sa)$;
where:

■ *Conditions* is a list of rule conditions in the form: wl_a ***func*** wl_b ***func*** … wl_d, where ***func*** are the operators from the set=$\{\vee, \wedge\}$ and $\{wl_a, wl_b, \ldots, wl_d\}$ are facts (non negated or negated by a negation as failure).

■ *Inf* is a function changing the value of the evaluation of security attribute *sa* by adding value *V* (security influence) to the security attribute evaluation, when V is an integer number which represents the evaluation of a given security attribute.

In the case of the security attribute evaluation, the resulting value cannot be lower than 0. The special function $Inf^0(sa)$ indicates the security attribute sa evaluation is reduced to 0. Regardless of sa's current value, sa is reduced to 0 by this function. When this operator is used, it means that this sa is not guaranteed. Independent of other evaluation rules increasing V value, the V value of sa will be equal to 0. We will describe this mechanism in more detail.

It is important to note that evaluation rules are not in fact rules in a traditional sense of the term. They are conditionals in which satisfaction of their conditions causes the value of the evaluation attribute to change.

ER denotes the set of evaluation rules. An example is given below:

$$f_1 \wedge f_2 \Rightarrow Inf^{10}(Confidentiality)$$
$$f_3 \wedge \sim f_4 \Rightarrow Inf^0(Integrity)$$

If the evaluation rule conditions are satisfied, the appropriate change of the security attribute evaluation value occurs. If we have the above rules and the case $P = \{f_1, f_2, f_3\}$, then the value of the security attribute *Confidentiality* should increase by 10 points and that of the security attribute *Integrity* should decrease to 0 points.

Defeasible implication is used in the evaluation rule as such a rule may be defeated by another one.

Definition 3.6 Strict satisfaction of rule conditions
Satisfaction of rule conditions in a strict way is possible when positive (non-negated) conditions are true and negative conditions (facts negated with a negation as failure) are false or cannot be concluded to be true.

The example of the rule is:

$$f_1 \wedge f_2 \wedge \sim f_3 \rightarrow f_4.$$

As follows from the above rule that if f_1 and f_2 are true and f_3 is false (it is not declared, it cannot be concluded from other rules, it is declared that $\neg f_3$ or there is a rule with the conclusion $\neg f_3$ and its conditions are satisfied) then f_4 is true.

Orders between facts

One can see easily that building a large set of rules is required for the evaluation of complex systems. This should make evaluation of any real system possible. There is still another possibility, that for some reasons a set of rules can be incomplete so there may be facts not used in any rule or evaluation rule.

As a result, misleading consequences of the evaluation process originating from the lack of evaluation of potentially important facts can arise. Moreover, such new facts, unpredicted in the rule base, can be somehow connected to the other ones already regulated. For example, better satisfaction of a condition of a chosen rule may be represented by them. However, it may be easier to declare, for instance, that fact f_1 means more than f_2 and can better satisfy the conditions of a chosen rule.

As follows from the above, it is possible to declare the orders between facts. The partial order $f_1 > f_2$ denotes that f_1 means more than f_2. If there is a rule in which one of the conditions is f_2, and f_1 is known to be satisfied, then it can be concluded that f_2 should be also satisfied (even if it is not literally true). The rule condition satisfaction is represented better by such an order. The example can be the statement, that if f_2 is a cipher with the default key length, then f_1 can indicate a cipher with a longer key length.

One should mention that the above relations may not be the same for every security attribute. Thus in the case of confidentiality, a longer key length is better while it is worse in the case of efficiency. Based on the above, additional information about security attributes concerning this reasoning should be added.

Also the relation of order between facts is assumed to be transitive:

$$\forall_{(X,Y,Z)}((X > Y) \wedge (Y > Z) \to (X > Z))$$

Introducing the structure: $OF = \langle F, >_{SA} \rangle$, where $>_{SA}$ is a relation of strict partial order which represents preferences between various facts from the set F in the context of Security Attribute SA ($f_1 >_{sa} f_2$, denotes that f_1 means more than f_2 in the context of security attribute sa).

Definition 3.7 Unstrict satisfaction of rule conditions
Condition f_x of a given rule is satisfied in an unstrict way when f_x is not true, but:

■ there is a fact f_y;

■ It is not known that $\neg f_x$ ($\sim \neg f_x$);

■ we know that $f_y >_{SA} f_x$;

■ reasoning concerns the evaluation of security attribute SA.

That kind of satisfaction of the condition of rule is called unstrict satisfaction of rule conditions. Its root comes from *a fortiori* reasoning (reasoning from more to less), commonly used in the legal domain. Paper [90] presents an example of such reasoning.

Taking a more general view, it can be stated that falsehood of the condition is not enough for the assumption that it is not satisfied. Thus truthfulness of the condition should be distinguished from its satisfaction. The model assumes that in the above cases false conditions can be treated as satisfied.

Also of significant importance connected with the above is the necessity of preserving of the consistency of the system model (as a consistency we understand here exclusion of the possibility of existing complementary facts, for example: $f_1, \neg f_1$). The second clauses of this definition ($\sim \neg f_x$) controlling condition can be satisfied in the unstrict way in the case it is not known that it is false, or it is impossible to derive that it is false. Accordingly, unstrict satisfaction may be defeated by strict declaration of another fact or by another rule.

Definition 3.8 Satisfaction of the conditions of the rule
If there is given a case C described by a set of literals $C = \{l_x, l_y, \dots, l_z\}$ which satisfies in a strict or unstrict way conditions (*Conditions*) of a rule $rf \in RF$, then we denote it as: $C \bullet Conditions$.

3.3 Inference rule

The significant characteristic of the system discussed above is a distinction between truthfulness of the condition and its satisfaction. It is necessary to modify the classic *Modus Ponens* rule to create an inference mechanism.

Definition 3.9 Inference rule
An inference rule is meant to be:
$$\frac{(Conditions \rightarrow Conclusions) \wedge f \bullet Conditions}{Conclusions};$$

where $\rightarrow$ is a strict implication and $f \bullet Conditions$ mean that fact f satisfies (in a strict or unstrict way) conditions of a given rule.

Rule conclusion can be treated as true and, consequently, satisfied as a result of strict or unstrict satisfaction of the rule's antecedents.

3.4 Inference mechanism

The inference mechanism is defined based on the inference rule defined above.

Definition 3.10 Fact based inference mechanism
The forward chaining mechanism based on the inference rule defined previously is considered to be a fact based inference mechanism. A set of conclusions whose inference mechanisms concludes from a case C, a set of rules RF and a set of orders OF are denoted $C \vdash C'$. Complete description of the case denoted P is called the union of sets: $C \cup C'$.

3.5 Security attributes

As follows from the above, the security attributes' set *SA* is composed of an unlimited but finite number of security attributes. A positive integer number expresses the evaluation value of each of them.

Definition 3.11 Set of security attributes pairs.
S is a set of pairs $O = \langle sa, o \rangle$, where $sa \in SA$ is a security attribute and o is its evaluation value.

For example, there are three security attributes possessing their evaluation value:

$$SA = confidentiality, integrity, authorization;$$
$$S = \{(confidentiality, 10), (integrity, 20), (authorization, 30)\}.$$

It is worth mentioning that security attributes can be positive or negative meaning that a larger value security attribute evaluation is better (positive) or worse (negative) evaluation.

3.6 Conflicts between rules

Conflicts between evaluation rules may result from some specific conditions.

Definition 3.12 Conflicting rules
A conflict between two or more evaluation rules occurs when they can not be executed together.

When the antecedents of two rules are satisfied, a conflict may take place. As the rules are somehow connected, their execution can affect improperly the security attribute evaluation.

Utilization of a defeasible implication results from the conflicting and subsuming rules. Here defeasibility of the evaluation rules is meant as possible exclusion from the evaluation process of a chosen rule by another rule. In the case of satisfying antecedents of two conflicting rules, only one of them can be executed. However, it is possible for such a rule to be defeated by another one.

Partial order between rules from a set *ER* is assumed in order to represent priorities between the evaluation rules. It makes it possible to express that $r_1 > r_2$ and $r_1, r_2 \in ER$; then rules r_1 and r_2 are in conflict. Moreover, in the case where there is satisfaction of both rules, the rule r_1 should be defeated by the rule r_2.

Reasoning about orders between conflicting rules

The mechanisms of the abovementioned conflicting rules recognition constitute the main problem. The basis of such recognition should be common sense reasoning.

However, this can be concluded in one situation when there are two rules and there is a more general set of conditions in one of them than in the other one. So it can be stated that every case satisfying the conditions of rule r_2 also satisfies conditions of the rule r_1. As follows from that, rule r_2 is a specific case of the rule r_1. Thus r_2 should defeat rule r_1 when the antecedents of both rules are satisfied. In a more general sense, there is a conflict between these two rules when the list of conditions of both of them results in modification of the same evaluation value attribute.

Definition 3.13 Subsuming rules
In the case of two rules:

$$r_x : Condition_x \Rightarrow Inf^{V1}(sa);$$
$$r_y : Condition_y \Rightarrow Inf^{V2}(sa);$$

where
$Condition_x$ and $Condition_y$ are the lists of antecedents of these rules. Both rules influence the same security attribute evaluation value sa (but they may have a different level of the influence), and if for any case P represented by a set of literals:

$$\forall_{P \in L}((P \bullet Condition_x) \rightarrow (P \bullet Condition_y));$$

then we recognize the rules r_x and r_y as subsuming and conflicting ones and in a view of more restrictive character of the rule r_x we may conclude that the rule r_x has priority over the rule r_y, which we denote: $r_x > r_y$ and while conditions of both rules are satisfied, rule r_x should defeat rule r_y.

The highest possible priority is for the rules with the function $Inf^0(sa)$ on the consequent part. There is a conflict between them and all the rules related to the security attribute sa. All evaluation rules related to the security attributes sa are excluded from reasoning whenever they satisfy conditions.

The reason for a more general rule to be replaced by a more specific one is another significant issue requiring explanation. It can be explained by a theory of law called *lex specialis derogat legi genrali*. This is one of the tools used to find a solution when legal rules are in conflict. According to it, a specific act (provision) derogates from (prevails over) the general regulation. Modeling legal rules encounters difficulties in deciding which rules are more or less specific [53]. In the case of the presented model it is much simpler because the hierarchy of generality of antecedents of the rules is easy to establish based on a finite number of possible facts and their explicitness.

3.7 Evaluation rules system

Definition 3.14 Evaluation of rules system
The evaluation of a rules system RO is a structure described by: a set of evaluation rules ER and relation OR= $\langle ER, > \rangle$.

The partial order between the rules from a set *ER* is represented by the relation *OR*, and it maps preferences between conflicting rules. Their source can be a strict declaration or a previously defined mechanism of finding or resolving a problem of subsuming rules. Two rules, between which there is a partial order relation, are treated as conflicting ones. They are conflict free if they are not comparable. The relation of order between rules is also assumed to be transitive:

$$\forall_{r_x, r_y, r_z}((r_x > r_y) \wedge (r_y > r_z) \rightarrow (r_x > r_z)).$$

3.8 QoP evaluation process of security mechanisms

Evaluation of security attributes is the means for qop evaluation of security mechanisms. The *SA* values depend on security mechanisms represented by facts F in the model.

The evaluation process of security mechanisms can be presented as a sequence of steps and proceeds according to Algorithm 3.1. Table 3.1 includes the parameters and variables used in this algorithm.

3.9 Background of the model

Generally viewed, the model under discussion includes some elements taken from the formal models of legal reasoning, which are of a specific character. It requires mechanisms to deal with incomplete knowledge and to resolve conflicts between legal rules and arguments, as well as various ways to interpret rules, etc. In order to support human reasoning computer systems must encounter similar problems and that is why the *a fortiori* rule or the *lex specialis...* rule is utilized in this system. Other computer science utilization also exploited similar models of legal reasoning [87] and it was necessary to implement one of the methods to resolve the conflicts between rules in the multiagent systems.

The model is based on proposition logic with some additions allowing better representation of specific features of the problem in question. First of all, the distinction between two kinds of negation is introduced: classical negation (strong) and negation as failure. By negation as failure there is meant one used in the conditional part of the rule. The negated condition is satisfied when it can not be fulfilled (it is false, it is not declared or it is impossible to derive that it is satisfied). In some logical systems e.g., in the Prakken and Sartor logic [73] or the Kowalski and Toni logic [72] there

Algorithm 3.1:
Algorithm of security attributes evaluation

1: SET C
2: **for** $i = 1$ to n **do**
3:      $o_i \leftarrow 0$
4:      SET $OF[i]$
5:      SET $C'[i] = RES(C, OF[i], R)$
6:      $P[i] = C[i] \cup C'[i]$
7:      SET $ER[i]$
8:
9:      **if** $ER[i] = \emptyset$ **then**
10:        $o_i \leftarrow 0$
11:        CONTINUE
12:        **for** $k = 1$ to $NER[i]$ **do**
13:          **for** $m = 1$ to $NER[i]$ **do**
14:            **if** $(er[k][i], er[m][i] \wedge er[k][i] > er[m][i])$ **then**
15:              EXCLUDE $er[m][i]$ from $ER[i]$
16:            **end if**
17:          **end for**
18:        **end for**
19:      **end if**
20:
21:      **for** $l = 1$ from $NER[i]$ **do**
22:        **if** exists $er[l][i]$ in $ER[i]$ such that conclusion is $Inf^0(i)$ **then**
23:          $o_i \leftarrow 0$
24:          CONTINUE
25:        **else**
26:          READ $V[l][i]$
27:          $o_i = o_i + V[l][i]$
28:        **end if**
29:      **end for**
30: **end for**

were two kinds of negation applied. In this model the way of negation utilization as failure is like the one given by H. Prakken and G. Sartor in [73] but the construction like $\sim \neg P$ is not allowed to be used because negation as failure is forbidden in the consequence part of the rule. The use of the classical negation antecedent part of the rule is not allowed either. Another significant aspect of our model is the conception of orders between facts based on a simplified version of an *a fortiori* reasoning (reasoning from more to less: If norm N1 is obliged to do more is binding, then norm N2 is obliged to do less is binding all the more). Here, this way of reasoning is somehow modified: when condition X of a rule r_1 is not satisfied literally, but there is a fact Y which satisfies this condition in a better way, we may treat such a condition as

Table 3.1: The parameters and variables for the security attributes evaluation algorithm.

SET	-	make a choice indication
$EXCLUDE$	-	excluding from the ER indication
$READ$	-	reading indication
$CONTINUE$	-	processing statement will be skipped
$RES(C, OF[i], R)$	-	the reasoning function based on a set of facts C and order of facts $OF[i]$ for the security attribute i and rules R(inference mechanisms)
$OF[i]$	-	orders between facts referred to security attribute i
C	-	a case expressed by a set of facts
C'	-	set of facts obtained from the inference mechanism
$P[i]$	-	full description of a case for a security attribute i
R	-	set of rules
k, m, l	-	indicators of current evaluation rule
o_i	-	evaluation of i-th security attribute
$ER[i]$	-	set of evaluation rules with satisfied conditions for the security attribute i
$NER[i]$	-	the number of rules with satisfied conditions for the security attribute i
$er[x][i]$	-	evaluation rule x for the security attribute i
i	-	the index of the current security attribute
n	-	quantity of Security Attributes
$V[l][i]$	-	the value of the security influence of the security mechanisms represented by the evaluation rule l for the security attribute i

satisfied. The more profound analysis and model of *a fortiori* reasoning can be found in [90].

This model has another important characteristic, namely, the utilization of defeasible implication in evaluation rules. Distinction of two kinds of implication is based on the formal models of legal argumentation with wide discussion of defeasibility of the rules. All arguments are defeasible in the Prakken and Sartor logic [73]. Two kinds of implication (material $\supset$ and defeasible $>$) are applied by Vreeswijk in the Abstract Argumentation System [89]. According to him, in defeasible implication utilization separate defeasible inference rules must be defined. However, Jaap Hage in his Reason Based Logic [37] expresses a different point of view about defeasibility of the rules. He treats it as a problem of applicability of the rule which could be satisfied but not applicable caused by e.g., a conflict with another rule. Kowalski and Toni [72] developed an interesting model of argumentation using defeasible and strict implication. According to them each defeasible rule r has the condition: $\sim defeated(r)$ (where $\sim$ is a negation as failure and $defeated(r)$ is a predicate indicating that this rule is defeated by another one only if it is conflict with another rule r' and its priority is lower than r'.

In the model under consideration defeasible rules are insignificantly different from those in the previously presented models. In this model the most important aspect is that only evaluation rules (strictly speaking not being rules) are defeasible. It is possible to defeat such a rule only if its conditions are satisfied, there is a conflict with another rule with satisfied conditions, and its priority is lower compared to the other one. Such a defeated rule does not undergo the reasoning process.

A few types of defeasibility are defined by L. Torre in [86] and the one used in this model is the closest to the overridden defeasibility formalizing cancelling of a rule by another one.

H. Prakken and G. Sartor discussed how to deal with conflicts between rules and orders within these rules [73, 71] where they developed their formal model of legal argumentation. In our approach the notion of conflict between rules is different from that presented by them but there is similarity in the way of resolving it by a declaration of orders between rules and assumptions of their defeasibility. In the logic of Kowalski and Toni there is a conflict between two rules where their complementary conclusions and conditions are satisfied. In their model they use two kinds of implication and two kinds of negation but their way of dealing with conflict is a bit different from that used in presented system. A few new predicates are defined by them to show that the condition of the rule r satisfied ($holds(r)$), rule r is defeated ($defeated(r)$) or two rules are in conflict ($conflict(r,r')$).

3.10   Method of QoP evaluation of security mechanisms

The QoP evaluation of security mechanisms includes four stages: QoP modeling, linking, configuration, and QoP evaluation. The method of the process is presented in Figure 3.1.

QoP modeling stage.
The first stage includes using one of the QoP models. It depends on the chosen QoP approach, but it gives the same result, modeling of the system must be done with QoP meaning (*System abstraction in the QoP model*). Different QoP modeling methods can make use of that model.

Linking stage.
In the next stage, the linking system, is modeled using the QoP model with the structure defined in the proposed model. First, all parameters used in the QoP model related to factors influencing QoP parameters must be extracted (*Extraction of the QoP parameters*). In the next step the atomic facts, which are explicit to those extracted from the model (*Atomic facts definition*) are created in the proposed model. The parameters in the QoP model can have different names from those defined in the model and they have to be linked together (*Linking QoP parameters with atomic facts*).

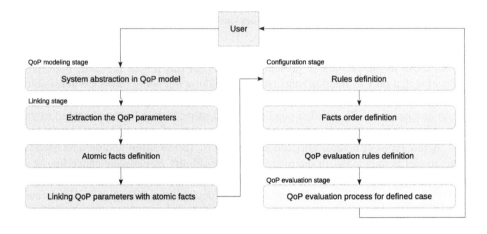

Figure 3.1: The method of QoP evaluation of security mechanisms.

Configuration stage.

The main phase is the stage in which there are defined all structures meant for QoP evaluation of security mechanisms in the model. The following can be mentioned: *Rules definition*, *Facts order definition* and *QoP evaluation rules definition*. In the previous sections all these structures are described.

QoP evaluation stage.

In the last stage, which is responsible for QoP evaluation of security mechanisms, the specified system configuration is evaluated (*Case Study*). The specification in question can be defined in the QoP model and the transfer of atomic facts into the QoP evaluation proceeds owing the links which were defined previously. Eventually, the QoP evaluation of security mechanisms is made, after the indication of the system version.

3.11   Case study: TLS handshake protocol

The case study of QoP evaluation of security mechanisms for the TLS Handshake protocol is discussed in this section. This protocol was described in the previous chapter in detail. Different security measures can be undertaken to accomplish the security requirements. Six versions of the protocol were analyzed in the previous chapter. Here, the quality of protection analysis of these protocol versions is analyzed.

The previous section included the methodology of QoP evaluation of security mechanisms using the model under discussion. Whereas this section deals with the methodology for analyzing the TLS handshake cryptographic protocol.

3.11.1   QoP modeling

In the first step one has to model the system in one of the QoP models. In the case study presented, the TLS protocol is analyzed as the full system. The QoP modeling process is presented in the previous chapter.

3.11.2   Linking stage

Extraction of the QoP parameters First, all parameters in the QoP model must be extracted and this is related to the factors affecting QoP parameters whose form is dependent on the QoP model chosen. In the QoP-ML the functions modifying the states of the variables and passing the objects by communication channels change the system behavior. This structure is decisive for the parameters influencing the QoP system.

Let qp be assumed to be the QoP parameter in the QoP model that affects system security. As the QoP parameter is atomic, it cannot be split into other atomic QoP parameters. The QP is the set of the following QoP parameters:

$QP = \{qp_1, qp_2, qp_3, \ldots qp_n\};$
where:
$qp_1, qp_2, qp_3, \ldots qp_n$ - QoP parameters which influence the system security;
QP - the set of QoP parameters.

For the TLS protocol which was presented in the previous chapter the following qop parameters are defined (3.2).

Atomic facts definition

Next, declare a set of all the possible facts F, which will represent features of the system being analyzed.

Here the atomic facts are defined in the model of the TLS cryptographic protocol. They come from the official specification of the TLS protocol [8] with all its possible versions defined and they are included in three groups related to the different factors: symmetric encryption (Table 3.3), message digest (Table 3.4), asymmetric encryption, and common facts (Table 3.5).

Linking QoP parameters with atomic facts

The QoP parameters used in the QoP model have different names from those of the atomic facts defined in the model. Here the QoP parameters are explicitly linked with the facts in the model under consideration.

Definition 3.15 Linking operator
The fact that one set of objects is explicitly mapped to another one is marked by the linking operator $\mapsto$.

Table 3.2: The QoP parameters for TLS protocol.

qop label	qop parameter name	function	value
qp_1	bitlength	enc	2048
qp_2	algorithm	enc	RSA
qp_3	bitlength	enc	128
qp_4	algorithm	enc	RC4
qp_5	type	enc	stream
qp_6	algorithm	hmac	MD5
qp_7	algorithm	enc	3DES
qp_8	bitlength	enc	112
qp_9	algorithm	hmac	SHA1
qp_{10}	mode	enc	CBC
qp_{11}	algorithm	enc	AES
qp_{12}	bitlength	enc	256
qp_{13}	algorithm	hmac	SHA512
qp_{14}	algorithm	com	DEFLATE - bin
qp_{15}	algorithm	com	DEFLATE - txt

Table 3.3: The group of facts refers to symmetric encryption.

facts
Group name: cipher (symmetric encryption algorithm)
$f_1(cipher) = RC4$
$f_2(cipher) = 3DES$
$f_3(cipher) = AES$
Group name: bs (block size in bytes)
$f_1(bs) = 8$
$f_1(bs) = 16$
Group name: IV (initiate vector in bytes)
$f_1(IV) = 8$
$f_1(IV) = 16$
Group name: key (key length in bytes)
$f_1(key) = 16$
$f_2(key) = 24$
$f_3(key) = 32$
$f_4(key) = 14$

The QP is assumed to be the set of QoP parameters used in the QoP model for the TLS protocol abstraction and F is assumed to be the set of all atomic facts defined in the model. Generally, the set of QoP parameters QP is considered to be a subset of

Table 3.4: The group of facts refers to message digest.

facts
Group name: mac (message authentication code algorithm)
$f_1(mac) = HMAC - MD5$
$f_2(mac) = HMAC - SHA1$
$f_3(mac) = HMAC - SHA256$
$f_4(mac) = HMAC - SHA512$
Group name: mac-len (message digest length in bytes)
$f_1(mac - len) = 16$
$f_2(mac - len) = 20$
$f_3(mac - len) = 32$
$f_4(mac - len) = 64$
Group name: k-len (mac key length in bytes)
$f_1(k - len) = 16$
$f_2(k - len) = 20$
$f_3(k - len) = 32$

Table 3.5: The group of facts refers to asymmetric cryptography and common facts.

facts
Group name: PK (key exchange algorithm scheme)
$f_1(PK) = RSA$
$f_2(PK) = DH - DSS$
$f_3(PK) = DH - RSA$
$f_4(PK) = DHE - DSS$
$f_5(PK) = DHE - RSA$
$f_6(PK) = DH - anon$
Group name: key-a(key length in bytes for asymmetric cryptography)
$f_1(key - a) = 1024$
$f_2(key - a) = 2048$
$f_3(key - a) = 4096$
Group name: type (type of bits computation)
$f_1(type) = Stream$
$f_1(type) = Block$
Group name: mode (mode of operation)
$f_1(mode) = CBC$
Group name: com (bit compression before encryption)
$f_1(com) = Compression - bin$
$f_2(com) = Compression - txt$

facts in the model F. However, in a particular case it can be equal to:

$QP = \{qp_1, qp_2, qp_3, \ldots qp_n\};$
$F = \{f_1, f_2, f_3, \ldots f_n\};$
$Z \in F;$
where:
$qp_1, qp_2, qp_3, \ldots qp_n$ - QoP parameters which influence the system security;
QP - the set of QoP parameters;
$f_1, f_2, f_3, \ldots f_n$ - facts in the formal model;
F - the set of all facts in the model;
Z - the subset of all facts in the model.

The linking operator $\mapsto$ links the QoP parameters from the QoP model with the subset of facts explicitly defined in the model.

$QP \mapsto Z.$

In Table 3.6 the QP parameters are mapped to Z for the analyzed TLS protocol.

Table 3.6: The linking QP parameters with Z.

qop parameter	operator	fact
qp_1	$\mapsto$	$f_2(key - a)$
qp_2	$\mapsto$	$f_1(PK)$
qp_3	$\mapsto$	$f_1(mac - len)$
qp_4	$\mapsto$	$f_1(cipher)$
qp_5	$\mapsto$	$f_1(type)$
qp_6	$\mapsto$	$f_1(mac)$
qp_7	$\mapsto$	$f_2(cipher)$
qp_8	$\mapsto$	$f_4(key)$
qp_9	$\mapsto$	$f_2(mac)$
qp_{10}	$\mapsto$	$f_1(mode)$
qp_{11}	$\mapsto$	$f_3(cipher)$
qp_{12}	$\mapsto$	$f_3(key)$
qp_{13}	$\mapsto$	No fact
qp_{14}	$\mapsto$	$f_1(com)$
qp_{15}	$\mapsto$	$f_2(com)$

3.11.3 Configuration stage

In the next stage, which is the main phase, all structures proposed in the model for the QoP evaluation of security factors are defined. These are, among others: rules, facts order and QoP evaluation rules.

Rules definition

The rules related to possible accomplishment of the protocol are specified based on the TLS cryptographic protocol specification [8]. The rules defining the TLS protocol are included in Appendix A.3.1.

Facts order definition

It is necessary to define the facts order for the same security attributes (SA) in the next step. The example shows evaluation of the QoP of security mechanisms in the case of three based security attributes: integrity (I), confidentiality (C) and availability (A). According to the expert knowledge facts order is defined in the field of cryptographic protocol. One can find the defined facts order in Appendix A.3.2.

QoP evaluation rules definition

Defining the QoP evaluation rules is the last step in the configuration. Considering the TLS protocol, the evaluation rules are related to the same security attributes: integrity (I), confidentiality (C) and availability (A). The evaluation of the QoP of security mechanisms of the TLS protocol proceeds according to these rules. As given in the literature the influence of specific security mechanisms is determined from expert knowledge in the field of cryptography and system security [13, 57]. Here the same expert knowledge analysis related to the TLS cryptographic protocol is concluded. The QoP evaluation rules determined are included in Appendix A.3.3.

3.11.4 QoP evaluation stage

The QoP evaluation process can be executed when the configuration stage is finished. Here six versions of the TLS protocol are taken which were defined in previous chapter and they are given in the Table 2.4. The TLS specification is applied for detailed description of these cipher suits [8]. Based on the TLS specification versions presented here, the fourth, the fifth, and the sixth, are modified. In the fourth version the case when the new cryptographic modules are possible from the defined ones is analyzed. This constitutes the implementation of HMAC-SHA512 [66]. In the fifth version the compression for binary data is analyzed. In the sixth one the textual data are compressed.

As six cases represent six different realizations of TLS protocol, they are analyzed as six versions characterized by the following set of facts:

■ Case 1: $C_1 = \{f_1(PK), f_2(key-a), f_1(cipher), f_1(key), f_1(mac)\}$;

■ Case 2: $C_2 = \{f_1(PK), f_2(key-a), f_2(cipher), f_1(mode), f_4(key), f_2(mac)\}$;

■ Case 3: $C_3 = \{f_1(PK), f_2(key-a), f_3(cipher), f_3(key), f_1(mode), f_2(mac)\}$;

■ Case 4: $C_4 = \{f_1(PK), f_2(key-a), f_1(cipher), f_1(key), f_1(mode), f_4(mac)\}$;

■ Case 5: $C_5 = \{f_1(PK), f_2(key-a), f_3(cipher), f_3(key), f_2(mac), f_1(com)\}$;

■ Case 6: $C_6 = \{f_1(PK), f_2(key-a), f_3(cipher), f_3(key), f_2(mac), f_2(com)\}$.

When the facts describing case (C) are defined, other atomic or complex facts (C') : $C \vdash C'$ must be derived $(\vdash)$ applying the inference mechanism and rules defined in Appendix A.3.1. From the above, the final evaluation of security mechanisms, represented as the security attributes, can be made. The evaluations of the six cases are given below.

QoP evaluation of Case 1:
$C_1 \vdash C_1'$;
$C_1' = \{\neg f_2(PK), \neg f_3(PK), \neg f_4(PK), \neg f_5(PK), \neg f_6(PK), f(PK), f(cipher), \neg f_1(IV),$
$\neg f_2(IV), \neg f_1(bs), \neg f_2(bs), \neg f_2(cipher), \neg f_3(cipher), f_1(mac-len), f_1(k-len),$
$\neg f_2(mac), \neg f_3(mac), \neg f_4(mac), f(mac), \neg f_2(key), \neg f_3(key), \neg f_4(key), f(key),$
$\neg f_2(mac-len), \neg f_3(mac-len), \neg f_4(mac-len), f(k-len), f(mac-len),$
$\neg f_2(k-len), \neg f_3(k-len)\}$.

Case 1 is denoted as P_1 and is a union of sets C_1 and C_1':
$P_1 = (C_1 \cup C_1')$.
The QoP evaluation of the security attributes:
$O_1 = \{\langle confidentiality, 2\rangle, \langle integrity, 3\rangle, \langle availability, 7\rangle\}$.

QoP evaluation of Case 2:
$C_2 \vdash C_2'$;
$C_2' = \{\neg f_2(PK), \neg f_3(PK), \neg f_4(PK), \neg f_5(PK), \neg f_6(PK), f(PK), f(cipher), \neg f_1(IV),$
$\neg f_1(bs), \neg f_1(cipher), \neg f_3(cipher), f_2(mac-len), f_2(k-len), \neg f_1(mac), \neg f_3(mac),$
$\neg f_4(mac), f(mac), f(IV), \neg f_2(IV), f(bs), \neg f_2(bs), \neg f_2(key), \neg f_3(key),$
$\neg f_1(key), f(key), \neg f_1(mac-len), \neg f_3(mac-len), \neg f_4(mac-len), f(k-len),$
$f(mac-len), \neg f_1(k-len), \neg f_3(k-len)\}$.

Case 2 is denoted as P_2 and is a union of sets C_2 and C_2':
$P_2 = (C_2 \cup C_2')$.
The QoP evaluation of the security attributes:
$O_2 = \{\langle confidentiality, 5\rangle, \langle integrity, 6\rangle, \langle availability, 11\rangle\}$.

QoP evaluation of Case 3:
$C_3 \vdash C_3'$;
$C_3' = \{\neg f_2(PK), \neg f_3(PK), \neg f_4(PK), \neg f_5(PK), \neg f_6(PK), f(PK), f(cipher), f_2(IV),$
$f_2(bs), \neg f_1(cipher), \neg f_2(cipher), f_2(mac-len), f_2(k-len), \neg f_1(mac), \neg f_3(mac),$
$\neg f_4(mac), f(mac), f(IV), \neg f_1(IV), f(bs), \neg f_1(bs), \neg f_1(key), \neg f_2(key),$
$\neg f_4(key), f(key), \neg f_1(mac-len), \neg f_3(mac-len), \neg f_4(mac-len), f(k-len),$
$f(mac-len), \neg f_1(k-len), \neg f_3(k-len)\}$.

Case 3 is denoted as P_3 and is a union of sets C_3 and C_3':
$P_3 = (C_3 \cup C_3')$.
The QoP evaluation of the security attributes:
$O_3 = \{\langle confidentiality, 10 \rangle, \langle integrity, 6 \rangle, \langle availability, 14 \rangle\}$.

QoP evaluation of Case 4:
$C_4 \vdash C_4'$;
$C_4' = \{\neg f_2(PK), \neg f_3(PK), \neg f_4(PK), \neg f_5(PK), \neg f_6(PK), f(PK), f(cipher), \neg f_1(IV),$
$\neg f_2(IV), \neg f_1(bs), \neg f_2(bs), \neg f_2(cipher), \neg f_3(cipher), f_4(mac - len), f_3(k - len),$
$\neg f_1(mac), \neg f_2(mac), \neg f_3(mac), f(mac), \neg f_2(key), \neg f_3(key), \neg f_4(key),$
$f(key), \neg f_1(mac - len), \neg f_2(mac - len), \neg f_3(mac - len), f(k - len), f(mac - len),$
$\neg f_1(k - len), \neg f_2(k - len)\}$.

Case 4 is denoted as P_4 and is a union of sets C_4 and C_4':
$P_4 = (C_4 \cup C_4')$.
The QoP evaluation of the security attributes:
$O_4 = \{\langle confidentiality, 2 \rangle, \langle integrity, 11 \rangle, \langle availability, 11 \rangle\}$.

QoP evaluation of Case 5:
$C_5 \vdash C_5'$;
$C_5' = \{\neg f_2(PK), \neg f_3(PK), \neg f_4(PK), \neg f_5(PK), \neg f_6(PK), f(PK), f(cipher), f_2(IV),$
$f_2(bs), \neg f_1(cipher), \neg f_2(cipher), f_2(mac - len), f_2(k - len), \neg f_1(mac), \neg f_3(mac),$
$\neg f_4(mac), f(mac), f(IV), \neg f_1(IV), f(bs), \neg f_1(bs), \neg f_1(key), \neg f_2(key),$
$\neg f_4(key), f(key), \neg f_1(mac - len), \neg f_3(mac - len), \neg f_4(mac - len), f(k - len),$
$f(mac - len), \neg f_1(k - len), \neg f_3(k - len)\}$.

Case 5 is denoted as P_5 and is a union of sets C_5 and C_5':
$P_5 = (C_5 \cup C_5')$.
The QoP evaluation of the security attributes:
$O_5 = \{\langle confidentiality, 10 \rangle, \langle integrity, 6 \rangle, \langle availability, 18 \rangle\}$.

QoP evaluation of Case 6:
$C_6 \vdash C_6'$;
$C_6' = \{\neg f_2(PK), \neg f_3(PK), \neg f_4(PK), \neg f_5(PK), \neg f_6(PK), f(PK), f(cipher), f_2(IV),$
$f_2(bs), \neg f_1(cipher), \neg f_2(cipher), f_2(mac - len), f_2(k - len), \neg f_1(mac), \neg f_3(mac),$
$\neg f_4(mac), f(mac), f(IV), \neg f_1(IV), f(bs), \neg f_1(bs), \neg f_1(key), \neg f_2(key),$
$\neg f_4(key), f(key), \neg f_1(mac - len), \neg f_3(mac - len), \neg f_4(mac - len), f(k - len),$
$f(mac - len), \neg f_1(k - len), \neg f_3(k - len)\}$.

Case 6 is denoted as P_6 and is a union of sets C_6 and C_6':
$P_6 = (C_6 \cup C_6')$.
The QoP evaluation of the security attributes:
$O_6 = \{\langle confidentiality, 10 \rangle, \langle integrity, 6 \rangle, \langle availability, 14 \rangle\rangle\}$.

Table 3.7: The QoP evaluation of the analyzed versions of TLS protocol.

version	C	I	A
1	2	3	7
2	5	6	11
3	10	6	14
4	2	11	11
5	10	6	18
6	10	6	15

Table 3.7 includes the quantitative results obtained by the QoP evaluation of security mechanisms.

3.11.5 Qualitative estimation

The results are regarded as a quantitative evaluation of the security attributes. In the process of QoP evaluation of security mechanisms, qualitative interpretation of the results can be made for all security attributes.

Here there are presented 5 levels of evaluation: very low, low, medium, high and very high. The fact that correlations between the quantitative and qualitative results are not only of theoretical character but also of real one, is of significant importance. Calculation of the possible minimal and maximal values of the security attributes for a given version of the protocol under analysis results in the practical character of their qualitative estimation. It is worth mentioning that quantitative evaluation of the availability security attribute should be interpreted in reverse order (very low will be very high, low will be high etc.), because the higher value of this parameter refers to larger computational requirements for the system.

The parameters for the qualitative evaluation are determined using the formulas:

$$very\,low = (Q_{min}, Q_{min} + X);$$
$$low = (Q_{min} + X, Q_{min} + 2X);$$
$$medium = (Q_{min} + 2X, Q_{min} + 3X);$$
$$high = (Q_{min} + 3X, Q_{min} + 4X); \qquad (3.1)$$
$$very\,high = (Q_{min} + 4X, Q_{min} + 5X);$$
$$where$$
$$X = \frac{Q_{max} - Q_{min}}{5};$$
$$where$$

Q_{max} - the maximum value for the security attribute among all analyzed versions of the protocol;

Q_{min} - the minimum value for the security attribute among all analyzed versions of the protocol.

Table 3.8: The qualitative interpretation of QoP evaluation of the analyzed versions of TLS protocol.

version	C	I	A
1	very low	very low	very high
2	low	low	high
3	very high	low	low
4	very low	very high	high
5	very high	low	very low
6	very high	low	low

Based on formula 3.1 it is possible to estimate the TLS protocol qualitatively, as given in Table 3.8.

Interpretation of the results follows the QoP evaluation of the security mechanisms. The most effective versions of the TLS protocol are the first, second, and fourth ones for the CPU performance, which is shown by the availability attribute. This results from the fact that the security mechanisms being applied are the most efficient. On the other hand, these attributes are accomplished on the lowest level as follows from the analysis of confidentiality.

Data integrity is another security attribute which can be guaranteed by the TLS protocol. The highest level is guaranteed by the fourth version, and this is a result of using the SHA512 algorithm as the par of the HMAC function. The other analyzed versions guarantee integrity on a low or a very low level.

The fifth and sixth versions are the similar ones. There is one difference which refers to the availability attribute because in the fifth version this attribute is realized on a very low level when the sixth is on a low level. It is caused by the type of data which are compressed; in the fifth one the data are binary, whereas in the sixth one data are textual. The compression time is similar but the compression ratio for the textual data are much more effective than for the binary one. The result of that is that the input data for the symmetric encryption, which is the next cryptographic operation in TLS protocol, will be smaller, so the encryption time will be decreased.

3.12   Formal model goals evaluation

The model goals were presented at the beginning of the formal model definition. This section will present the goals achieved.

1. *Goal 1: Automatic QoP evaluation of the not directly defined scenarios.*
   QoP security evaluation based on not directly defined scenarios is one of the most important features of the model. Thus in the process of analysis the QoP evaluation of one of the not directly defined cryptographic protocol versions can be prepared. The model has the inference mechanism and rules defined

so that the set of facts describing the analyzed version of the protocol can be automatically derived. In the case of the not directly defined protocol versions, conflicting facts can be obtained during their derivation. The model has the rules order indicating which of the conflicting facts are to be considered. Based on the structures described, it is possible to prepare the QoP analysis from the security mechanisms.

2. *Goal 2: Quality of Protection evaluation of all security mechanisms.*
   The model allows evaluation of any of the security mechanisms in the case of the quality of protection factor. The model under consideration enables the security mechanisms, modeled in one of the QoP models, to be mapped to the atomic facts or complex facts. It is possible to define the kind of facts represented by any security mechanism. The mapping process is executed using the linking stage described in methodology. Finally, it is possible to prepare the QoP evaluation of security mechanisms from the QoP evaluation rules and their order.

3. *Goal 3: Analysis refers to all security attributes.*
   In the case of information security requirements the system behavior can be described by the security attribute. It can be changed by the security mechanisms, modifying the modeled system. The model can represent any of security mechanisms and it enables the analysis of any security attribute.

4. *Goal 4: The model can be used for any QoP models.*
   The systems created in any of the QoP models can use this model. The linking operator which links the QoP parameters from the QoP model with the subset of facts defined in the model enables achievement of the goal. The objects are explicitly mapped.

Chapter 4

Advanced communication and energy efficiency modeling

CONTENTS

There are a few limitations of the QoP-ML basic communication model due to the channels which represent the link between each pair of hosts. The first one consists in the fact that it is impossible to identify the message receiver when the same channel is used by many hosts. Then the first host waiting for a message on the channel receives it. Another limitation is that it is not possible to identify the message sender to send back a response.

New mechanisms and structures must be created in the QoP-ML model to remove the limitations discussed above. These mechanisms were first discussed in [77]. In this chapter three new mechanisms: topology, routing, and packet filtering are presented. The methodology providing the time analysis of communication steps in the network is introduced. The time of delivering a message from the sender to the receiver depends on the chosen path in the network. Based on the model, characteristics of the channel can be determined and the transmission time can be calculated.

The energy analysis module is another level of analysis which can be performed. In [77] the basis of the energy aware analysis were first discussed, and in this chapter the energy consumption module is further discussed.

The BNF (BackusNaur Form) [16] standard is used for presentation of all structures in Appendix A, whereas Appendix A.4 presents the algorithms used by the proposed network analysis module.

4.1   Topology

The graph where the vertices are the hosts and the edges are the connections between them defines topology. All connections are defined and a weight represents their quality (the lower the weight, the better the quality). For broadcasting messages, a link between the host and the medium is used as a type of connection which does not have the quality parameter.

The topology structure is a (from line 16 to 32 in Listing 4.1) part of the communication structure which is applied in the description of the communication characteristics of mediums (channels). The definition of topology and default topology parameters for all mediums are included in the communication structure, which can be located in two places. It can be one of the main structures (like hosts, functions, etc.) affecting the whole model and all versions, or it can be placed in the version structure after the run structure, thus affecting only a selected version. If the element of the *communication* structure (e.g., topology) for a given medium is defined in the *version* structure, then it overrides the main *communication* structure (i.e., the topology is determined on basis of the version *communication* structure only).

4.1.1   Connection definition

The connections between the hosts or between the hosts and the medium (used in broadcasting) are defined by the rules making the topology. The rule is composed of two sets of hosts (left and right), the direction and optionally, after the colon, the connection-specific values of parameters. Three types of direction can be distinguished.

1. A → B, the connection is created from the host A to B;

2. A ← B, the connection is created from the host B to A;

3. A ↔ B, the connection is created in both ways.

```
1  communication {
2
3    medium[cable] {
4      default_q = 0.1;
5      default_time = 1ms;
6
7      topology {
8        Gateway -> Sensor[0];
9      }
10   }
11
12   medium[air_channel] {
13     default_q = 1;
14     default_time = 18ms;
15
16     topology {
17       Sink <-> Gateway : t=wsn_time[ms];
18
19       Sensor -> * : time=17ms;
20
21       Sensor[0] -> Gateway , time = 5ms;
22       Sensor[0] <- Gateway : q=2.5, time = 5ms;
23       Sensor[1] <- Sensor[2] : q=3.5, time = 5ms;
24
25       Sensor[2:5] -> Sensor[3];
26       Sensor[2:] -> Sensor[4] : time = 15ms;
27       Sensor[:2] -> Sensor[5] : q=3.5, time = 15ms;
28
29       Sensor -> Server[i+1] : q=2;
30       Sensor[0:5] <- Server[i-2];
31       Sensor[4:] <- Server[i-3];
32     }
33   }
34 }
```

Listing 4.1: The example of a topology definition connected with *channel_name* tag.

Three possible ways of declaring the left set of hosts are presented in Listing 4.1.

1. The first way (without indices) covers all hosts with a given name. The rules are presented in lines 17 and 29 (Listing 4.1). They can be applied in the main communication structure as it does not specify the index of the repeated hosts.

2. The second way (with one index in square brackets) has to do with selection of only one host that with a given index. The rules are presented in lines 21, 22 and 23 (Listing 4.1).

3. The third way (with indices and colon in square brackets) refers to the selection of the range of hosts with the indices larger than or equal to the first index and lower than or equal to the second one. Zero is used if the first index is not specified. A number of hosts is made use of if the second index is not specified. The rules in lines 25, 26, 27, 30 and 31 (Listing 4.1) are given as an example.

Besides the above described methods, two other methods can also be used for declaration of the right set of hosts.

1. Specification of the hosts can be made using a special i index and its increased or decreased value. Then there are selected hosts with the indices shifted by given values toward all hosts from the left. The example rules are in lines 29, 30, and 31 in Listing 4.1. The first rule (line 29) defines the links between all Sensors and their next neighbors (forming a line) while the second one (line 30) defines the links between Sensors with the indices 0, 1, 2, 3, 4, and 5 and their second predecessor. The last rule (line 31) creates the link between Sensors with the index larger than or equal to 4 and their third predecessors. When a host does not have a selected neighbor, the link is not created. This type of rule can be used only in the version structure when the indices are used on the left side.

2. As star sign (*) representing the medium can replace the hosts. Then the quality parameter is not defined. The direction can be only right (from the left hosts to the medium). The parameters for broadcasting a message are defined by means of this type of rule. The example rule is in line 19 in Listing 4.1.

4.1.2 Quality of connections

Parametrization is necessary in topology for each connection. Parameters are applied for communication steps analysis. A default value characterizes each parameter. The default value is defined by preceding its name with *default_* and placing it in the *medium* structure. The default value is used in case the parameter is not defined for a particular connection.

Parameter **q** is the one required for representing the quality (weight) of connection between the hosts (the lower the value, the better the quality). The routing algorithm uses the quality parameter for finding the best route between two hosts in a multi-hop communication. This value is the result of the environmental factors (e.g., distance, barriers, etc.). The algorithm in question defines this parameter statically or estimates dynamically. The structure presented in the next section is the one where this algorithm can be defined.

4.1.3 Transmission time

The time analysis introducing the **time** parameter is another essential factor in communication analysis. The time of data transmission between the hosts or between the host and the medium (used for the broadcast) is represented by the proposed parameter. One can specify its value as:

- a constant or random number from a specified range in seconds or milliseconds;

- a value depending on the size of data: mspb, mspB, kbps, mbps (constant or random value from a specified range per bit or byte);

- a constant or random value from a specified range in seconds or milliseconds per each block of data (e.g., 100ms per each 16 bytes);

- the result of an algorithm in seconds or milliseconds (the algorithms are described in Section 4.1.4).

The communication time depends on the number of receivers. Below are the main rules:

- In the case where a message is sent to one receiver, the communication time equals the result of the time parameter. With the result the time of sender and receiver is increased.

- In the case where a message is sent to zero receivers (nobody is waiting for a message), the communication time equals the result of the **time** parameter between the host and the medium (broadcast time). The increase is found only in the time of the receiver.

- The communication time differs for all hosts when a message is sent to many receivers and is equal to the result of time parameter between the sender and the given receiver result. With the varying times of communication between the sender and receiver, receiving times can be different.

4.1.4 Transmission time – Algorithms structure

Taking the transmission time bandwidth in a medium is the easiest way to determine it. Yet there is some inaccuracy connected with it. For a more precise determination, the algorithm structure is added, enabling the addition of non-linear values of metrics.

Listing 4.2 gives an example of such an algorithm. The transmission time between two TelosB motes [60] is calculated and it is equal to constant 18 ms plus 0.12 ms per each byte. In order to handle messages the while loop is used with a payload larger than 110 bytes being the maximal size of the payload in ZigBee. Then it is divided into many packets, each with 110 bytes payload size.

```
 1  algorithms {
 2      alg wsn_time(msg) {
 3          sending = 18;
 4          size_factor = 0.12;
 5          full_time = 0.0;
 6          msg_size = size(msg);
 7          while (msg_size > 0) {
 8              current_size = 110;
 9              if (msg_size < 110) {
10                  current_size = msg_size;
11              }
12              full_time += sending + current_size * 0.12;
13              msg_size = msg_size - 110;
14          }
15          return full_time;
16      }
17  }
```

Listing 4.2: The example of algorithm for communication time.

An algorithm (started with a word *alg*) is considered to be a function. It possesses one parameter – a message sent during the communication step or the function call expression during an operation process.

The algorithm is built of arithmetic operations, constructions form the C language: **if, while** and the two predefined function calls:

- *quality* – applied only in the algorithm to calculate the communication the step and returning the quality of the link between the sender and the receiver (parameter **q**);

- *size* – taking one argument and returning its size.

With the algorithm parameter the function size is called the argument to get the sent message size which is called the function or its indexed element.

One can find the exemplary algorithm as the value of the communication parameter in Listing 4.1 (line 17). The time of message transmission between the sensor and the gateway hosts is calculated using the **wsn_time** algorithm. The return value is expressed in milliseconds.

4.2 Packet filtering

Packet filtering determines which packets are to be sent to the selected host. The kind of packet is specified by the receiver, and the type of packet transmitted is determined by the sender. Thus many hosts can communicate on the same channel.

4.2.1 Channels

Listing 4.3 gives the channel's structure. A tag determining channel characteristics, the medium name is the value in the square brackets at the end of the channel definition. It is used for linking the channel with the medium. One medium can have many channels and each of them is treated independently as having the same characteristics (topology, topology parameters, etc.).

Listing 4.3 presents the example. There is a channel structure which contains one channel named channel WSN. It has an unlimited buffer of messages (the star sign) and is connected with the medium by a communication structure called an air channel.

```
1  channels { channel channel_WSN (*)[air_channel]; }
```

Listing 4.3: Definition of one channel called channel_WSN with *air_channel* characteristics.

4.2.2 Input and output messages

The example of the packet filtering introducing a new (optional) part of the **in** instruction in QoP-ML (input message) is given in Listing 4.4.

```
1  in(channel_name : var_name : |*, id(), init_cmd()|);
```

Listing 4.4: Example of the extended in instruction.

The message from the channel *channel_name* is expected by this instruction and it is saved in a *var_name* variable. The beginning of a new part is marked with the second colon. The first three values of an incoming message are specified by the values between | signs. In the case of different values of the message, the instruction **in** will still wait for delivery of the message with three specified values.

This feature can be used to reject the packets not addressed to the host (or process). Then new, predefined functions: *id* (Listing 4.4) and *pid* executed with one optional parameter must be used. The identification number of host (id) or process (pid) with the same name as the passed argument is returned when the parameter is specified. Otherwise the identification of host or process in which the function is executed is returned.

The designer can use four types of elements as the filtering value in the *in* instruction:

■ simple function call, the *init_cmd()* in Listing 4.4;

■ functions *id* and *pid*, described above;

■ variable name when its value should be used to filter the packet;

■ sign * (star) that states any value is accepted.

Listing 4.4 shows the host waiting for the message having any value in the first element, its identification in the second. The third is the **init_cmd** function. The host can wait for many messages from many other hosts. In order to distinguish these messages the third parameter has been used as the message type. In Listing 4.4 the host waits for a message that is in some way understood as the initial command (**init_cmd()**). However, the number of parameters is not fixed and the designer can use a different number of filtering parameters than the three used in the above example.

As regards the sending host, the filtered values must be included in the packet filtering. Message **MSG**, as an example, is presented in Listing 4.5. It is sent through the channel *channel_name*. Being 4-tuple it contains: the sender's identification, the receiver's identification, the message type, and the data. The instruction in Listing 4.4 can filter this type of message.

```
1  MSG = (id(), id(Sensor), init_cmd(), data());
2  out(channel_name : MSG);
```

Listing 4.5: Example of out instruction sending a message with the header.

Based on the QoP-ML the syntax and semantics of our instruction do not change and it accepts any variable. In the case of the packet filtering feature used, the variable values must be tuples due to the fact that the **in** instruction needs access to their indexed elements.

When the hosts are replicated it is possible to send back a message to the sender introducing the **id** and **pid** predefined functions.

4.3 Routing

The routing, which is an integral part of all networks, can be defined as static with all connections defined in advance, and not possible to change or dynamic with the path from the host A to B modified in time. Topology is used to find the shortest path between a pair of hosts (using the Dijkstra algorithm) in the model of communication presented. The connection qualities defined in the topology are used for comparing the edges. The QoP-ML multi-hop communication problem is solved using the routing feature. It is possible for the sender to check which host is the next hop in the path between the sender and receiver by applying the new, predefined function - *routing_next* with three parameters. The first parameter is the topology name, the second is the receiver's identification, and the third is the sender's identification (that of the host which calls the function by default). The sender's next hop host identification is returned by the function.

Listing *routing_next* gives the example of the *routing_next* function use. The identification of the next two hops in the path to the Gateway host is obtained by the host, and a message with the information as to who is the second hop is sent by him.

```
1 FIRST_NEXT_ID = routing_next(air_channel, id(Sensor));
2 SECOND_NEXT_ID = routing_next(air_channel, id(Sensor), ↵
    FIRST_NEXT_ID);
3 MSG = (id(), FIRST_NEXT_ID, init_cmd(), data(), SECOND_NEXT_ID);
4 out(channel_name : MSG);
```

Listing 4.6: Obtaining the addresses of the next two hops and sending the message.

4.4 Energy analysis

The energy analysis module is used for evaluating the energy consumption of the system being modeled. To do this, the performance analysis process must contain the time analysis module because its task is to track operation times and communication steps. The total energy used by simple operations based only on the CPU (security operations, other arithmetic operations, etc.) and communication operations (listening, receiving and sending) using the radio is defined as the energy consumption. It is calculated from:

$$E_{op} = T * I * V \tag{4.1}$$

where:

- E_{op} is the energy consumption of the operation,

- T is the time of the operation,

- I is the electric current of the operation,

- V is the voltage of the host.

The time analysis module is used for time retrieval and the constant is the voltage defined for each host. Current, which is the last factor, is defined either independently or for a group operations. A metric with the current header is used for specification of its value. The medium structure is used to define current in communication steps.

Then the energy consumption for each host is evaluated by the energy module analysis based on:

$$E_H = E_{H_{CPU}} + E_{H_{COMM}} \tag{4.2}$$

where:

- E_H is the host energy consumption,

- $E_{H_{CPU}}$ is the sum of energy consumption of all CPU operations plus those with separately specified electric current,

- $E_{H_{COMM}}$ is the sum of energy consumption of all the communication steps (sending, receiving, and listening).

The three parameters: **sending_current receiving_current**, and **listening_current** describing the electric current in three different states, are included in the energy analysis module. When the host is waiting for a message on the channel, the electric current is defined by the listening current. In the transmission state it is divided into: **sending_current** and **receiving_current** as data can be sent by the hosts with different electric current than received (e.g., depending on the signal strength the sending current in sensors can vary).

The constant in milliamps or the result of an algorithm in milliamps can specify the current value. The electrical current of the sending message process can be calculated using the *wsn_sending_current* algorithm (line 10, Listing 4.7). Milliamps – the unit defined in square brackets – are used for determination of the value. The algorithm's structure must contain the *wsn_sending_current* algorithm which returns the current value. Listing 4.7 presents an example of this kind of algorithm.

```
1  communication {
2    medium[wsn] {
3      default_q = 1;
4      default_t = 20ms;
5      default_sending_current = 14.8 mA;
6      default_receiving_current = 22.4 mA;
7      default_listening_current = 1.8 mA;
8
9      topology {
10       Sensor <-> Gateway : sending_current=wsn_sending_current[↩
             mA];
11     }
12   }
13 }
```

Listing 4.7: Algorithm used to calculate the value of metric.

4.5   Case study – Multihop authentication protocols for WSN

In [60] several protocols, enabling joining a node to a multihop WSN in a secure way was proposed. These protocols can be modeled and energy can be analyzed thanks to the advanced communication module and energy module which were described in the previous section. In this section these protocols will be described and after this the QoP-ML model will be presented. These protocols can be divided into two classes:

1. Direct Join to the Sink (DJS): a node joins directly through the sink.

2. Indirect Join to the Sink (IJS): a node joins the network through intermediate nodes in order to reach the sink.

The public key Elliptic Curve Cryptography (ECC) with the parameters secp160r1 from Standards for Efficient Cryptography Group [81] is used. In the next section the main idea of the ECC standard is presented.

Let us assume that each node N knows the public key $pk(S)$ of the sink S and also its own pair of private and public keys, denoted $(pk(N), sk(N))$ respectively, before deployment. As follows from ECC, we have that $pk(N) = sk(N) \times G$, where G is a generator point of the elliptic curve. Based on this, a shared key with the sink S can be computed by each node N by means of a variation of the Diffie–Hellman key exchange without interaction between the nodes, denoted $K_{DH}(N, S)$. In order to preserve energy the computations can be performed by the sink and by all nodes before deployment.

■ The sink knows its own secret key $sk(S)$ and the public key $pk(N)$ of a node N. The sink computes $K_{DH}(N, S) = sk(S) \times pk(N)$.

■ Node N multiplies his secret key $sk(N)$ by the public key of the sink $pk(S)$ to get $K_{DH}(N, S)$.

Both computations obtain the same shared key since:

$$
\begin{aligned}
K_{DH}(N, S) &= sk(N) \times pk(S) = sk(N) \times (sk(S) \times G) = (sk(N) \times G) \times sk(S) \\
&= pk(N) \times sk(S)
\end{aligned}
$$

Notations

Next, to describe exchanged messages in order protocols the following notations are used:

■ I: a new node that initiates the protocol,

■ R: a neighbor of node I,

■ S: the sink of the network (also called base station),

■ J_i: the i-th intermediate node between R and S,

■ n_A: a nonce generated by node A,

■ $pk(A)$: the public key of node A,

■ $sk(A)$: the secret (private) key of node A,

■ $K(I, S)$: the session key between I and S,

■ NK: the symmetric network key between all the nodes of the network,

■ $K_{DH}(N, S)$: the shared symmetric key between N and S using the Diffie–Hellman key exchange without the above described interaction.

■ $\{x\}_k$: the encryption of message x with the symmetric or asymmetric key k.

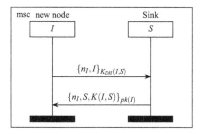

Figure 4.1: DJS_{orig}: **Direct Join to Sink. The node I joins directly to the network by communicating directly with the sink S.**

4.5.1 Direct join to sink: DJS_{orig}

The DJS_{orig} protocol is the original one from [59]. Based on it new nodes in the range of sink, join the network directly as shown in Figure 4.1. A direct request is sent to S by the new node to establish a session key with it. The process is joined with the sink S computing the symmetric key $K_{DH}(I,S)$. Next a nonce n_I, is generated and its identity added to form the request $\{n_I, I\}$ which is encrypted with $K_{DH}(I,S)$ and sent to S. After reception, $K_{DH}(I,S)$ is computed in order to decrypt the request. Next the identity of I is verified and a new session key $K(I,S)$ is generated. The joint response contains n_I, the identity of S, and the new symmetric session key. The response is encrypted using $pk(I)$ and is sent to I. The response with its secret key $sk(I)$ can be decrypted only by I. It is noted that n_I helps I to authenticate S.

4.5.2 Indirect protocols to join the sink

Four different protocols enabling joining the network by a new node out of range S are discussed in this section. The network can be joined by a new node through a neighbor node already authenticated in the network. The difference between these protocols consists in the ways of establishing the authentication of nodes between R and S and forwarding messages between them. Each proposed protocol can be described. The main difference between the proposed protocols is presented in Table 4.1.

The main idea included in protocols is to make it possible for the application to choose a protocol according to its constraints concerning capacities and the need for a security level. As for a number of cryptographic operations, it is less time consuming to use the IJS_{orig} protocol on the condition that all nodes in the network are trusted ones. The $IJS_{NK,dec/enc}$ and $IJS_{K,dec/enc}$ protocols are similar in terms of the number of operations but the latter is more resilient to node capture as it uses different keys along the route to the sink. Most cryptographic operations for the authentication process on the sink are done by the network using $IJS_{NK,onion}$ which reduces the computation time on intermediate nodes.

Table 4.1: Operations on intermediate nodes for the indirect join protocols.

Protocol name	Authentication	Key type	from R to S		from S to R	
			Encrypt	Decrypt	Encrypt	Decrypt
IJS_{orig}	no	DH with S	no	no	no	no
$IJS_{NK,dec/enc}$	yes	network key	yes	yes	yes	yes
$IJS_{K,dec/enc}$	yes	session key	yes	yes	yes	yes
$IJS_{NK,onion}$	yes	network key	yes	no	no	yes

4.5.2.1 Protocol: IJS_{orig}

The protocol presented in [59] is original, allowing the network to be joined by a new node through the neighbor node R. As can be seen in Figure 4.2 an indirect request is sent to S by the new node to establish a session key with R, which sends the request to S through the intermediate node J_i. It should be noted that the request and response are not modified when being forwarded by J_i. No message can be decrypted by node J_i because of the key used for encryption. The messages encrypted with $K_{DH}(I,S)$ can be decrypted only by nodes I and S, and those encrypted with $K_{DH}(R,S)$ only by R and S.

In this protocol the intermediate nodes are assumed to be trusted. Thus there is no resilience against attacks from inside by the intermediate nodes. An intruder playing the role of an intermediate node cannot be detected by either the sink or the new node.

Here, three protocols that allow joining a new node to the network without trusting any intermediate node are proposed. Each solution uses a different approach for solving this question and has been proven secure using the Scyther Tool [23].

4.5.2.2 Protocol: $IJS_{NK,dec/enc}$

The aim of this protocol is to ensure authentication between all nodes adding a nonce on each hop as well as decrypting and encrypting the exchanged messages in the following way.

The $IJS_{NK,dec/enc}$ protocol presented in Figure 4.3 enables new nodes to join the network through a neighbor node R by means of the network key for encryption/decryption on intermediate nodes. A request containing a nonce with its own identity or the identity of R is sent by the node I. Then a nonce is generated and added to the initial request by the node R before being encrypted with NK and forwarded to J. After reception, the request is decrypted by node n_J, and a new nonce n_J is generated and added to the received request. Finally, the results is encrypted using NK. After the response message is received by J, it is decrypted using NK and n_J is extracted. The response message is sent to R while keeping n_R in it. It should be noted that the nonce values n_I, n_R and n_J contributed to I, R and J authentication by S and secured, forwarding the request by previously authenticated nodes.

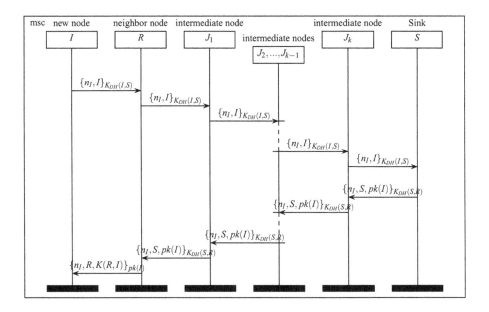

Figure 4.2: IJS_{orig}: **Indirect Join to Sink, the original version. The intermediate node between R and S forwards messages without any encryption or decryption.**

As proved by the Scyther Tool [23] this protocol is secure. However, a message has to be decrypted and encrypted by each intermediate node with the same key that is the network key. Yet there are some drawbacks, namely, these cryptographic operations are resource consuming, and with the same key a node capture attack is moire dangerous, for the attacker is able to decrypt the authentication process of all nodes. The next protocol avoids such a risk by using a session key.

4.5.2.3 Protocol: $IJS_{K,dec/enc}$

$IJS_{K,dec/enc}$ protocol is presented in Figure 4.4. $IJS_{K,dec/enc}$ and $IJS_{NK,dec/enc}$ differ in the following.

■ The request and response are encrypted and decrypted between R and S with the symmetric session key $K(J_i, J_{i+1})$ which was established in the process of the earlier join phases.

■ All identities of intermediate nodes are also added to the initial request sent by I.

The node I is assumed to be able to obtain a secure path to S from R, which is already known by R, as it was able to join the network and to build it using its routing protocol.

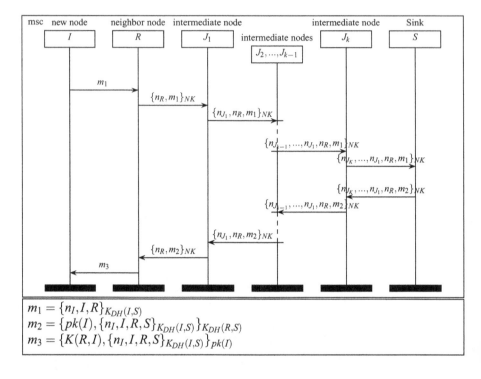

$$m_1 = \{n_I, I, R\}_{K_{DH}(I,S)}$$
$$m_2 = \{pk(I), \{n_I, I, R, S\}_{K_{DH}(I,S)}\}_{K_{DH}(R,S)}$$
$$m_3 = \{K(R,I), \{n_I, I, R, S\}_{K_{DH}(I,S)}\}_{pk(I)}$$

Figure 4.3: $IJS_{NK,dec/enc}$**: Indirect Join to Sink. The intermediate nodes** J_i **decrypt, add a nonce value and encrypt the result message before forwarding it. It uses the network key to encrypt/decrypt this message.**

The previous protocol is enhanced by this one by means of session keys. However, there are some problems doing cryptographic operations on intermediate nodes. The attempt is made to avoid overcharging intermediate nodes in the next protocol performing most operations on the sink.

4.5.2.4   Protocol: $IJS_{NK,onion}$

The description of the $IJS_{NK,onion}$ protocol in Figure 4.5 is an enhancement over $IJS_{NK,dec/enc}$ as for a number of operations performed by intermediate nodes.

Intermediate nodes should be helped to save time and energy. A nonce can be added to the initial request and the result can be encrypted before forwarding it by an intermediate node J_i using NK. When received, the response message can be decrypted, the nonce n_{J_i} can be extracted and retrieved, and the rest of the message can be forwarded to R by J_i. However, the encryption/decryption operations not done by J_i are accomplished by S, which is assumed to be more efficient in computing and possesses more energy than the other nodes of the network.

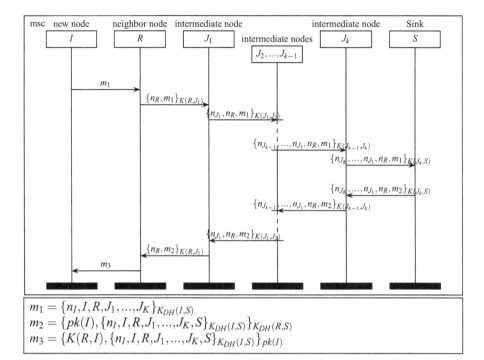

Figure 4.4: $IJS_{K,dec/enc}$: **Indirect Join to Sink. The intermediate nodes J_i decrypt, add a nonce value and encrypt the result message before forwarding it. They use the session key to encrypt/decrypt this message.**

The advantage of this protocol is the fact that it is more energy efficient for intermediate nodes but the disadvantage is its exposure because of node capture attack as in the case of the $IJS_{NK,dec/enc}$ protocol as the same network key is applied from the source node to the sink.

4.6   The WSN protocols modeling in QoP-ML

The five steps: protocol modeling, security metrics definition, process instantiation, QoP-ML processing and QoP evaluation are used in the QoP analysis process (Figure 2.2). They are described during the modeling of the WSN protocols in the next section. The four operations: function defining, equation defining, channel defining, and protocol flow description are included in the protocol modeling step.

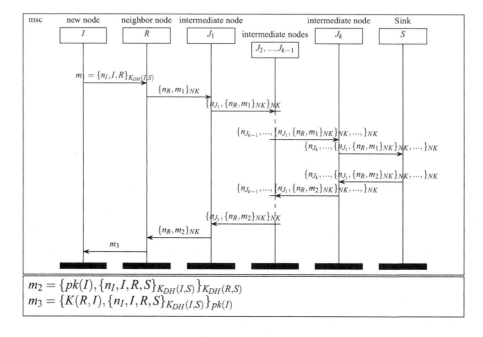

$$m_2 = \{pk(I), \{n_I, I, R, S\}_{K_{DH}(I,S)}\}_{K_{DH}(R,S)}$$
$$m_3 = \{K(R,I), \{n_I, I, R, S\}_{K_{DH}(I,S)}\}_{pk(I)}$$

Figure 4.5: $IJS_{NK,onion}$: **Indirect Join to Sink. The intermediate nodes J_i add a nonce and encrypt the request message, and forward it to S.**

4.6.1 Functions

The functions referring to the cryptographic operations required in the protocol are defined for the modeling of TLS. They are discussed below (Listing 4.8) and their description is presented in Table 4.2.

```
 1  functions
 2  {
 3      % List operations
 4      fun empty_list ();
 5      fun add_to_list (list , element );
 6      fun get_from_list (list );
 7      fun pop_list (list );
 8
 9      % Messages types
10      fun request_msg ();
11      fun response_msg ();
12
13      fun is_enc_with (K, D);
14
15      fun check_node (nodeID );
16      fun nonce ();
17      fun network_key ();
18      fun session_key ();
19      fun gen_new_session_key ();
```

```
20    fun sk(host_id);
21    fun pk(sk)[Time: key_size];
22    fun ecies_kdf_mac()[Time: key_size];
23    fun ecies_kdf()[Time: key_size];
24    fun ecies_enc(data, PK)[Time: inside_algorithm,key_size];
25    fun ecies_dec(data, SK)[Time: inside_algorithm,key_size];
26    fun ecies_temp_key()[Time: key_size];
27    fun ecies_mac();
28    fun s_enc(data, K)[Time: algorithm,key_size];
29    fun s_dec(data, K)[Time: algorithm,key_size];
30    fun dh_key(PK_ID1, SK_ID2);
31  }
```

Listing 4.8: The functions for WSN protocols.

Table 4.2: QoP-ML's functions for WSN protocols model – Description.

Function	Description
empty_list()	creates empty list
add_to_list(list, element)	adds element to the list
get_from_list(list)	gets element from the list
pop_list(list)	pops the list
request_msg()	requests the message
response_msg()	response the message
is_enc_with(K, D)	states that element D is encrypted by key K
check_node(nodeID)	checks if node nodeID can join network
nonce()	generates nonce
network_key()	returns the network key used by all nodes
session_key()	returns the session key between two nodes - in this model it is simplified to the same form as the network key
gen_new_session_key()	generates session key for new node
sk(host_id)	secret key of id
pk(sk)	public key for sk secret key
ecies_kdf_mac()	ecies key derivation function and MAC calculation before encryption
ecies_kdf()	ecies key derivation function before decryption
ecies_enc(data, PK)	assymetric encryption using ECIES algorithm
ecies_dec(data, SK)	assymetric decryption using ECIES algorithm
ecies_temp_key()	generates temporary key for encryption
ecies_mac()	generates MAC for encrypted message
s_enc(data, K)	symmetric encryption
s_dec(data, K)	symmetric decryption
dh_key(PK_ID1, SK_ID2)	generates Diffie-Hellman key between two nodes ID1 and ID2 using their public and secret keys

Table 4.3: QoP-ML's equations for WSN protocols – Description.

Function	Description
pop_list(add_to_list(L, E)) = L	pop/add element to list
get_from_list(add_to_list(L, E)) = E	get/add element to list
is_enc_with(K, s_enc(data, K)) = true	check if the data is encrypted
ecies_enc(ecies_dec(data, SK), pk(SK)) = data	asymmetric encryption/decryption
ecies_dec(ecies_enc(data, pk(SK)), SK) = data	asymmetric encryption/decryption
s_enc(s_dec(data, K), K) = data	symmetric encryption/decryption
s_dec(s_enc(data, K), K) = data	symmetric encryption/decryption
s_dec(s_enc(data, dh_key(pk(sk(ID1)), sk(ID2))), dh_key(pk(sk(ID2)), sk(ID1))) = data	symmetric decryption by the key generated by DH scheme
s_enc(s_dec(data, dh_key(pk(sk(ID1)), sk(ID2))), dh_key(pk(sk(ID2)), sk(ID1))) = data	symmetric encryption by the key generated by DH scheme

4.6.2   Equations

After defining the functions one can describe the relations between them (Listing 4.9). The description of this equation is presented in Table 4.3.

```
1  equations
2  {
3      % List equations
4      eq pop_list(add_to_list(L, E)) = L;
5      eq get_from_list(add_to_list(L, E)) = E;
6
7      % Cryptographic equations
8      eq is_enc_with(K, s_enc(data, K)) = true;
9      eq ecies_enc(ecies_dec(data, SK), pk(SK)) = data;
10     eq ecies_dec(ecies_enc(data, pk(SK)), SK) = data;
11     eq s_enc(s_dec(data, K), K) = data;
12     eq s_dec(s_enc(data, K), K) = data;
13     eq s_dec(s_enc(data, dh_key(pk(sk(ID1)), sk(ID2))), dh_key(←
           pk(sk(ID2)), sk(ID1))) = data;
14     eq s_enc(s_dec(data, dh_key(pk(sk(ID1)), sk(ID2))), dh_key(←
           pk(sk(ID2)), sk(ID1))) = data;
15 }
```

Listing 4.9: The equations for WSN protocols.

4.6.3   Channels

In the wireless sensor networks all nodes are using a wireless network in the ZigBee standard (IEEE 802.15.4), that is why one channel is defined (4.10).

```
1  channels
2  {
3      channel ch_WSN(*)[wsn];
4  }
```

Listing 4.10: The channels for WSN protocols.

4.6.4 Protocol flow

Abstracting the protocol flow is the last and the most important operation in modeling. Four types of nodes must by modeled for all WSN protocols presented in the case study.

1. The first type is the **New Node** which is the one which would like to join the network.

2. The second one is the **Neighbor** which is the node near the new node.

3. The third one is the **Sink** node which is the one to which all data are routed.

4. The fourth one is the **Forwarder** node which is one which is between the neighbor and the sink.

The number of forwarders can be changed and depends on the size of the network. In the protocol flow all types of nodes must modeled. This section will describe in detail the high hierarchy processes which refer to all nodes.

4.6.4.1 Host NewNode (Listing 4.11)

In Listing 4.11 one can see the model of **New Node** which will join to the network. The *host NewNode* includes one main process (*process Main*) which has ten subprocesses. The subprocess *Init160b* is responsible for creating asymmetric keys for yourself. The subprocess *MakeRequestWithNewNodeIdOnly* creates a request for authentication when the new node is next to the sink (no neighbors). The subprocess *MakeRequestWithNewNodeAndNeighborId* creates the request for authentication when a new node has one neighbor which is between the new node and the sink. The next subprocess *MakeRequestWithNewNode_NeighborAndIntermediateNodesIds* creates a request for authentication when the forwarders are located between the neighbor and the sink. The next subprocess *DecryptResponse_160b* decrypts the response for an authentication request. The next set of five subprocesses handles the received response but the type of operation which must be executed depends on the type of WSN protocols used. These subprocesses are named according to the version of the protocols analyzed and one can enumerate them: *HandleResponse_Direct_Original*, *HandleResponse_Indirect_Original*, *HandleResponse_Indirect_NK_EncDec*, *HandleResponse_Indirect_SessKey_EncDec*, *HandleResponse_Indirect_Onion*.

```
1  host NewNode(rr)(*)
2      {
3          #SK_NewNode = sk(id());
4          process Main(*)
5          {
6              nNN = nonce();
7
8              subprocess Init160b()
9              {
10                 PK_S       = pk(sk(id(Sink)))[160];
11                 PK_NewNode = pk(SK_NewNode)[160];
12                 D_NN_S = dh_key(PK_S, SK_NewNode);
13             }
14             subprocess MakeRequestWithNewNodeIdOnly(*)
15             {
16                 REQ = (nNN, add_to_list(empty_list(), id()));
17             }
18             subprocess MakeRequestWithNewNodeAndNeighbourId(*)
19             {
20                 L = empty_list();
21                 L = add_to_list(L, id());
22                 L = add_to_list(L, routing_next(wsn, id(Sink)));
23                 REQ = (nNN, L);
24             }
25             subprocess MakeRequestWithNewNode ←
                   _NeighbourAndIntermediateNodesIds(*)
26             {
27                 L = empty_list();
28                 L = add_to_list(L, id());
29                 NEXT_ID = routing_next(wsn, id(Sink));
30                 while (NEXT_ID != id(Sink))
31                 {
32                     L = add_to_list(L, NEXT_ID);
33                     NEXT_ID = routing_next(wsn, id(Sink), ←
                           NEXT_ID);
34                 }
35                 L = add_to_list(L, id(Sink));
36                 REQ = (nNN, L);
37             }
38             NEXT_ID = routing_next(wsn, id(Sink));
39             ENC_REQ = s_enc(REQ, D_NN_S)[AES-CTR,128];
40             ENC_REQ = (id(), NEXT_ID, request_msg(), ENC_REQ);
41             out(ch_WSN: ENC_REQ);
42             in(ch_WSN: NN_RESP_MSG: |*, id(), response_msg()|);
43             NN_RESP_PAYLOAD_WITH_MAC = NN_RESP_MSG[3];
44             NN_RESP_PAYLOAD = NN_RESP_PAYLOAD_WITH_MAC[0];
45             subprocess DecryptResponse_160b()
46             {
47                 ecies_kdf()[160];
48                 RESP = ecies_dec(NN_RESP_PAYLOAD, SK_NewNode)[←
                       AES,160];
49             }
50             subprocess HandleResponse_Direct_Original(*)
51             {
52                 nNN_from_response = RESP[0];
53                 SymKey_NN_N = RESP[2];
```

```
54|      }
55|      subprocess HandleResponse_Indirect_Original (*)
56|      {
57|          nNN_from_response = RESP[0];
58|          SymKey_NN_N = RESP[2];
59|      }
60|      subprocess HandleResponse_Indirect_NK_EncDec (*)
61|      {
62|          SymKey_NN_N = RESP[0];
63|          E_DH_RESP = RESP[1];
64|          DH_RESP = s_dec(E_DH_RESP, D_NN_S)[AES-CTR,128];
65|          nNN_from_response = DH_RESP[0];
66|      }
67|      subprocess HandleResponse_Indirect_SessKey_EncDec (*)
68|      {
69|          SymKey_NN_N = RESP[0];
70|          E_DH_RESP = RESP[1];
71|          DH_RESP = s_dec(E_DH_RESP, D_NN_S)[AES-CTR,128];
72|          nNN_from_response = DH_RESP[0];
73|      }
74|      subprocess HandleResponse_Indirect_Onion (*)
75|      {
76|          SymKey_NN_N = RESP[0];
77|          E_DH_RESP = RESP[1];
78|          DH_RESP = s_dec(E_DH_RESP, D_NN_S)[AES-CTR,128];
79|          nNN_from_response = DH_RESP[0];
80|      }
81|      if (nNN == nNN_from_response)
82|      {
83|          end;
84|      }
85|      else
86|      {
87|          stop;
88|      }
89|      }
90|  }
```

Listing 4.11: The host NewNode.

4.6.4.2 *Host Neighbor (Listing 4.12)*

In Listing 4.12 one can see the model of the **Neighbor** node near the new node, which will join to the network. The *host Neighbor* includes one main process (*process Main*) which has nine subprocesses. The subprocess *Init160b* is responsible for creating asymmetric keys for yourself. The next three subprocesses: *Forward_NK_EncDec_To_Sink*, *Forward_SessKey_EncDec_To_Sink*, and *Forward_Onion_To_Sink* forward received data to the sink. The difference between them refers to the type of WSN protocol used. The next four subprocesses are responsible for forwarding received messages to the new node, which differ of the used WSN protocol. Among them one can enumerate: *Forward_Original_To_NewNode*,

Forward_NK_EncDec_To_NewNode, Forward_SessKey_EncDec_To_NewNode, Forward_Onion_To_NewNode. The last subprocess *ECIESEncryptNRESP_160b* is responsible for asymmetric encryption of the data received.

```
 1  host Neighbour (rr)(*)
 2      {
 3          #MY_ID = id();
 4          #SK_Neighbour = sk(MY_ID);
 5          #NK  = network_key();
 6          #SessKey_J = session_key();
 7          process Main(*)
 8          {
 9              in(ch_WSN: MSG: |*, id(), request_msg()|);
10              MSG_PAYLOAD = MSG[3];
11              subprocess Init160b()
12              {
13                  PK_S = pk(sk(id(Sink)))[160];
14                  PK_Neighbour = pk(SK_Neighbour)[160];
15              }
16              DH_Neighbour_S = dh_key(PK_S, SK_Neighbour);
17              subprocess Forward_NK_EncDec_To_Sink(*)
18              {
19                  NONCES_LIST = empty_list();
20                  N = nonce();
21                  NONCES_LIST = add_to_list(NONCES_LIST, N);
22                  MSG_PAYLOAD_RAW = (NONCES_LIST, MSG_PAYLOAD);
23                  MSG_PAYLOAD = s_enc(MSG_PAYLOAD_RAW, NK)[AES-CTR←
                        ,128];
24              }
25              subprocess Forward_SessKey_EncDec_To_Sink(*)
26              {
27                  NONCES_LIST = empty_list();
28                  N = nonce();
29                  NONCES_LIST = add_to_list(NONCES_LIST, N);
30                  MSG_PAYLOAD_RAW = (NONCES_LIST, MSG_PAYLOAD);
31                  MSG_PAYLOAD = s_enc(MSG_PAYLOAD_RAW, SessKey_J)[←
                        AES-CTR,128];
32              }
33              subprocess Forward_Onion_To_Sink(*)
34              {
35                  N = nonce();
36                  MSG_PAYLOAD_RAW = (N, MSG_PAYLOAD);
37                  MSG_PAYLOAD = s_enc(MSG_PAYLOAD_RAW, NK)[AES-CTR←
                        ,128];
38              }
39              NEXT_ID = routing_next(wsn, id(Sink));
40              M_WITH_HEADER = (id(), NEXT_ID, request_msg(), ←
                    MSG_PAYLOAD);
41              out(ch_WSN: M_WITH_HEADER);
42              in(ch_WSN: MSG: |*, id(), response_msg()|);
43              MSG_PAYLOAD = MSG[3];
44              subprocess Forward_Original_To_NewNode(*)
45              {
46                  MSG_PAYLOAD_RAW = s_dec(MSG_PAYLOAD, ←
                        DH_Neighbour_S)[AES-CTR,128];
47                  SessionKey_NN_N = gen_new_session_key();
```

```
48      PK_NewNode = MSG_PAYLOAD_RAW [2];
49      MSG_PAYLOAD_TO_ENCRYPT = (MSG_PAYLOAD_RAW [0], id←
           (), SessionKey_NN_N);
50   }
51   subprocess Forward_NK_EncDec_To_NewNode(*)
52   {
53      MSG_PAYLOAD_RAW = s_dec(MSG_PAYLOAD, NK)[AES-CTR←
           ,128];
54      M2 = MSG_PAYLOAD_RAW [1];
55      SessionKey_NN_N = gen_new_session_key();
56      M2_RAW = s_dec(M2, DH_Neighbour_S)[AES-CTR,128];
57      PK_NewNode = M2_RAW [0];
58      MSG_PAYLOAD_TO_ENCRYPT = (SessionKey_NN_N, ←
           M2_RAW [1]);
59   }
60   subprocess Forward_SessKey_EncDec_To_NewNode(*)
61   {
62      MSG_PAYLOAD_RAW = s_dec(MSG_PAYLOAD, SessKey_J)[←
           AES-CTR,128];
63      M2 = MSG_PAYLOAD_RAW [1];
64      SessionKey_NN_N = gen_new_session_key();
65      M2_RAW = s_dec(M2, DH_Neighbour_S)[AES-CTR,128];
66      PK_NewNode = M2_RAW [0];
67      MSG_PAYLOAD_TO_ENCRYPT = (SessionKey_NN_N, ←
           M2_RAW [1]);
68   }
69   subprocess Forward_Onion_To_NewNode(*)
70   {
71      MSG_PAYLOAD_RAW = s_dec(MSG_PAYLOAD, NK)[AES-CTR←
           ,128];
72      M2 = MSG_PAYLOAD_RAW [1];
73      SessionKey_NN_N = gen_new_session_key();
74      M2_RAW = s_dec(M2, DH_Neighbour_S)[AES-CTR,128];
75      PK_NewNode = M2_RAW [0];
76      MSG_PAYLOAD_TO_ENCRYPT = (SessionKey_NN_N, ←
           M2_RAW [1]);
77   }
78   subprocess ECIESEncryptNRESP_160b()
79   {
80      ecies_kdf_mac()[160];
81      M = ecies_enc(MSG_PAYLOAD_TO_ENCRYPT, PK_NewNode←
           )[AES,160];
82      ECIES_RESP = (M, ecies_temp_key()[160], ←
           ecies_mac()[160]);
83      M_PAYLOAD = ECIES_RESP;
84   }
85   NEXT_ID = routing_next(wsn, id(NewNode));
86   M_WITH_HEADER = (id(), NEXT_ID, response_msg(), ←
           M_PAYLOAD);
87   out(ch_WSN: M_WITH_HEADER);
88   }
89 }
```

Listing 4.12: The host Neighbor.

4.6.4.3 Host Sink (Listing 4.13)

In Listing 4.13 one can see a model of the **Sink** node which is the node where the new node is authenticated. The *host Sink* includes one main process (*process Main*) which has ten subprocesses. The subprocess *Init160b* is responsible for creating asymmetric keys for the Sink. The next four subprocesses: *HandleRequest_Original*, *HandleRequest_NK_EncDec*, and *HandleRequest_SessKey_EncDec*, *HandleRequest_Onion* handle the requests from the new node (the operations executed depend on the version of the WSN protocols). The next subprocess (*MakeResponseToNewNodeDirectly_160b*) responds to the new node when it is located near the new node. The next four subprocesses respond to the neighbor, and type of the subprocess depends on the version of the WSN authentication protocol. Among them one can enumerate: *MakeResponseToNeighbour_Original*, *MakeResponseToNeighbour_NK_EncDec*, *MakeResponseToNeighbour_SessKey_EncDec*, and *MakeResponseToNeighbour_Onion*.

```
 1  host Sink(rr)(*)
 2      {
 3          #SK_S  = sk(id(Sink));
 4          #NK = network_key();
 5          #SessKey_J = session_key();
 6          process Main(*)
 7          {
 8              PREV_ID = id();
 9              NEXT_ID = routing_next(wsn, id(NewNode), PREV_ID);
10              while (NEXT_ID != id(NewNode)) {
11                  PREV_ID = NEXT_ID;
12                  NEXT_ID = routing_next(wsn, id(NewNode), PREV_ID↩
                        );
13              }
14              subprocess Init160b()
15              {
16                  PK_NewNode = pk(sk(id(NewNode)))[160];
17                  PK_Neighbour = pk(sk(PREV_ID))[160];
18              }
19              DH_S_Neighbour = dh_key(PK_Neighbour, SK_S);
20              DH_S_NewNode = dh_key(PK_NewNode, SK_S);
21              in(ch_WSN: M: |*, id(), request_msg()|);
22              M_PAYLOAD = M[3];
23              subprocess HandleRequest_Original(*)
24              {
25                  REQ = s_dec(M_PAYLOAD, DH_S_NewNode)[AES-CTR↩
                        ,128];
26                  NN_NONCE = REQ[0];
27                  IDS_LIST = REQ[1];
28              }
29              subprocess HandleRequest_NK_EncDec(*)
30              {
31                  M_PAYLOAD_RAW = s_dec(M_PAYLOAD, NK)[AES-CTR↩
                        ,128];
32                  NONCES_LIST = M_PAYLOAD_RAW[0];
33                  E_REQ = M_PAYLOAD_RAW[1];
34                  REQ = s_dec(E_REQ, DH_S_NewNode)[AES-CTR,128];
```

```
35      NN_NONCE = REQ[0];
36      IDS_LIST = REQ[1];
37  }
38  subprocess HandleRequest_SessKey_EncDec(*)
39  {
40      M_PAYLOAD_RAW = s_dec(M_PAYLOAD, SessKey_J)[AES-↩
            CTR,128];
41      NONCES_LIST = M_PAYLOAD_RAW[0];
42      E_REQ = M_PAYLOAD_RAW[1];
43      REQ = s_dec(E_REQ, DH_S_NewNode)[AES-CTR,128];
44      NN_NONCE = REQ[0];
45      IDS_LIST = REQ[1];
46  }
47  subprocess HandleRequest_Onion(*)
48  {
49      TMP_NONCES_LIST = empty_list();
50      E_DATA = M_PAYLOAD;
51      while (is_enc_with(NK, E_DATA) == true)
52      {
53          DATA = s_dec(E_DATA, NK)[AES-CTR,128];
54          TMP_NONCES_LIST = add_to_list(↩
                TMP_NONCES_LIST, DATA[0]);
55          E_DATA = DATA[1];
56      }
57      E_REQ = E_DATA;
58      REQ = s_dec(E_REQ, DH_S_NewNode)[AES-CTR,128];
59      NN_NONCE = REQ[0];
60      IDS_LIST = REQ[1];
61  }
62  check_node(newNodeId);
63  subprocess MakeResponseToNewNodeDirectly_160b(*)
64  {
65      SessionKey_NN_S = gen_new_session_key();
66      RESP = (NN_NONCE, id(), SessionKey_NN_S);
67      ecies_kdf_mac()[160];
68      E_RESP = ecies_enc(RESP, PK_NewNode)[AES,160];
69      ECIES_RESP = (E_RESP, ecies_temp_key()[160], ↩
            ecies_mac()[160]);
70      M_PAYLOAD = ECIES_RESP;
71  }
72  subprocess MakeResponseToNeighbour_Original(*)
73  {
74      RESP = (NN_NONCE, id(), PK_NewNode);
75      E_RESP = s_enc(RESP, DH_S_Neighbour)[AES-CTR↩
            ,128];
76      M_PAYLOAD = E_RESP;
77  }
78  subprocess MakeResponseToNeighbour_NK_EncDec(*)
79  {
80      IDS_LIST = add_to_list(IDS_LIST, id());
81      RESP_TO_NN_RAW = (NN_NONCE, IDS_LIST);
82      RESP_TO_NN = s_enc(RESP_TO_NN_RAW, DH_S_NewNode)↩
            [AES-CTR,128];
83      M2 = (PK_NewNode, RESP_TO_NN);
84      E_M2 = s_enc(M2, DH_S_Neighbour)[AES-CTR,128];
85      RESP = (NONCES_LIST, E_M2);
86      E_RESP = s_enc(RESP, NK)[AES-CTR,128];
```

```
 87              M_PAYLOAD = E_RESP;
 88          }
 89          subprocess MakeResponseToNeighbour_SessKey_EncDec(*)
 90          {
 91              IDS_LIST = add_to_list(IDS_LIST, id());
 92              RESP_TO_NN_RAW = (NN_NONCE, IDS_LIST);
 93              RESP_TO_NN = s_enc(RESP_TO_NN_RAW, DH_S_NewNode)↩
                    [AES-CTR,128];
 94              M2 = (PK_NewNode, RESP_TO_NN);
 95              E_M2 = s_enc(M2, DH_S_Neighbour)[AES-CTR,128];
 96              RESP = (NONCES_LIST, E_M2);
 97              E_RESP = s_enc(RESP, SessKey_J)[AES-CTR,128];
 98              M_PAYLOAD = E_RESP;
 99          }
100          subprocess MakeResponseToNeighbour_Onion(*)
101          {
102              IDS_LIST = add_to_list(IDS_LIST, id());
103              RESP_TO_NN_RAW = (NN_NONCE, IDS_LIST);
104              RESP_TO_NN = s_enc(RESP_TO_NN_RAW, DH_S_NewNode)↩
                    [AES-CTR,128];
105              M2 = (PK_NewNode, RESP_TO_NN);
106              E_M2 = s_enc(M2, DH_S_Neighbour)[AES-CTR,128];
107              M_PAYLOAD = E_M2;
108              while (TMP_NONCES_LIST != empty_list())
109              {
110                  N = get_from_list(TMP_NONCES_LIST);
111                  TMP_NONCES_LIST = pop_list(TMP_NONCES_LIST);
112                  M_PAYLOAD = (N, M_PAYLOAD);
113                  M_PAYLOAD = s_enc(M_PAYLOAD, NK)[AES-CTR↩
                        ,128];
114              }
115          }
116          NEXT_ID = routing_next(wsn, id(NewNode));
117          M = (id(), NEXT_ID, response_msg(), M_PAYLOAD);
118          out(ch_WSN: M);
119      }
120  }
```

Listing 4.13: The host Sink.

4.6.4.4   Host J_OriginalForwarder (Listing 4.14)

In Listing 4.14 one can see the model of the **Forwarder** node, which is located between the neighbor of the new node and the sink. This type of forwarder is used in the WSN authentication protocol named: *IJS*$_{orig}$. The *host J_OriginalForwarder* includes one main process (*process Main*) which has no subprocesses.

```
1  host J_OriginalForwarder(rr)(*)
2  {
3      process Main(*)
4      {
5          in(ch_WSN: M: |*, id(), request_msg()|);
6          M_PAYLOAD = M[3];
```

```
 7    NEXT_ID = routing_next(wsn, id(Sink));
 8    M = (id(), NEXT_ID, request_msg(), M_PAYLOAD);
 9    out(ch_WSN:M);
10    in(ch_WSN: M: |*, id(), response_msg()|);
11    M_PAYLOAD = M[3];
12    NEXT_ID = routing_next(wsn, id(NewNode));
13    M = (id(), NEXT_ID, response_msg(), M_PAYLOAD);
14    out(ch_WSN:M);
15         }
16    }
```

Listing 4.14: The forwarder in the WSN protocol – IJS_{orig}.

4.6.4.5 Host J_NK_EncDec (Listing 4.15)

In Listing 4.15 one can see the model of the **Forwarder** node which is located between the neighbor of the new node and the sink. This type of the forwarder is used in the WSN authentication protocol named: $IJS_{NK,dec/enc}$. The *host J_NK_EncDec* includes one main process (*process Main*) which has no subprocesses.

```
 1  host J_NK_EncDec(rr)(*)
 2    {
 3        #NK = network_key();
 4        process Main(*)
 5        {
 6            in(ch_WSN: M: |*, id(), request_msg()|);
 7            M_PAYLOAD = M[3];
 8            M_PAYLOAD_RAW = s_dec(M_PAYLOAD, NK)[AES-CTR,128];
 9            NONCES_LIST = M_PAYLOAD_RAW[0];
10            N = nonce();
11            NONCES_LIST = add_to_list(NONCES_LIST, N);
12            M_PAYLOAD_RAW = (NONCES_LIST, M_PAYLOAD_RAW[1]);
13            M_PAYLOAD = s_enc(M_PAYLOAD_RAW, NK)[AES-CTR,128];
14            NEXT_ID = routing_next(wsn, id(Sink));
15            M = (id(), NEXT_ID, request_msg(), M_PAYLOAD);
16            out(ch_WSN: M);
17            in(ch_WSN: M: |*, id(), response_msg()|);
18            M_PAYLOAD = M[3];
19            M_PAYLOAD_RAW = s_dec(M_PAYLOAD, NK)[AES-CTR,128];
20            NONCES_LIST = M_PAYLOAD_RAW[0];
21            NONCES_LIST = pop_list(NONCES_LIST);
22            M_PAYLOAD_RAW = (NONCES_LIST, M_PAYLOAD_RAW[1]);
23            M_PAYLOAD = s_enc(M_PAYLOAD_RAW, NK)[AES-CTR,128];
24            NEXT_ID = routing_next(wsn, id(NewNode));
25            M = (id(), NEXT_ID, response_msg(), M_PAYLOAD);
26            out(ch_WSN: M);
27         }
28    }
```

Listing 4.15: The forwarder in the WSN protocol – $IJS_{NK,dec/enc}$.

4.6.4.6   Host J_SessKey_EncDec (Listing 4.16)

In Listing 4.16 one can see the model of the **Forwarder** node which is located between the neighbor of the new node and the sink. This type of the forwarder is used
in the WSN authentication protocol named: $IJS_{K,dec/enc}$. The *host J_SessKey_EncDec*
includes one main process (*process Main*) which has no subprocesses.

```
 1  host  J_SessKey_EncDec(rr)(*)
 2      {
 3          #SessKey_J = session_key();
 4          process Main(*)
 5          {
 6              in(ch_WSN: M: |*, id(), request_msg()|);
 7              M_PAYLOAD = M[3];
 8              M_PAYLOAD_RAW = s_dec(M_PAYLOAD, SessKey_J)[AES-CTR↩
                    ,128];
 9              NONCES_LIST = M_PAYLOAD_RAW[0];
10              N = nonce();
11              NONCES_LIST = add_to_list(NONCES_LIST, N);
12              M_PAYLOAD_RAW = (NONCES_LIST, M_PAYLOAD_RAW[1]);
13              M_PAYLOAD = s_enc(M_PAYLOAD_RAW, SessKey_J)[AES-CTR↩
                    ,128];
14              NEXT_ID = routing_next(wsn, id(Sink));
15              M = (id(), NEXT_ID, request_msg(), M_PAYLOAD);
16              out(ch_WSN: M);
17              in(ch_WSN: M: |*, id(), response_msg()|);
18              M_PAYLOAD = M[3];
19              M_PAYLOAD_RAW = s_dec(M_PAYLOAD, SessKey_J)[AES-CTR↩
                    ,128];
20              NONCES_LIST = M_PAYLOAD_RAW[0];
21              NONCES_LIST = pop_list(NONCES_LIST);
22              M_PAYLOAD_RAW = (NONCES_LIST, M_PAYLOAD_RAW[1]);
23              M_PAYLOAD = s_enc(M_PAYLOAD_RAW, SessKey_J)[AES-CTR↩
                    ,128];
24              NEXT_ID = routing_next(wsn, id(NewNode));
25              M = (id(), NEXT_ID, response_msg(), M_PAYLOAD);
26              out(ch_WSN: M);
27          }
28      }
```

Listing 4.16: The forwarder in the WSN protocol – $IJS_{K,dec/enc}$.

4.6.4.7   Host J_Onion (Listing 4.17)

In Listing 4.17 one can see the model of the **Forwarder** node which is located between the neighbor of the new node and the sink. This type of the forwarder is used
in the WSN authentication protocol named: $IJS_{NK,onion}$. The *host J_Onion* includes
one main process (*process Main*) which has no subprocesses.

```
 1  host  J_Onion(rr)(*)
 2      {
 3          #NK = network_key();
```

```
 4    process Main(*)
 5    {
 6         in(ch_WSN: M: |*, id(), request_msg()|);
 7         M_PAYLOAD = M[3];
 8         N = nonce();
 9         M_PAYLOAD_RAW = (N, M_PAYLOAD);
10         M_PAYLOAD = s_enc(M_PAYLOAD_RAW, NK)[AES-CTR,128];
11         NEXT_ID = routing_next(wsn, id(Sink));
12         M = (id(), NEXT_ID, request_msg(), M_PAYLOAD);
13         out(ch_WSN: M);
14         in(ch_WSN: M: |*, id(), response_msg()|);
15         M_PAYLOAD = M[3];
16         M_PAYLOAD_RAW = s_dec(M_PAYLOAD, NK)[AES-CTR,128];
17         MY_N = M_PAYLOAD_RAW[0];
18         M_PAYLOAD = M_PAYLOAD_RAW[1];
19         NEXT_ID = routing_next(wsn, id(NewNode));
20         M = (id(), NEXT_ID, response_msg(), M_PAYLOAD);
21         out(ch_WSN: M);
22    }
23    }
```

Listing 4.17: The forwarder in the WSN protocol – *IJS$_{NK,onion}$*.

4.6.5   The algorithm structure

The time of message transmission between sensors is calculated using the **wsn_time** algorithm. Listing 4.18 presents the algorithm structure which is used in the case study. The transmission time between two nodes which are using *CC2420 radio* [6] is calculated and it is equal to constant 18 ms plus 0.12 ms per each byte. The time of message transmission between the sensor and the gateway hosts is calculated using the **wsn_time** algorithm. The return value is expressed in milliseconds.

```
1  algorithms {
2      alg wsn_time(msg) {
3          sending_headers = 18.28;
4          sending_data = size(msg[3]) * 0.12;
5          return sending_headers + sending_data;
6      }
7  }
```

Listing 4.18: The algorithm's structure for WSN protocols.

4.6.6   Security metrics

In the case study presented, three scenarios are analyzed. The architecture of the wireless sensor networks is the same, but three different types of sensors are used.

1. In the first scenario all the nodes are *MicaZ* [25]. They have *8MHz* CPU and 4-kbit of RAM memory.

2. In the second scenario all the nodes are *Imote2* [24] They have *13MHz* CPU and 256-kbit of RAM memory.

3. In the third scenario all the nodes are also *Imote2* [24] but with *104MHz* CPU and 256-kbit of RAM memory.

All the sensors use the same *CC2420 radio* [6].

Here four types of the host configuration (conf()) are defined. The first three refer to three types of scenarios. The first one is denoted as MicaZ, the second one as Imote_13Mhz and the third one as Imote_104Mhz. The fourth one, denoted as PC, refers to the Personal Computer which is used for **Protocol:** $IJS_{NK,onion}$. The security metrics for all operations required for these motes one can take from benchmarks presented in the literature. In our case study, benchmarks for the AES algorithm for MicaZ and Imote2 motes were taken from [30] and the ECIES encryption and decryption for MicaZ and Imote2 motes were from [55]. The benchmarks of the PC Computer are omitted (the times equal 0) because they are several orders of magnitude smaller than the sensors' motes.

Listing 4.19 presents the full security metrics for *MicaZ* mote.

```
1
2  metrics {
3
4  conf (MicaZ) {
5      CPU = 8MHz;
6      RAM = 4-kbit;
7  }
8
9  conf (Imote2_13Mhz) {
10     CPU = 13MHz;
11     RAM = 256-kbit;
12 }
13
14 conf (Imote2_104Mhz) {
15     CPU = 104MHz;
16     RAM = 256-kbit;
17 }
18
19 conf (PC) {
20     CPU = Pentium Dual-Core T4200 2GHz;
21 }
22
23 data(MicaZ) {
24     primhead[function][size:exact(B)];
25     primitive[nonce][4];
26     primitive[id][1];
27     primitive[gen_new_session_key][16];
28     primitive[session_key][16];
29     primitive[network_key][16];
30     primitive[dh_key][16];
31     primitive[empty_list][0];
32     #
33     primhead[function][key_size][size:exact(b)];
34     primitive[pk][160][320];
```

```
35    primitive[ecies_temp_key][160][160];
36    primitive[ecies_mac][160][160];
37    #
38    primhead[function][size:sum_ratio];
39    primitive[add_to_list][1:1,2:1];
40    #
41    primhead[function][size:ratio];
42    primitive[pop_list][1:1];
43    #
44    primhead[function][alg][key_size][time:block(ms,B)][size:←
          ratio];
45    primitive[s_enc][AES-CTR][128][1:25.2:16][1:1];
46    #
47    primhead[function][alg][key_size][time:block(ms,B)][size:←
          nested];
48    primitive[s_dec][AES-CTR][128][1:25.2:16][1:1];
49    #
50    primhead[function][key_size][time:exact(ms)];
51    primitive[ecies_kdf_mac][160][61376.63];
52    primitive[ecies_kdf][160][31847.08];
53    #
54    primhead[function][inside_algorithm][key_size][time:block(ms←
          ,B)][size:ratio];
55    primitive[ecies_enc][AES][160][1:25.2:16][1:1];
56    #
57    primhead[function][inside_algorithm][key_size][time:block(ms←
          ,B)][size:nested];
58    primitive[ecies_dec][AES][160][1:25.2:16][1:1];
59    #
60    primhead[function][current:exact(mA)];
61    primitive[cpu][8];
62 }
63
64 }
```

Listing 4.19: The metrics for WSN.

Most of the security metrics are the same for all type of motes. This is because the standard size of the different data structures is defined there, as well as the ratio of the operations, etc. For *Imote2* only the part of the security metrics which refers to the CPU operation is presented and they are unique for this mote. Listing 4.20 presents the unique part of the security metrics for an *Imote2* mote with 13Mhz CPU.

```
1
2 metrics {
3
4 data(Imote2_13Mhz) {
5
6    primhead[function][key_size][time:exact(ms)];
7    primitive[ecies_kdf_mac][160][5498.89];
8    primitive[ecies_kdf][160][2796.47];
9    #
10   primhead[function][inside_algorithm][key_size][time:block(ms←
          ,B)][size:ratio];
```

```
11    primitive[ecies_enc][AES][160][1:15.4:16][1:1];
12    #
13    primhead[function][inside_algorithm][key_size][time:block(ms←
          ,B)][size:nested];
14    primitive[ecies_dec][AES][160][1:15.4:16][1:1];
15    #
16    primhead[function][current:exact(mA)];
17    primitive[cpu][44];
18 }
19
20 \begin{lstlisting}[caption=The metrics for WSN., label=l.wsn.sm]
```

Listing 4.20: The metrics for WSN.

Listing 4.21 presents the unique part of the security metrics for an *Imote2* mote with 104Mhz CPU.

```
1
2 metrics {
3
4
5 data(Imote2_104Mhz) {
6
7     primhead[function][key_size][time:exact(ms)];
8     primitive[ecies_kdf_mac][160][687.33];
9     primitive[ecies_kdf][160][349.55];
10    #
11    primhead[function][inside_algorithm][key_size][time:block(ms←
          ,B)][size:ratio];
12    primitive[ecies_enc][AES][160][1:1.9:16][1:1];
13    #
14    primhead[function][inside_algorithm][key_size][time:block(ms←
          ,B)][size:nested];
15    primitive[ecies_dec][AES][160][1:1.9:16][1:1];
16    #
17    primhead[function][current:exact(mA)];
18    primitive[cpu][66];
19 }
```

Listing 4.21: The metrics for WSN.

Listing 4.22 presents the unique part of the security metrics for a PC with 2GHz CPU.

```
1
2
3 data(PC) {
4     primhead[function][alg][key_size][time:exact(ms)][size:ratio←
          ];
5     primitive[s_enc][AES-CTR][128][0][1:1];
6     #
```

```
 7     primhead [function][alg][key_size][time:exact(ms)][size:↩
           nested];
 8     primitive[s_dec][AES-CTR][128][0][1:1];
 9     #
10     primhead [function][size:sum_ratio];
11     primitive[add_to_list][1:1,2:1];
12     #
13     primhead [function][size:ratio];
14     primitive[pop_list][1:1];
15     #
16     primhead [function][current:exact(mA)];
17     primitive[cpu][0];
18     }
19
20  }
```

Listing 4.22: The metrics for WSN.

4.6.7   *Process instantiation*

In the case study five WSN authentication protocols are modeled, one for direct join-ing to the sink (Listing 4.23) and four where intermediate nodes are located be-tween new node and sink(Listings 4.24, 4.25, 4.26, 4.27). Moreover, three scenarios are taken into account, which differ on the types of sensor motes used. In all the listings presented the protocol instantiation for *MicaZ* motes is presented (scenario 1). For other scenarios (different types of motes) only the argument of the func-tion: set host must be changed, where the Sink mote *MicaZ* is defined as set host Sink(MicaZ). For an Imote2 with 13MHz CPU the set host function for Sink should be defined according to the security metrics structure as: set host Sink(Imote2_13Mhz).

In the advanced communication modeling and energy efficiency analysis one has to define communication and topology structure. It must be defined for all defined versions. In our case study in the communication structure the communication qual-ity is equal to 1 and the wsn_time algorithm will be used for calculating the time of data transmission. Also, the default current for three types of radio states must be defined: sending, receiving and listening. The current for these motes can be taken from a datasheet of the motes [25, 24]. After defining the communication parameters the topology is defined. In the direct joint to sink protocol (Listing 4.23) only one communication path is defined between a new node and the sink. For the indirect join to sink protocols, the additional paths in the topology are defined, which join a new node with neighbors, the neighbors with forwarders, and the forwarders with the sink.

Additionally, the simulations for the different number of forwarders (interme-diate nodes) can be calculated for indirect join to sink protocols. For example, in Listing 4.24 processes were executed which simulated the original indirect join to sink protocol with 10 forwarders located between the new node and the sinks (`run host J_OriginalForwarder(*)10`).

```
1
2
3   version DirectJoinToSink_160b {
4
5       set host Sink(MicaZ);
6       set host NewNode(MicaZ);
7
8       run host Sink(*) {
9           run Main(Init160b,HandleRequest_Original ,←
                MakeResponseToNewNodeDirectly_160b)
10      }
11      run host NewNode(*) {
12          run Main(Init160b,MakeRequestWithNewNodeIdOnly ,←
                DecryptResponse_160b ,HandleResponse_Direct_Original)
13      }
14
15      communication
16      {
17          medium[wsn] {
18              default_q = 1;
19                  default_time = wsn_time [ms];
20              default_sending_current = 17.4 mA;
21              default_receiving_current = 19.7 mA;
22              default_listening_current = 0.02 mA;
23
24          topology
25          {
26              Sink <-> NewNode;
27          }
28      }
29  }
30 }
```

Listing 4.23: The version structure for direct join to sink protocol.

In Listing 4.24 the indirect join to sink protocol is presented in its original version.

```
1
2   version IndirectJoinToSink_Original_160b_10 {
3
4   set host Sink(MicaZ);
5   set host Neighbour(MicaZ);
6   set host NewNode(MicaZ);
7   set host J_OriginalForwarder(MicaZ);
8
9   run host Sink(*) {
10      run Main(Init160b,HandleRequest_Original ,←
            MakeResponseToNeighbour_Original)
11  }
12  run host Neighbour(*) {
```

```
13    run Main(Init160b,Forward_Original_To_NewNode,←
          ECIESEncryptNRESP_160b)
14  }
15  run host J_OriginalForwarder(*){10} {
16    run Main(*)
17  }
18  run host NewNode(*) {
19    run Main(Init160b,MakeRequestWithNewNodeIdOnly,←
          DecryptResponse_160b,HandleResponse_Indirect_Original)
20  }
21
22  communication
23  {
24    medium[wsn] {
25      default_q = 1;
26      default_time = wsn_time [ms];
27      default_sending_current = 17.4 mA;
28      default_receiving_current = 19.7 mA;
29      default_listening_current = 0.02 mA;
30
31      topology
32      {
33      NewNode <-> Neighbour;
34      Neighbour <-> J_OriginalForwarder[0];
35      J_OriginalForwarder <-> J_OriginalForwarder[i+1];
36      J_OriginalForwarder[9] <-> Sink;
37      }
38    }
39  }
40 }
```

Listing 4.24: The version structure for the indirect join to sink protocol is presented in its original version.

In Listing 4.25 the indirect join to sink protocol is presented with the network key version.

```
1
2  version IndirectJoinToSink_NK_EncDec_160b {
3
4    set host Sink(MicaZ);
5    set host Neighbour(MicaZ);
6    set host NewNode(MicaZ);
7    set host J_NK_EncDec(MicaZ);
8
9    run host Sink(*) {
10     run Main(Init160b,HandleRequest_NK_EncDec,←
           MakeResponseToNeighbour_NK_EncDec)
11   }
12   run host Neighbour(*) {
13     run Main(Init160b,Forward_NK_EncDec_To_Sink,←
           Forward_NK_EncDec_To_NewNode,ECIESEncryptNRESP_160b)
14   }
15   run host J_NK_EncDec(*){10} {
```

```
16      run Main(*)
17   }
18   run host NewNode(*) {
19      run Main(Init160b,MakeRequestWithNewNodeAndNeighbourId,←↵
            DecryptResponse_160b,HandleResponse_Indirect_NK_EncDec)
20   }
21
22   communication
23   {
24     medium[wsn] {
25        default_q = 1;
26        default_time = wsn_time [ms];
27        default_sending_current = 17.4 mA;
28        default_receiving_current = 19.7 mA;
29        default_listening_current = 0.02 mA;
30
31        topology
32        {
33     NewNode <-> Neighbour;
34     Neighbour <-> J_NK_EncDec[0];
35     J_NK_EncDec <-> J_NK_EncDec[i+1];
36     J_NK_EncDec[9] <-> Sink ;
37        }
38     }
39   }
40 }
```

Listing 4.25: The version structure for the indirect join to sink protocol is presented with the network key version.

In Listing 4.26 the indirect join to sink protocol is presented with the session key version.

```
1
2  version IndirectJoinToSink_SessKey_EncDec_160b {
3
4    set host Sink(MicaZ);
5    set host Neighbour(MicaZ);
6    set host NewNode(MicaZ);
7    set host J_SessKey_EncDec(MicaZ);
8
9    run host Sink(*) {
10      run Main(Init160b,HandleRequest_SessKey_EncDec,←↵
            MakeResponseToNeighbour_SessKey_EncDec)
11   }
12   run host Neighbour(*) {
13      run Main(Init160b,Forward_SessKey_EncDec_To_Sink,←↵
            Forward_SessKey_EncDec_To_NewNode,ECIESEncryptNRESP_160b←↵
            )
14   }
15   run host J_SessKey_EncDec(*){10} {
16      run Main(*)
17   }
18   run host NewNode(*) {
```

```
19     run Main(Init160b,↩
            MakeRequestWithNewNode_NeighbourAndIntermediateNodesIds,↩
            DecryptResponse_160b,↩
            HandleResponse_Indirect_SessKey_EncDec)
20   }
21
22   communication
23   {
24     medium[wsn] {
25        default_q = 1;
26        default_time = wsn_time [ms];
27        default_sending_current = 17.4 mA;
28        default_receiving_current = 19.7 mA;
29        default_listening_current = 0.02 mA;
30
31        topology
32        {
33     NewNode <-> Neighbour;
34     Neighbour <-> J_SessKey_EncDec[0];
35     J_SessKey_EncDec <-> J_SessKey_EncDec[i+1];
36     J_SessKey_EncDec[9] <-> Sink ;
37        }
38     }
39   }
40 }
```

Listing 4.26: The version structure for the indirect join to sink protocol is presented with the session key version.

In Listing 4.27 the indirect join to sink protocol is presented in the onion version.

```
1
2  version IndirectJoinToSink_Onion_160b {
3
4     set host Sink(PC);
5     set host Neighbour(MicaZ);
6     set host NewNode(MicaZ);
7     set host J_Onion(MicaZ);
8
9     run host Sink(*) {
10       run Main(Init160b,InFromIntermediateNode,HandleRequest_Onion↩
             ,CheckNode,MakeResponseToNeighbour_Onion,↩
             OutToIntermediateNode)
11    }
12    run host Neighbour(*) {
13       run Main(Init160b,Forward_Onion_To_Sink,↩
             Forward_Onion_To_NewNode,ECIESEncryptNRESP_160b)
14    }
15    run host J_Onion(*){10} {
16       run Main(*)
17    }
18    run host NewNode(*) {
19       run Main(Init160b,MakeRequestWithNewNodeAndNeighbourId,↩
             DecryptResponse_160b,HandleResponse_Indirect_Onion)
20    }
```

```
21
22    communication
23    {
24      medium[wsn] {
25        default_q = 1;
26        default_time = wsn_time [ms];
27        default_sending_current = 17.4 mA;
28        default_receiving_current = 19.7 mA;
29        default_listening_current = 0.02 mA;
30
31        topology
32        {
33      NewNode <-> Neighbour;
34      Neighbour <-> J_Onion[0];
35      J_Onion <-> J_Onion[i+1];
36      J_Onion[9] <-> Sink ;
37        }
38      }
39    }
40 }
```

Listing 4.27: The version structure for the indirect join to sink protocol is presented in the onion version.

4.6.8   WSN protocols evaluation – Results

In the case study presented, five WSN authentication protocols and three types of sensors motes (scenarios) are analyzed. Two types of results are presented in this section, the first one is the execution time of the protocols and the second one is the energy consumption of the nodes taking part in the protocols. The simulated execution time and energy consumption is obtained with the AQoPA tool.

4.6.8.1   Execution time – Scenario 1 – (MicaZ motes)

The first set of tests refer is to the protocol execution time prediction. In Table 4.4 the estimated execution time using the AQoPA tool for all five protocols for the MicaZ mote are presented. All indirect join protocols were executed and simulated with one intermediate node.

In Figure 4.6 and Table 4.5 the time execution for all protocols in both scenarios for 20, 40, 60, 80 and 100 intermediate nodes is presented. One can notice that for a small number of intermediate nodes the difference between the two scenarios is insignificant; then it gets bigger when the number of intermediate nodes becomes more important.

Note that the number of intermediate nodes provides a rough idea of the radius of the network and not the size of the network. Indeed, when evaluating a scenario with 20 intermediate nodes, it means that the furthest point of the network is 20 hops away from the sink. The total number of nodes in the network in that case will depend on

Table 4.4: Total times of joining new node with one intermediate node for MicaZ mote.

ECIES - 160b key length	
Protocol name	Estimated time in QoP-ML (AQoPA) [s]
DJS	93.41939
IJS_{orig}	93.65571
$IJS_{NK,dec/enc}$	94.21407
$IJS_{K,dec/enc}$	94.26591
$IJS_{NK,onion}$	93.83607

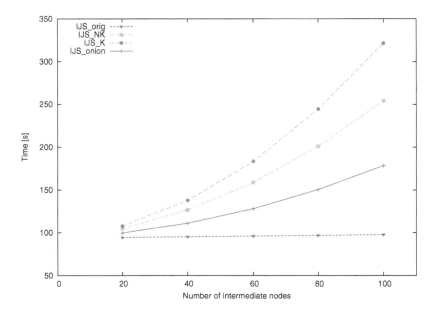

Figure 4.6: The execution time (in s) depending on the protocol and number of intermediate nodes for MicaZ motes (scenario 1).

the density of nodes. Keep in mind that simultaneous join requests can be generated in the network, and can take place at the same time.

It is important to note that the time consumption of the original protocol is almost invariant when the number of intermediate nodes rises. Indeed, the main advantage of this protocol is that cryptographic operations are only done on the new node and the sink, while the intermediate node only forwards the request and response without doing any cryptographic operation.

The $IJS_{NK,dec/enc}$ protocol is more efficient than the $IJS_{K,dec/enc}$. Indeed, for the $IJS_{K,dec/enc}$ protocol, the join request has the list of all the intermediate nodes starting

Table 4.5: The execution time (in s) depending on the protocol and number of intermediate nodes for MicaZ motes.

ECIES key length 160b				
No. of intermediate nodes	IJS_{orig}	$IJS_{NK,dec/enc}$	$IJS_{K,dec/enc}$	$IJS_{NK,onion}$
20	94.46435	105.07643	108.06011	99.78443
40	95.31555	126.69963	137.89851	111.32763
60	96.16675	158.78683	183.53371	128.29483
80	97.01795	201.33803	244.76411	150.68603
100	97.86915	254.35323	321.69051	178.50123

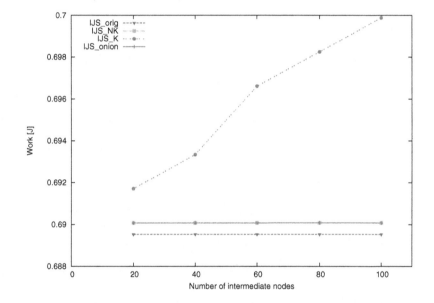

Figure 4.7: Energy consumption analysis (in J) of a new node depending on the protocol and the number of intermediate nodes for MicaZ motes (scenario 1).

from the first hop, whereas for $IJS_{NK,dec/enc}$ each intermediate node adds its identifier as it forwards the requests. This makes the request message bigger for $IJS_{K,dec/enc}$ and thus it needs more time for encryption and decryption along the route to the sink.

Finally, as expected, the protocol IJS_{onion} is more efficient than $IJS_{NK,dec/enc}$ and $IJS_{K,dec/enc}$ because the global number of cryptographic operations is less important in intermediate nodes. Note that the time consumption at the base station for the IJS_{onion} protocol is not included, so this protocol is proposed for applications where sensor nodes are energy constrained but the base station is not.

Table 4.6: The energy consumption (in J) of a new node depending on the protocol and number of MicaZ intermediate nodes.

No. of intermediate nodes	\multicolumn{4}{c}{ECIES key length 160b}			
	IJS_{orig}	$IJS_{NK,dec/enc}$	$IJS_{K,dec/enc}$	$IJS_{NK,onion}$
20	0.6895355115	0.6900804216	0.6917137908	0.6900801358
40	0.6895355575	0.6900815892	0.6933485981	0.6900807591
60	0.6895356034	0.6900833219	0.6966172144	0.6900816754
80	0.6895356494	0.6900856197	0.6982537169	0.6900828845
100	0.6895356954	0.6900884825	0.699891067	0.6900843865

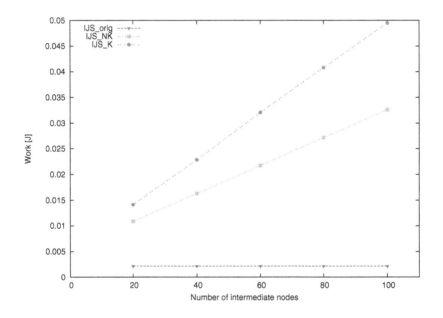

Figure 4.8: Energy consumption analysis (in J) of a sink, depending on the protocol and the number of intermediate nodes for MicaZ motes (scenario 1).

4.6.8.2   *Energy consumption – Scenario 1 (MicaZ motes)*

The energy consumption of a new node joining the network is presented in this paragraph. One of the reasons for the new node energy consumption examination is that it takes part in the protocol from the beginning to the end, and its radio is in the listening mode most of the time. In Figure 4.7 and Tables 4.6 the energy consumption of the *new node*, depending on the protocol, is presented. The results for 20, 40, 60, 80

Table 4.7: The energy consumption (in J) of a sink depending on the protocol and number of MicaZ intermediate nodes.

ECIES key length 160b			
No. of intermediate nodes	IJS_{orig}	$IJS_{NK,dec/enc}$	$IJS_{K,dec/enc}$
20	0.0021794195	0.0108897711	0.0141560172
40	0.0021794399	0.0163344386	0.0228670612
60	0.0021794603	0.0217793885	0.0321228491
80	0.0021794807	0.027224621	0.0408347394
100	0.002179501	0.032670136	0.0495470535

Table 4.8: Total times of joining a new node with one intermediate node for Imote2, 13MHz mote.

ECIES - 160b key length	
Protocol name	Estimated time in QoP-ML (AQoPA) [s]
DJS	8.43224
IJS_{orig}	8.60976
$IJS_{NK,dec/enc}$	8.95252
$IJS_{K,dec/enc}$	8.98476
$IJS_{NK,onion}$	8.72152

and 100 intermediate nodes are presented in linear topology indicating that a request is processed by all intermediate nodes.

In Figure 4.8 and Table 4.7 the energy consumption of *sink*, depending on the protocol, is presented. The results for 20, 40, 60, 80 and 100 intermediate nodes are presented in a linear topology indicating that a request is processed by all intermediate nodes.

4.6.8.3   Execution time – Scenario 2 (Imote2, 13MHz motes)

The first set of tests refers to the protocol execution time prediction. In Table 4.8 the estimated execution time using the AQoPA tool for all five protocols for the Imote2 13MHz mote are presented. All indirect join protocols were executed and simulated with one intermediate node.

In Figure 4.9 and Table 4.9 the time execution for scenario 2 (Imote2 13MhZ CPU) and for 20, 40, 60, 80 and 100 intermediate nodes is presented. The same as in the scenario 1, for a small number of intermediate nodes the difference between the two scenarios is insignificant; it gets bigger when the number of intermediate nodes becomes more important.

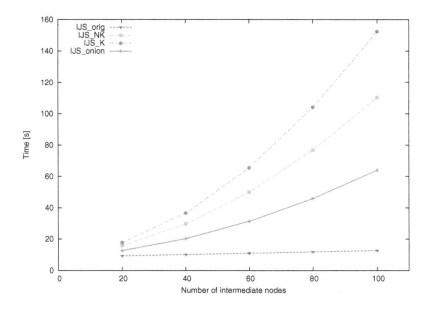

Figure 4.9: The execution time (in s) depending on the protocol, and the number of intermediate nodes for MicaZ motes (scenario 2).

Table 4.9: The execution time (in s) depending on the protocol and number of intermediate nodes for Imote2, 13MHz motes.

	ECIES key length 160b			
No. of intermediate nodes	IJS_{orig}	$IJS_{NK,dec/enc}$	$IJS_{K,dec/enc}$	$IJS_{NK,onion}$
20	9.4184	15.99288	17.85936	12.75888
40	10.2696	29.77608	36.78056	20.38208
60	11.1208	50.10328	65.57936	31.46928
80	11.972	76.97448	104.1325	46.02048
100	12.8232	110.38968	152.50176	64.03568

4.6.8.4   *Energy consumption – Scenario 2 (Imote2, 13MHz motes)*

In Figure 4.10 and Table 4.10 the energy consumption of a new node depending on the protocol is presented. The results for 20, 40, 60, 80 and 100 intermediate nodes are presented in a linear topology indicating that a request is processed by all intermediate nodes.

In Figure 4.11 and Table 4.11 the energy consumption of a *sink*, depending on the protocol, is presented. The results for 20, 40, 60, 80 and 100 intermediate nodes are presented in a linear topology indicating that a request is processed by all the intermediate nodes.

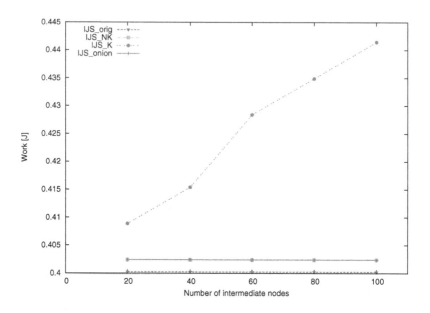

Figure 4.10: The energy consumption (in J) of a new node, depending on the protocol and the number of Imote2, 13MHz intermediate nodes.

Table 4.10: The energy consumption (in J) of a new node depending on the protocol and number of Imote2, 13MHz intermediate nodes.

ECIES key length 160b				
No. of intermediate nodes	IJS_{orig}	$IJS_{NK,dec/enc}$	$IJS_{K,dec/enc}$	$IJS_{NK,onion}$
20	0.4002510191	0.4024197806	0.408925156	0.4024195737
40	0.4002510735	0.4024206628	0.4154316086	0.4024200615
60	0.400251128	0.4024219637	0.4284436504	0.4024207711
80	0.4002511825	0.4024236835	0.4349513595	0.4024217024
100	0.400251237	0.402425822	0.4414596968	0.4024228554

4.6.8.5 Execution time – Scenario 3 (Imote2, 104MHz motes)

The first set of tests refers to the protocol execution time prediction. In Table 4.12 the estimated execution time using the AQoPA tool for all five protocols for the Imote2 104MHz mote is presented. All indirect join protocols were executed and simulated with one intermediate node.

In Figure 4.12 and Table 4.13 the time execution for scenario 3 (Imote2 104MhZ CPU) and for 20, 40, 60, 80 and 100 intermediate nodes is presented. The same as in scenario 1 and 2, for small number of intermediate nodes the difference between the

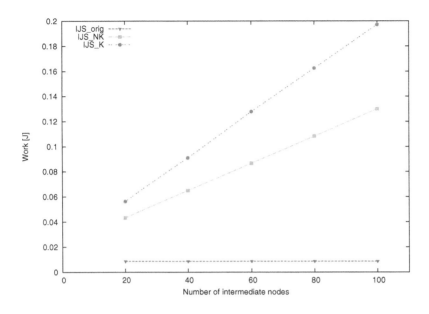

Figure 4.11: The energy consumption (in J) of a sink depending on the protocol and the number of Imote2, 13MHz intermediate nodes.

Table 4.11: The energy consumption (in J) of a sink depending on the protocol and number of Imote2, 13MHz intermediate nodes.

ECIES key length 160b			
No. of intermediate nodes	IJS_{orig}	$IJS_{NK,dec/enc}$	$IJS_{K,dec/enc}$
20	0.0086758151	0.0433703032	0.056380577
40	0.0086758392	0.065055026	0.0910756651
60	0.0086758634	0.0867399582	0.1279393872
80	0.0086758876	0.1084250998	0.1626351025
100	0.0086759117	0.1301104509	0.1973311319

two scenarios is insignificant; it gets bigger when the number of intermediate nodes becomes more important.

4.6.8.6   Energy consumption – Scenario 3 (Imote2, 104MHz motes)

In Figure 4.13 and Table 4.14 the energy consumption of a new node, depending on the protocol, is presented. The results for 20, 40, 60, 80 and 100 intermediate nodes are presented in a linear topology indicating that a request is processed by all intermediate nodes.

In Figure 4.14 and Table 4.15 the energy consumption of a *sink*, depending on the protocol, is presented. The results for 20, 40, 60, 80 and 100 intermediate nodes

Table 4.12: Total time of joining a new node with one intermediate node for Imote2, 104MHz mote.

ECIES - 160b key length	
Protocol name	Estimated time in QoP-ML (AQoPA) [s]
DJS	1.09276
IJS_{orig}	1.18928
$IJS_{NK,dec/enc}$	1.23504
$IJS_{K,dec/enc}$	1.24028
$IJS_{NK,onion}$	1.20654

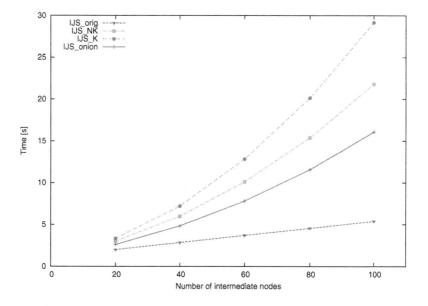

Figure 4.12: The execution time (in s) depending on the protocol and the number of intermediate nodes for Imote2, 104MHz motes (scenario 3).

are presented in a linear topology indicating that a request is processed by all intermediate nodes.

4.6.8.7 Energy consumption – Motes comparisons

One of the most important sensors in the wireless sensor network is the sink (gateway). During an evaluation of the WSN protocols the key issue is to choose the appropriate sensor motes for a sink. In this section the comparison of sink energy consumption according to the type of authentication protocol is presented. Based on

Table 4.13: The execution time (in s), depending on the protocol and the number of intermediate nodes for Imote2, 104MHz motes.

	ECIES key length 160b			
No. of intermediate nodes	IJS_{orig}	$IJS_{NK,dec/enc}$	$IJS_{K,dec/enc}$	$IJS_{NK,onion}$
20	1.99792	3.0104	3.33788	2.6114
40	2.84912	5.9936	7.22008	4.8346
60	3.70032	10.1208	12.82588	7.8218
80	4.55152	15.392	20.14008	11.573
100	5.40272	21.807	29.17028	16.0882

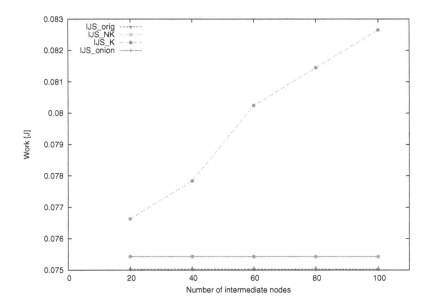

Figure 4.13: The energy consumption (in J) of a new node, depending on the protocol and the number of Imote2, 104MHz intermediate nodes.

the results one can calculate the lifetime of the sink and then one can make a choice. In this section the energy consumption of the sink with regard to the authentication protocol is presented.

In Figure 4.15 the energy consumption of a *sink* for the origin protocol is presented. The results for 20, 40, 60, 80 and 100 intermediate nodes are presented in a linear topology, indicating that a request precedes all intermediate nodes. One can see that energy consumption does not depend on the number of intermediate nodes and is equal for any number of intermediate nodes. The most energy efficient is the imote2 104MHz CPU mote; the less energy efficient is the imote2 13MHz CPU. It

Table 4.14: The energy consumption (in J) of a new node, depending on the protocol and the number of Imote2, 104MHz intermediate nodes.

ECIES key length 160b				
No. of intermediate nodes	IJS_{orig}	$IJS_{NK,dec/enc}$	$IJS_{K,dec/enc}$	$IJS_{NK,onion}$
20	0.0750315673	0.0754329338	0.0766370933	0.0754329083
40	0.0750316218	0.0754331247	0.077841466	0.0754330506
60	0.0750316763	0.0754333889	0.0802497886	0.0754332417
80	0.0750317308	0.0754337262	0.081454381	0.0754334818
100	0.0750317853	0.0754341368	0.0826590832	0.0754337708

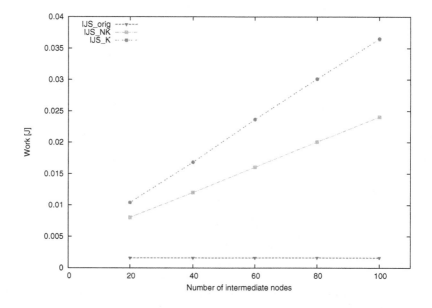

Figure 4.14: The energy consumption (in J) of a sink depending on the protocol, and the number of Imote2, 104MHz intermediate nodes.

is worth mentioning that the energy consumption for the imote2 104MHz CPU and the MicaZ 8MHz are similar.

In Figure 4.16 the energy consumption of a *sink* for an authentication protocol with a network key is presented. The results for 20, 40, 60, 80 and 100 intermediate nodes are presented in a linear topology, indicating that a request precedes all intermediate nodes. In this case, energy consumption depends on the number of intermediate nodes. Similar to the original protocol the most energy efficient is the

Table 4.15: The energy consumption (in J) of a sink, depending on the protocol and the number of Imote2, 104MHz intermediate nodes.

	ECIES key length 160b		
No. of intermediate nodes	IJS_{orig}	$IJS_{NK,dec/enc}$	$IJS_{K,dec/enc}$
20	0.0016076542	0.0080293762	0.0104373651
40	0.0016076784	0.0120434009	0.0168593828
60	0.0016077025	0.0160574622	0.0236827355
80	0.0016077267	0.0200715602	0.030104863
100	0.0016077509	0.0240856947	0.0365270454

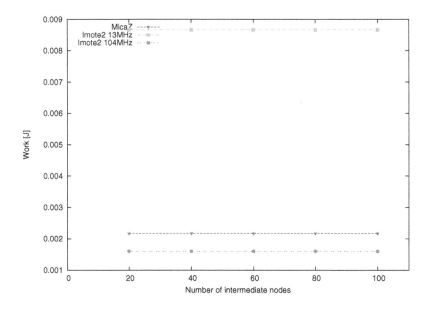

Figure 4.15: The energy consumption (in J) of a sink, depending on the motes for the origin protocol.

imote2 104MHz CPU mote; the less energy efficient is the imote2 13MHz CPU. The energy consumption of the imote2 104MHz CPU and the MicaZ 8MHz is similar.

In Figure 4.17 the energy consumption of a *sink* for the authentication protocol with a session key is presented. The results for 20, 40, 60, 80 and 100 intermediate nodes are presented in a linear topology, indicating that a request precedes all intermediate nodes. These results are similar to the authentication protocol with a network key. Energy consumption depends on the number of intermediate nodes. The most energy efficient is the imote2 104MHz CPU mote; the less energy efficient is the imote2 13MHz CPU. The energy consumption for imote2 104MHz CPU and MicaZ 8MHz is similar.

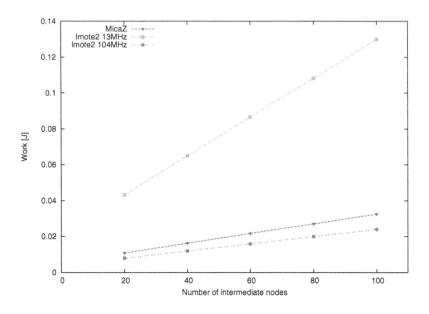

Figure 4.16: The energy consumption (in J) of a sink, depending on the motes for a WSN protocol with a network key.

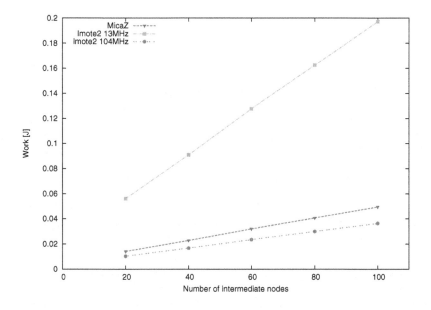

Figure 4.17: The energy consumption (in J) of a sink, depending on the motes for a WSN protocol with a session key.

Chapter 5

Environmental impact and financial costs analysis

CONTENTS

5.1   The financial and economic analyses

The crucial role of the finances in IT is the reason a new stage is introduced in the analysis scheme. Because the most financially concentrated asset in every organization is the data center, a standardized method to measure the total cash outlay for its physical infrastructure is in high demand. Companies can get more purchasing power and preserve cash for operational issues by designing IT budgets, identifying IT budget items, developing appropriate pricing strategies, and implementing and operating financial management. Effective management of the power utilized is an essential part of an enterprise's economic policy. This chapter focuses on presenting the financial, economic and environmental stages in the analysis process. The first analysis was presented in [63].

5.1.1   Cost of energy consumption of the infrastructure

The data center uses electricity from an electric company, which is measured in kilowatt-hours. Being aware of the price of one kWh, and knowing that a server works χ hours through ρ days, utilizing κ kilowatt-hours, it is fairly straightforward to calculate the total financial cost (ς_{CPU}) of its work:

$$\varsigma = \kappa \cdot \chi \cdot \rho \cdot \sigma \tag{5.1}$$

where:

κ is the total number of kilowatt-hours utilized

χ is the total number of hours when the server is busy

ρ is the total number of days when the server is busy

σ is the cost of one kWh

However, total power consumption of a single server is a sum of the power utilized by all its working components. In such case, $\kappa = \kappa_{CPU} + \kappa_{RAM} + \kappa_{HDD} + \dots$. Therefore, to assess the real cost of a single working machine, the approximate amount of the energy utilized by all its elements should be estimated.

As we have briefly described the server's power consumption, let us now focus on CPU energy utilization in more detail, since this component is the largest energy consumer in a typical computer.

Some assumptions should be made about energy use before evaluating its consumption by the CPU. Here is a simplified CPU utilization formula:

$$U = R/C \tag{5.2}$$

where:

U is the CPU utilization, expressed in a percentage

R defines our requirements, the actual busy time of the CPU [seconds]

C stands for the CPU capacity, the total time spent on analysis [seconds]

The CPU consumption is usually expressed in a percentage. As follows from the formula, time known as busy time to perform an action is required from the CPU. So the sum of the busy and idle time (i.e., the total time available for the CPU) is the CPU capacity. Based on that, the CPU capacity should be multiplied by the number of the CPU cores ($C = C \cdot cores$) when going multi-core. This formula can be transformed into a more detailed one:

$$load\,[\%] = \frac{time_{session} \cdot users}{time_{total}} \tag{5.3}$$

where $time_{total}$ is expressed as $time_{session} \cdot users + time_{idle}$.

Let us recall that when *idle* the CPU voltage is $0.600V$, and while solving cryptographic operations, it is equal to $1.350V$ (according to [34]). Simply, one can say that over a 1 minute interval, the CPU can provide a maximum of 60 of its seconds (power). The CPU *capacity* can be understood as *busy time + idle time* (the time which was used, plus the time which was left over). However, the CPU capacity is assumed to include both busy and idle states. Even in an idle state the CPU uses some power. With a specified CPU load and on the assumption that the server can handle a defined number of users in a given time, it is possible to calculate the idle time from equation (5.3).

When the idle time is defined, it is quite simple to calculate power consumed by estimating the work needed to produce one watt of power for one second:

$$J = W \cdot time_{idle} = V \cdot A \cdot time_{idle} = V_{min} \cdot A_{idle} \cdot time_{idle}$$

where $time_{idle}$ refers to the *idle* state of the CPU, expressed in seconds.

Thus the sum of energy used in the busy time (obtained by the AQoPA tool) and the used when the CPU was idle (calculated manually based on formulas) is the power consumed. Only the busy time of the CPU is taken into account in the analysis. The leftover time is neglected and the focus is on the power consumed during security operations. From equation (5.1) it is possible to estimate the daily, weekly, monthly, and annual cost of each server's power consumption to the company.

Here the focus is on the energy use of the CPU which is the main unit in cryptographic operations. Its influence on other energy consumers is briefly discussed. One can find power consumption of other server components on the producer's web sites and those performing independent hardware benchmarks and tests. Further investigations will deal with the analysis of the optimal energy consumption of a single server together with its components. The research proves that the reduction of CPU use and as a result, reduction of the amount of energy used, produces a large economic profit. As mentioned earlier, saving of costs is even larger than estimated, because CPU power use saving reduces the amount of energy used for the cooling system and decreases power consumption of the server's physical components. As follows from the study, power consumption and cost can be reduced when the required security is ensured.

5.1.2 Cost of cooling infrastructure utilization

The work of servers, routers, switches and other key data center equipment is ensured by providing sufficient cooling. As the cooling infrastructure function consumes energy, its cost must be included in the total cost of the server maintenance. The heat generated by all the machines rapidly increases the temperature which exceeds that of equipment specifications in the enclosed space of a server room. This, in turn, results in hardware failure, data loss, etc. In the daily performance of servers and other equipment a large amount of heat is generated because each watt of power used by a server is dissipated into the air as heat. The amount of heat output per server depends on the server configuration. To make servers operate, cooling takes up a defined amount of watts for every watt powering it, depending on the cooling efficiency. As in the case of power delivery, an additional back-up cooling solution is necessary to keep the server room's temperature within the listed tolerance. So the additional costs generated by back-up chillers must be taken into account. To obtain the power needed for cooling, equipment must be used with heat dissipation specifications expressed in British Thermal Units, obtainable in either the system user's guide or on the manufacturer's website. They define the number of BTUs generated by the individual machine each hour. Thus the cooling cost needed to keep the equipment in operation can be calculated from the formula:

$$\varsigma_{cooling} = BTU_{cooling} \cdot \sigma \cdot \chi \cdot \rho \qquad (5.4)$$

where:

$BTU_{cooling}$ is the number of the BTUs generated by the cooling system (per server);

χ is the total number of hours when the cooling system is busy;

ρ is the total number of days when the cooling system is busy;

σ is the cost of one kWh.

5.2 CO_2 emissions analysis

Design and development of effective IT environments are of significant importance nowadays. Green computing has stopped being a boardroom discussion and has become a reality for many enterprises. More energy-efficient servers must be designed because of recent data center growth. However, saving money on energy bills is desirable, but reducing CO_2 is a more important goal. As data centers constitute a large part of IT, decreasing CO_2 emission (and as a result, bills) by reducing power consumption is highly demanded. Implementation of best practices such us energy efficient central units (CPUs), peripherals, and servers is connected with green computing. What's more, the aim of green technology is the reduction of resource consumption and the improvement of electronic waste disposal.

CO_2 emission reduction is of essential importance particularly for large data centers. Data centers use not only servers but also storage and network components which produce enormous amounts of carbon dioxide. While estimating the amount of CO_2 emissions, it should be kept in mind that the total quantity depends on various factors, such as size of data centers (number of working components), server load (which translates into kilowatt-hours), and the type of resources used for electricity generation. Thus devices consuming much power have a negative environmental effect. As mentioned before, energy reduction using green computing techniques results in lower carbon dioxide emission due to the reduction of resources used by power plants. The annual environmental impact (ς_{co_2}) for the server (and the server room as well as the whole data center) can be easily estimated by means of a single formula. It should be remembered that while estimating possible emissions of carbon dioxide, only the busy state of the CPU was considered:

$$\varsigma_{co_2} = \kappa \cdot \chi \cdot \rho \cdot \delta \qquad (5.5)$$

where:

κ - is the total number of the utilized kilowatt-hours

χ - is the total number of hours when the server is busy

ρ - is the total number of days when the server is busy

δ - defines the number of pounds of CO_2 per kWh

The worst scenario is when electricity is created with conventional coal combustion, producing the largest amount of emitted CO_2. In fact, different energy sources such as coal, petroleum, natural gases etc. are used by power suppliers. However, CO_2 emissions are negligible if nuclear, hydro, or renewable resources (geothermal, hydropower, solar energy, tidal power, wave power, wind power etc.) are used for electricity supply.

5.3 Case study – Energy and environmental impact analysis of a data center

Apart from enhanced security and reduced administration costs, another important issue to be thoroughly evaluated in complex secure environments is system performance. It is challenging to model a complicated enterprise infrastructure and to apply the role-based access control. It was possible to model a simple RBAC in a real-life business situation and assess its activity using the Automated Quality of Protection Analysis tool instead of presenting a complex infrastructure abstraction and all possible operations. In order to model RBAC in the QoP-ML, the existence of an enterprise with many departments and of various responsibilities, as well as distinct permission and rights to the company's assets, was assumed. Five from the available enterprise roles were taken into account, and the influence of different permissions on the overall system performance was examined.

5.3.1 Scenario

The scenario presented in the case study refers to an real business situation and possible assignment of a role in an actual enterprise environment. Based on the enterprise network infrastructure in Figure 5.1 five roles: *role1*, *role2*, *role3*, *role4* and *role5* with *very low*, *low*, *medium*, *high* and *very high* security levels, respectively, were considered. The analysis performed here assumes that all of the defined applications are tunnelled by the TLS protocol. Table 5.1 presents the versions of the TLS protocol used, along with the equivalent cryptographic algorithms. One can find the scenarios in Table 5.2. The amount of data transferred between the server and the client during the session presented in Table 5.2 is the data size. In total, 50MB can be exchanged in a single session whereas each action performed during such a data transfer is of different sizes, as given in Table 5.2.

Table 5.1: TLS protocol versions with corresponding cryptographic algorithms.

TLS version 1 (*role1*)
RC4 128 + MD5
TLS version 2 (*role2*)
RC4 256 + SHA-256
TLS version 3 (*role3*)
3DES CBC + SHA-1
TLS version 4 (*role4*)
AES 128 + SHA-1
TLS version 5 (*role5*)
AES 256 + SHA-512

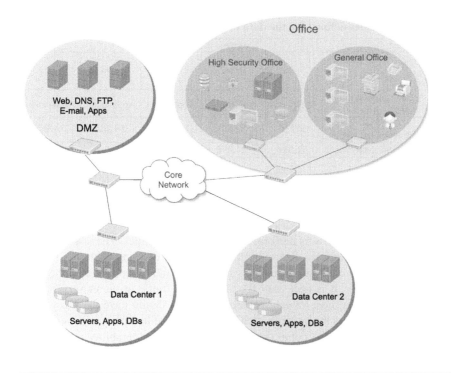

Figure 5.1: The storage center architecture.

In a real, complex company infrastructures, it is challenging to consider all the existing security connections and correlations, and to prove that the assignment of the roles matters when it comes to the system's performance (while it certainly does, it is just not so straightforward to notice significant performance differences and come up with appropriate conclusions). This scenario distinguishes five roles: *role1*, *role2*, *role3*, *role4*, *role5*. All the roles have the same permissions (meaning assigned users have access to the same subset of the enterprises assets), a single session between the client and the server can carry only a defined amount of data, (regardless of the session character - no matter if it is the e-mail or application traffic), but they vary in quality of protection and security mechanisms. Saying so, having defined our scenarios, and carefully analyzing gathered results, it is pretty easy to point out the impact of an assigned role on time, and so, on the energy consumption. Prepared scenarios are summarized in Table 5.2.

To examine the performance of miscellaneous roles in a real-life situation, we mapped the general rules proposed in the defined scenarios to the example segment

Table 5.2: The roles defined for the data center.

Scenario					
Role	*role1*	*role2*	*role3*	*role4*	*role5*
Application Access (single session)	Application	Application	Application	Application	Application
Data Size (for each action separately)	50 MB	50 MB	50 MB	50 MB	50 MB
Security Mechanisms	TLSv1	TLSv2	TLSv3	TLSv4	TLSv5

of the enterprise network in a storage center company. Considering the extended example, we can actually prove that the chosen role matters when it comes to the system performance and the energy usage. The case study shows that when they are assigned to a given role, users perform different responsibilities. The responsibilities within the company usually determine the user's role. Our approach: the need for the RBAC and different security levels is undeniable and is supported by the above extension. Generally, it is necessary for all network traffic in the enterprise to be secure. However, the most valuable enterprise assets should have the most secure network connections as the integrity, availability, and confidentiality of the enterprise – crucial resources can be compromised by a security vulnerability or weakness, exposing the enterprise to serious additional costs.

Users with defined roles apply the same types of enterprise resources (FTP, WWW, applications, databases). But actually they work with different physical assets. It should be added that a single session performed by the user includes operations appropriate for the user's role.

Some assumptions should be considered before the daily, weekly, monthly and annual server usage costs estimation. Let us take an example of a storage center company located in the United States, which manages a typical IT environment of 42U server racks (520 physical servers in total, 13 physical servers per rack). Based on a specified load capacity, the servers cope with enterprise traffic for 24 hours [1]. Taking the above example, there are 1000 CSR workstations (which automatically translates into the number of the users assigned the first role), 60 security managers (employees having role 3 permissions) [3] and 20 system operators – people with a second level of authorization. Each server in the example call center is equipped with an Intel Xeon X5675 processor, able to handle the required number of employees' connections, regardless of the assigned RBAC role.

5.3.2 Role-based access control model in QoP-ML

In the RBAC modeling approach, the QoP-MLs functions, equations, channels, processes, subprocesses, and hosts are defined. All the elements prepared for creating the role-based access control model are briefly discussed and the results obtained by means of the AQoPA tool are analyzed. It should be emphasized that QoP-ML is able to determine modeled system performance on machines with different hardware specifications. A fancy feature of the Quality of Protection Modeling Language is that the earlier described security metrics can be used to study the hardware's effect on access control management.

A security model of two communicating hosts was prepared: a client and a server for creating the role-based access control in the QoP-ML. Additionally, three asynchronous communication channels were prepared in order to facilitate the process of information exchange. The main process responsible for a secure connection with the server and the subprocess for generation of different types of network traffic based on the role received from the server was modeled on the client's site. The server abstracted in QoP-ML resembles the client as it also has main process for setting up the communication parameters but the difference is in the fact that it contains three subprocesses so it is able to manage clients with various levels of authorization.

5.3.2.1   The model

Modeling of the RBAC QoP-MLs functions, equations, channels, processes, and hosts were defined. Here all elements prepared for creation of the security model are presented and discussed.

The functions defined in the QoP-ML referring to the roles specified for the exemplary enterprise are demonstrated. Five roles: *role1, role2, role3, role4, role5* are represented by declared operations. The source code presented below does not include remaining functions which refer to the ordinary TLS operations because they are less important.

```
1  functions
2  {
3      fun getRole1();
4      fun getRole2();
5      fun getRole3();
6      fun getRole4();
7      fun getRole5();
8  }
```

Listing 5.1: QoP-ML's functions.

Some equation rules were declared with the functions. Similar to the case of the QoP-ML functions, there is no direct connection between defined equations and the specified RBAC roles.

A QoP-MLs channel must be defined to ensure communication between the processes running. The TLS and actual data traffic exchange is made using channels ch1 and ch2 but the assigned RBAC role is transferred using the rbacCH. The value in square brackets at the end of channel definition (the [ent_net]) indicates a medium name. This is used to link the channel with the medium, determining the channel characteristics. The same medium can have many channels. Though each channel is treated independently, the characteristics (topology, topology parameters, etc.) are the same for all channels.

```
1  channels
2  {
3      channel rbacCH(0)[ent_net];
4      channel ch1(0)[ent_net];
5      channel ch2(0)[ent_net];
6  }
```

Listing 5.2: Channels used for transferring the data.

Here, operations which can be done by users with different assigned RBAC roles, are expressed by subprocesses. The TLS handshake is modeled by client and server processes.

After being defined, processes and subprocesses can be grouped into host structures named Client and Server. They express communicating sites in the RBAC model. Below a subprocess of the client wanting to connect to an FTP server and the corresponding role is presented. However, distinct roles are handled differently by the server. The general concept taking into account role 5 management behavior is presented.

```
1   subprocess AccessFTPServer(rbacCH,ch1) {
2       in(rbacCH:role);
3       if(role == role1){
4           D1 = data()[ftpRole1];
5           D1E = enc(D1,K1)[128,RC4,stream];
6           D1MAC = hmac(D1E)[MD5];
7           M5 = (D1E,D1MAC);
8           out(ch1:M5);
9       }
10      if(role == role2){
11          D1 = data()[ftpRole2];
12          D1E = enc(D1,K1)[256, RC4, stream];
13          D1MAC = hmac(D1E)[SHA256];
14          M5 = (D1E,D1MAC);
15          out(ch1:M5);
16      }
17      if(role == role3){
18          D1 = data()[ftpRole3];
19          D1E = enc(D1,K1)[56,3DES,CBC];
20          D1MAC = hmac(D1E)[SHA1];
21          M5 = (D1E,D1MAC);
22          out(ch1:M5);
23      }
24      if(role == role4){
25          D1 = data()[ftpRole4];
26          D1E = enc(D1,K1)[128, AES, CBC];
27          D1MAC = hmac(D1E)[SHA1];
28          M5 = (D1E,D1MAC);
29          out(ch1:M5);
30      }
31      if(role == role5){
32          D1 = data()[ftpRole5];
33          D1E = enc(D1,K1)[256, AES, CBC];
34          D1MAC = hmac(D1E)[SHA512];
35          M5 = (D1E,D1MAC);
36          out(ch1:M5);
37      }
38  }
```

Listing 5.3: Client's subprocess responsible for accessing the FTP server.

```
1  subprocess HandleRole5(rbacCH,ch1) {
2      role3 = getRole5();
3      out(rbacCH:role5);
4      wait()[30];
5      in(ch1:Z);
6      K1E=Y[0];
7      D1E=Z[0];
8      D1MAC=Z[1];
9      K1=dec(K1E,SKS)[2048,RSA];
10     D1EVerif=hmac(D1E)[SHA512];
11     if (D1EVerif == D1MAC){
12         D1=dec(D1E,K1)[256, AES, CBC];
13     }else{
14         stop;
15     }
16 }
```

Listing 5.4: Server's subprocess responsible for handling clients' requests.

The above codes can be discussed as follows. The RBAC channel (rbacCH) is first read by a client's subprocess responsible for the FTP connection in order to get the assigned role from server. It is possible for the client to exchange (upload or download) files of various sizes with the enterprise FTP server depending on the obtained permission set. Taking the *role 5* permissions, using the data function, *data* of size *ftpRole5* (in security metrics) are created and assigned to the *D1* variable. In the next step, the data are encrypted. Next, the *hmac* of the encrypted message is generated and assigned to the *D1MAC* variable. Finally, the encrypted message along with its message authentication code is composed in a tuple, and sent through the *ch1* channel to the server. Considering the server's subprocess handling the client's request, one can see that the first instruction uses the *getRole5* QoP-ML's function to generate the permission set for the third RBAC role, and then sends it through the *rbacCH* to the client, using the *out* instruction. After a 30 second wait time, the server uses the *ch1* channel to receive the tuple *Z* (with the help of the *in* operation), consisting of the encrypted message (available in *Z[0]* and assigned to the *D1E* on the server's site), with its corresponding hmac (*Z[1]*). Next, the server computes its own message authentication code on the encrypted message received. After verifying that it is equal to the obtained message, it can be decrypted by the server. If it is not equal, the communication ends.

5.3.2.2   Security metrics

The data required by the security metrics structure using the methodology presented in Chapter 7 and by the Crypto Metrics Tool were collected. In the case study, the servers are equipped with the Intel Core i7-3930K Processor and the metrics' generation process for them was performed. Using CMT, metrics for all the security mechanisms proposed in the case study (Table 5.1) were gathered. One of the available base measures, the CPU time, was taken into consideration. The CPU time indicates the amount of time for which a central processing unit was used for processing the execution of the security operations (such as AES encryption/decryption, SHA-1

Table 5.3: Security metrics gathered by the Crypto-metrics tool for the purpose of the case study.

Security mechanism ⟍ Characteristics	*operation type*	*operation mode*	*key length*	*base measure (CPU time)*
3DES	encryption decryption	CBC	56 bytes	0.1476892300 ms
AES	encryption decryption	CBC	128 bytes	0.0315219700 ms
AES	encryption decryption	CBC	256 bytes	0.0440027556 ms
RC4	encryption decryption	stream	128 bytes	0.0058003700 ms
RC4	encryption decryption	stream	256 bytes	0.0058003600 ms
MD5	HMAC	-	-	0.0066404200 ms
SHA-1	HMAC	-	-	0.0061203800 ms
SHA-256	HMAC	-	-	0.0234414700 ms
SHA-512	HMAC	-	-	0.0183211400 ms

hashing and others available). The results yielded by the Crypto Metrics Tool represent the most reliable, accurate, and actual hardware benchmarks for all the cryptographic primitives used in our scenario. Results obtained, free of random errors values (along with their attributes) are gathered in Table 5.3.

Remaining characteristics needed for the analysis (such as the CPU voltage) were taken from the official documentation of the processor which was utilized for the metrics generation [34]. Since cryptographic operations utilized in the defined scenario are considered power-consuming, in our analysis, when evaluating energy utilized in the *busy* state of CPU, we decided to choose its maximum available voltage. Assessing the power consumed in the *idle* state of the CPU, one should assume the smallest available voltage value. All the values utilized are gathered in Table 5.4.

Table 5.4: Intel Core i7-3930K Processor.

power consumption	*voltage*$_{min}$	*voltage*$_{max}$	*current*$_{idle}$	*current*$_{busy}$
130 W	0.600 V	1.35 V	W/V ≈ 96.29 A ≈ 96 290 mA	W/V ≈ 216.67 A ≈ 216 670 mA

5.3.3 The analyses

During investigation the actual analysis was performed for only one client accessing the server in a single session. It was found that the remaining results grew linearly with the number of incoming session requests. Time spent on handling client connections, amount of kilowatt-hours, financial costs as well as carbon dioxide emissions were determined. Besides the result, the scheme used for evaluation of a chosen system is presented. The analysis of the IT environment under consideration requires following the steps given below, which focus on each important detail, making the analysis multilevel.

5.3.3.1 The time analysis

Role 1 is considered in the scenario. The maximum size of the traffic between the client and the server in a single session is 50 MB. The version 1 TLS protocol protects the communication channel. The performance takes only 0.318485 seconds (Table 5.5). However, under identical conditions it takes 0.748592 seconds (*role2*) to change only the channel protection type. The safest communication type is role 3 (conditions the same as in role 1 and role 2) and it takes the longest time (3.937527 seconds). In the role 4, the full session takes 0.963645 and in role 5 it takes 1.595493. Such analysis shows that the assigned role (protection level) can affect the performance of the whole system.

Supposing the time of the chosen security operation assessed by the time analysis module was equal to τ seconds and assuming that there was a given time interval equal to $\phi = 3\,600$ seconds), for the server working under $\varphi\%$ of machine load, it is quite straightforward to calculate the maximum number of users the server is able to manage within the given time interval:

$$users_{max} = \frac{\varphi \cdot \phi}{100 \cdot \tau},$$
(5.6)

where:

τ - is the total time of a single session in seconds,

φ - is the machine load in percentage,

ϕ - is the considered time interval in seconds.

Based on the results already obtained one can estimate the maximum number of clients (sessions) processing different authorization permissions. In the analysis it was assumed that during one hour the CPU load for server is equal to 90%. This estimation is as simple as knowing that it takes 0.318485 seconds for the existing server to handle role 1 assigned to the user and applying the simplified formula for CPU use, it is possible to calculate the number of clients served (taking given conditions into account).

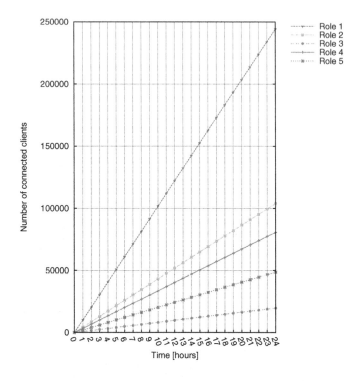

Figure 5.2: Server's performance (CPU load = 90%).

$$users = \frac{90 \cdot 3600}{100 \cdot 0.318485}$$

which gives about 10173 handled employees per hour (Figure 5.2). Taking into account the linear growth, it is easy to obtain that for two hours the machine can manage about $10173 \cdot 2 = 20346$ connections. For 3 hours it increases up to $5717 \cdot 3 = 30519$ users handled (and so on and so forth). For the other roles (role 2, role 3, role 4 and role 5) the same method of assessment was applied.

As follows from the results obtained and assumptions of a 90% machine load, it is possible for the server to handle clients faster with the first authorization level than those permitted to perform role 3 actions. It is also evident that the relationship between the role assigned and consumption of server resources is as follows: the longer time needed to accomplish the action, the more server resources are going to be used. The longer working server utilizes more resources, so a larger amount of energy is consumed.

Table 5.5: Server's performance results obtained by AQoPA suggest that the assigned role matters when it comes to the system's performance.

Scenario					
Role Total time	*role1*	*role2*	*role3*	*role4*	*role5*
Total time (full session)	0.318485 s	0.748592 s	3.937527 s	0.963645 s	1.595493 s

5.3.3.2   The energy usage analysis

Besides the time analysis presented, we modeled the energy usage for our two scenarios. We collected the data required by the AQoPA's Energy Analysis Module from the official documentation of the CPU which was used for the metrics generation [77]. Since cryptographic operations are considered power-consuming, in our analysis, when evaluating energy utilized in the *busy* state, we decided to choose the maximum available CPU voltage.

Table 5.6 contains the results in joules gathered by the AQoPA tool.

Due to the fact that the Energy Analysis Module provided by the AQoPA tool yields its results using *joules* as a unit, we can convert the values obtained to *kWh*. We know that one joule is equal to $2.777778 \cdot 10^{-7}$ kilowatt-hours:

$$1J = 2.777778 \cdot 10^{-7} kWh = 2.777778 \cdot 10^{-7} kWh = (1/3600000)kWh$$

So the energy in kilowatt-hour $E(kWh)$ is equal to the energy in joules $E(J)$ divided by 3600000:

$$E(kWh) = E(J)/3600000 = E(J) \cdot 2.777778 \cdot 10^{-7}$$

Conversion between the joules and kWh is required by the (to be implemented) AQoPA's module, the Finance Module. Here, having the total power consumption of each host, along with the current price of one kWh, we can calculate the total economic cost of the CPU usage. Knowing that, we can balance the security level against energy usage, which can be simply translated into cost savings.

Table 5.6: Server's energy analysis results obtained by the AQoPA's energy analysis module [J].

Scenario					
Role Total Power Usage	*role1*	*role2*	*role3*	*role4*	*role5*
Full session	46.58 J	109.48 J	575.87 J	140.94 J	233.34 J

5.3.3.3 The financial and economic analysis

In this section, a brief overview of predicting the total budget required to manage a data center is presented, focusing mainly on a method for measuring its total cost and indicating possible gains. Instead of focusing only on the CPU, dealing with the economic aspect of the data center, it is worth considering the server as a primary unit in our discussion. Performing the estimations, the formulas presented in Section 5.1 were utilized.

Determining the total cost of the working machine, the biggest attention should be drawn to the CPU, since this component is the largest energy consumer in a typical computer. Although the CPU is clearly the largest consumer of energy, total energy utilization of a single server consists of the power usage of all its components. To obtain the total power consumption of a single server, one needs to take into consideration the power usage of its HDDs, RAMs, network cards, video cards, and so forth. Depending on the server's workload, the energy utilized for the cooling system (the amount of the power needed to ensure a proper temperature for the busy machine and its components) must be covered as well. Let us have a closer look at, for instance, the CPU's fan power consumption. One should keep in mind that an *idle* server requires less energy, and thus cooling, than the *busy* one. In some certain scenarios CPU fans contribute much to the power requirements of PC components. Among the factors that affect fan energy usage one can enumerate the fan speed (measured in RPM), fan size (80 mm, 92 mm, 120 mm, 140 mm and 200 mm) and whether it has LED lights. Typical power consumption of a 80 mm case fan (3,000 RPM) ranks between 2.4 and 3 W [5]. As can be seen from the time analysis, to handle the exact number of incoming connections, the server needs to spend more time on serving users assigned *role3* privileges, than those having *role1* permissions. Based on Figure 5.2, to deal with about 20 000 users, the machine works for approximately 1 hour (*role1*), but considering *role3* accesses, this value increases to about 24 hours. Suppose our single server uses a CPU with a 3W fan (both working for 24 hours a day). During 24 *busy* hours, fan utilizes about $(24 \cdot 3 \text{ W})/1\,000 = 0.072$ kilowatt-hours (which costs approximately $0.004382069), while processing *role1* requests for 1 hour requires about twenty-four less money (approximately $(1 \cdot 3 \text{ W})/1000 = 0.003$ kWhs, $0.000182586).

The conclusion is, the role-switching (the security level switching) has undeniable impact not only on CPU energy utilization, but also on the amount of power consumed by cooling, and, in fact, on all the working components of the machine, which strictly translates into cost savings. In this section, however, we focused only on the energy usage of the CPU as the main unit utilized for the cryptographic operations and made only a brief note about its influence on remaining energy consumers. Power consumption of other server components can be found on the manufacturer's websites as well as on the websites which perform independent hardware benchmarks and tests. The analysis of the optimal energy consumption of a single server along with all its components is left for the future work. Nevertheless, research provides a serious argument for believing that reduction of the CPU usage, and thus the amount of the utilized energy, entails significant economic profits. As stated before, cost savings are in fact even higher than those estimated here, since saving the CPU power usage, we reduce the amount of energy utilized for the cooling system, as well as decrease power consumption of all the server's physical components. Our study showed, that ensuring required security, it is possible to reduce the power consumption and increase cost savings at the same time. At first glance, figures presented here may seem irrelevant; however, when put in the context of a large data center environment, they can quickly become very significant.

On the basis of the analyses performed, the total cost of the data center utilization depends not only on the power consumption of the server's CPU. Calculating the total cost of operating a data center one needs to take into account both fixed and variable costs, which are affected by complex and interrelated factors. From the economic analysis of the power consumed by the central processing unit, one can note that with the exact number of served users, it is possible to save money by switching the level of protection from the *strongest* to the *weakest* one. The financial analysis performed earlier proved that by reducing protection mechanisms, one can expect significant financial profits. Analyzing the results of our research, one can see that by changing the level of protection it is possible to handle the required number of users and increase financial profits even more (since the reduction of the CPU load implies the decrease of the power used by all server components, resulting in lower costs). However, in the economic stage of the analysis process, we need to look at power consumption, heating and cooling, and the data center footprint.

Determining the approximate total cost of a whole data center, servers with Intel Core i7-3930K Processors were assumed to be used. However, neither the network nor the storage footprint (nor its equipment) were included in the estimation. Server-specific numbers (such as BTU) utilized in our evaluation were obtained from the technical guide of the Intel Core i7-3930K Processors.

Although it does not seem to result directly from the economic analysis of a single machine, the solution presented can bring real, meaningful cost savings. In the approach presented, economic profits actually come from the number of working machines with their load factor. Modification in the configuration of security mechanisms lets one obtain significant benefits. This approach brings additional possibilities: by switching security mechanisms from the *strongest* to the *weakest*, it is possible to provide effective services and maximize the utilization of hardware resources at the same time. Since one can accomplish the same goal using *weaker* security mechanisms, in many situations it is wasteful to assign too many hardware resources to perform the given task. Applying the proposed solution to the existing IT environment, one can see a serious reduction in IT costs while increasing the efficiency, utilization, and flexibility of their existing computer hardware. Table 5.7 explores this concept in more detail.

If the *role5* will be taken into consideration where AES algorithm with 256 bit of key and SHA 512 algorithm is used then in an hour 2030 users can be handled having 90% of CPU load. Since we assumed that the number of users grows linearly, within 24 hours, it gives us $2030 \cdot 24 = 48\,720$ employees a day, resulting in $48\,720 \cdot 365 = 17\,782\,800$ connections a year per server. Assuming that we have the whole data center at our disposal, it will turn out that we can serve roughly $17\,782\,800 \cdot 520 =$

Table 5.7: CPU load equals 90%, number of connections to handle is given for the scenario. Estimated values represent the total annual cost of the energy and cooling usage, rounded up to the nearest dollar.

| | *Scenario* | |
| | *(users to handle ≈ 9 247 056 000)* | |
	server(s)	$S_{power+cooling}$
role1	104	23 894$
role2	244	56 161$
role3	1285	295 611$
role4	314	72 298$
role5	520	119 725$

9 247 056 000 users assigned *role5* permissions a year. To handle the same number of users assigned *role1* privileges with 90% of CPU load, and being aware that a *role1* permissions server is capable of dealing with 10 173 users within an hour, it is trivial to compute the number of physical machines capable of managing the same number of employees, with different security mechanisms applied:

$$users_{max_{S1R1}} \cdot \chi \cdot \rho \cdot \mu_{S1R1} \approx$$
$$users_{max_{S1R5}} \cdot \chi \cdot \rho \cdot \mu_{S1R5} , \tag{5.7}$$

where:

$users_{max_{S1R1}}$ is the maximum number of users assigned *role1* permissions, that can be handled within an hour by a single server,

$users_{max_{S1R5}}$ is the maximum number of users assigned *role5* permissions, that can be handled within an hour by a single server,

χ is the total amount of hours when a single server was busy,

ρ is the total amount of days when a single server was busy,

μ_{S1R1} is the number of servers being capable of dealing with the given traffic (supposing managing $users_{max_{S1R1}}$ employees an hour, having *role1* privileges through χ hours for ρ days),

μ_{S1R5} is the number of servers capable of dealing with the given traffic (supposing managing $users_{max_{S1R5}}$ employees an hour, having *role3* privileges through χ hours for ρ days), which, in our case, results in:

$$10\ 173 \cdot 24 \cdot 365 \cdot \mu_{_{S1R1}} \approx 2\ 030 \cdot 24 \cdot 365 \cdot 520,$$
$$\mu_{_{S1R1}} \approx 104.$$

From Table 5.7, it can be seen that to handle about 9 247 056 000 connections (a year) with *role5* permissions assigned, it is necessary to utilize all of the physical machines in the enterprise. However, the same amount of employees can be dealt with by about 104 servers, if we change the communication channel protection type to *role1* privileges.

As assumed earlier, performing day-to-day tasks, the energy consumption for a single server for the five analyzed roles is presented in Table 5.6. Table 5.8 comprises assessed costs for a single machine, a rack, and the whole data center.

Being aware of the annual usage cost of a single server, we were able to compute the amount of money spent on any number of working machines.

In conclusion, such security mechanism switching can offer a variety of economic advantages: it permits one to increase the scale of server infrastructure without purchasing additional pieces of hardware and allows resources to be used more efficiently. In addition to the savings in hardware costs, security level switching decreases the amount of floor space and maintenance costs. Such server consolidation also reduces the overall footprint of the entire data center. That means far fewer servers, less networking gear, a smaller number of racks needed – all of which translates into less data center floor space required. Consolidating servers means lowering monthly power and cooling costs in the data center.

5.3.3.4 *CO_2 emission analysis*

In a worst-case scenario, when electricity is created with conventional coal combustion, one deals with the highest values of the emitted CO_2. In reality, power suppliers use a mix of different energy sources, for instance coal, petroleum, natural gas and so forth. There is of course the alternative case of negligible emissions of CO_2, if the electricity supply is completely based on nuclear, hydro, or renewable energy resources (such as geothermal, hydro-power, solar energy, and wind power).

Table 5.8: Approximate annual cost of energy consumption (in US dollars). The number of handled users is equal to 7 884 000 per server a year, and the CPU load varies between the roles.

		Scenario				
	Role	*role1* (CPU load ≈ 7.96%)	*role2* (CPU load ≈ 18.71%)	*role3* (CPU load ≈ 98.44%)	*role4* (CPU load ≈ 24.09%)	*role5* (CPU load ≈ 39.89%)
Server(s)		$\varsigma_{power} + \varsigma_{cooling}$ $_{annual}$ $_{annual}$	$\varsigma_{power} + \varsigma_{cooling}$ $_{annual}$ $_{annual}$	$\varsigma_{power} + \varsigma_{cooling}$ $_{annual}$ $_{annual}$	$\varsigma_{power} + \varsigma_{cooling}$ $_{annual}$ $_{annual}$	$\varsigma_{power} + \varsigma_{cooling}$ $_{annual}$ $_{annual}$
1		333 $	349 $	474 $	358 $	382 $
13		4 323 $	4 541 $	6 158 $	4 650 $	4 970 $
520		172 908 $	181 633 $	246 324 $	185 996 $	198 813 $

Table 5.9: Approximate annual environmental impact (in pounds of CO_2). The number of users handled is equal to 7 884 000 per server a year; the CPU load varies between the roles.

	Scenario				
Server(s) \ Role	*role1* *(CPU load ≈ 7.96%)*	*role2* *(CPU load ≈ 18.71%)*	*role3* *(CPU load ≈ 98.44%)*	*role4* *(CPU load ≈ 24.09%)*	*role5* *(CPU load ≈ 39.89%)*
1	5 078	5 334	7 234	5 462	5 839
13	66 012	69 342	94 040	71 008	75 901
520	2 640 466	2 773 699	3 761 591	2 840 336	3 036 055

The energy usage estimation performed for the example storage center can be a good start for research on carbon dioxide emissions. The following further analysis confirms the statement that the more energy we save, the less CO_2 our machine will produce. When it comes to the emissions of CO_2 analysis of an example IT environment, we proposed to use Equation (5.5) to estimate the volume produced. Values estimated with the help of Equation (5.5) are summarized in Table 5.9. They refer to a single physical machine performing actions defined in our security-based data flow management RBAC model and represent the total annual environmental impact of the server's energy usage, rounded up to the nearest pound.

The same as in the case of the financial and economic analyses, it is possible to estimate the amount of the carbon dioxide which can be saved if we perform the proposed security-switching. As is apparent from Table 5.10, by changing protection mechanisms from the *strongest* to the *weakest*, ensuring required security at the same time, it is possible to significantly decrease the amount of the carbon dioxide released to the atmosphere.

According to [4], the average amount of carbon dioxide released to the atmosphere per kWh was about 0.84368kg (1.86 pounds) in April 2014. Therefore, handling 9 247 056 000 users by a data center annually where servers have ≈ 90% of the CPU load differs for the different roles significantly. Regarding the whole data center and privileges on *role1*, it released about 729 754 pounds of carbon dioxide to

Table 5.10: CPU load equals 90%, number of connections to handle is given for the defined scenario. Estimated values represent the total, approximate annual environmental impact (in pounds of CO_2), rounded up to the nearest pound.

	Scenario *(users to handle ≈ 9 247 056 000)*	
	server(s)	*pounds of CO_2*
role1	104	729 754
role2	244	1 715 260
role3	1285	9 028 501
role4	314	2 208 120
role5	520	3 656 617

the atmosphere, whereas *role2* released about 9 028 501 pounds of carbon dioxide. Comparing the above values estimated for *role3* to those assessed when dealing with the first one, it can be seen that by switching between the security mechanisms one can reduce the emissions of CO_2 12.3 times, that is, about 8 298 747 pounds per data center.

In accordance with the information in [2], the annual amount of released carbon dioxide saved by switching between the roles (from *role3* to *role1*) for the data center is equivalent to about 792 passenger vehicles, 423 568 gallons of gasoline consumed, 4 043 231 pounds of coal burned per year or 343 homes' electricity use for one year. However, bear in mind that the data presented here correspond to the average values. Let us have a closer look at, for instance number of gallons of gasoline consumed (for instance, by the passenger vehicles). Here, the number of gallons of gasoline consumed depends on many different factors, i.e., the type of the gearbox (automatic or manual), engine size, or even the weight and the shape of the car. More profound analysis requires consideration of all of these factors.

5.3.3.5   The QoP analysis

Another crucial aspect of the multi-level analysis is the assessment of the security quality (commonly referred to as the quality of protection). Such analysis is based on the evaluation of the impact of security mechanisms on system performance. In Chapter 3 the methodology of QoP assessment is described and based on the facts defined in Appendix A.3.1 using the framework (SMETool) which permits one to assess the quality of protection of previously predefined security mechanisms, the QoP evaluation is prepared. Five roles and five different versions of the TLS protocol were analyzed and their quality of protection was assessed in terms of confidentiality, integrity, and availability. In Table 5.11 the qualitative interpretation of QoP evaluation of the analyzed versions of TLS protocol in data center is presented.

Table 5.11: The qualitative interpretation of QoP evaluation of the analyzed versions of TLS protocol in data center.

Security mechanisms \ Security attribute	confidentiality	integrity	availability
RC4 128 + MD5	very low	very low	very high
RC4 256 + SHA-256	low	high	low
3DES CBC + SHA-1	low	low	medium
AES CBC 128 + SHA-1	high	low	low
AES CBC 256 + SHA-512	very high	very high	very low

Chapter 6

Reputation analysis in QoP-ML

CONTENTS

A formal approach in which the reputation system can be represented as a part of the protocol and all the operations and communication steps can be consistently modeled ensures analysis completeness. The QoP-ML is intended to represent a series of steps described as a cryptography protocol. The multilevel protocol introduced in the QoP-ML makes it possible to describe the state of the cryptographic protocol. Moreover, the QoP-ML makes it possible to perform the security economics analysis called adaptable security in the literature [43, 44].

Here we discuss the syntax and semantics of a new structure for the Quality of Protection Modeling Language (QoP-ML) needed in the analysis of a reputation system (reputation module). The first view of this module was presented in [46]. The essential achievement is introducing the ability of formally specifying the distributed reputation systems along with other protocols and functions of information security supporting the reputation systems. Based on the reputation module, it is possible to analyze the reputation system from the technical and information perspective. To calculate the reputation values of agents, defined algorithms are applied which are abstracted from the operating system by means of the host being defined as a part of the whole IT architecture, which is used for abstraction of distributed communities. In this infrastructure, defense mechanisms can be modeled and their impact on the reputation system can be analyzed. The reputation module proposed here is a part of the Quality of Protection Modeling Language and the first modeling language enabling abstraction and analysis of the reputation systems as regards the technical and information security perspective in a formal way.

Another aspect which should be taken into consideration is the influence of the reputation systems on the performance of IT architecture. One can imagine the scenario, when the reputation server will be flooded by requests for account creation, which will be the part of the Sybil attack. The efficiency analysis should be performed according to the usage of any defense mechanisms which protect the reputation systems. These mechanisms influence the performance of the IT systems which are responsible for calculating reputation values. Such an approach can be achieved by means of Quality of Protection systems where security mechanisms are evaluated according to their influence on the system security and performance. Among the Quality of Protection models one can enumerate Quality of Protection Modeling Language (QoP-ML).

The main contribution of the reputation module introduced is the possibility of analyzing a reputation system from a technical and information security perspective. The reputation values of the agents are calculated according to the defined algorithms which are abstracted as the process in the operating system which is realized by means of the host. This host is defined as the part of whole IT architecture by means of which distributed communities can be abstracted. In this infrastructure one can abstract different types of the adversaries which are performing attacks on reputation systems and one can analyze the defined reputation algorithms and the performance of IT architecture which realize the reputation systems. In the other side, one can model the defense mechanisms and analyze the impact on the reputation system and the IT architecture performance.

The five steps: protocol modeling, security metrics definition, process instantiation, QoP-ML processing and QoP evaluation [42] make up the base analysis in the

QoP-ML. Here we present a new reputation module to allow simultaneously preparation of the reputation analysis and that of standard of quality of protection of the security mechanisms. The reputation analysis being the sixth step, it is made at the same time as the QoP evaluation using the methodology given in [42].

Two structures, introduced in the QoP-ML, functions and security metrics, have to be applied for reputation modeling. Moreover, a new structure, namely the modules structure, will be used for reputation modeling. The semantics of all the structures needed in reputation modeling in the QoP-ML is discussed in next section.

6.1   Functions

The function can be defined as modification of the states of the variables and passing the objects by communication channels. With the reputation qop parameters it is declared as follows:

```
1  fun post(id)[Reputation: par1, par2, par3, par4, par5]
```

Listing 6.1: Function definition with reputation factor.

The phrase fun proceeds the function declaration. Post is the name of this function. Having the name of the function, its arguments have to be set and two types of factors should be described by them. The function is executed by means of the functional parameters written in round brackets, whereas the system quality of protection is affected by the additional parameters written in square brackets.

6.2   Security metrics

In the QoP-ML, the influence of the system behavior is represented by means of the functions. During the function declaration the quality of protection parameters is defined and the details about this function are described.

The data* structure should be used for representing the reputation metrics as reputation is modeled but not measured. The example of the metrics structure used for reputation modeling is following:

```
1  metrics
2  {
3      }
4  data*()
5      {
6          primhead[function][reputation:algorithm]
7          primitive[post][alg1]
8      }
9  }
```

Listing 6.2: Security metrics definition for the reputation modeling.

There are the two operators: `primhead` and `primitive` in the body of the `data*` structures. The parameters for agent actions influencing its reputation are defined by the `primhead` operator. In the for the `data*` the two parameters were defined of which the first one is the function name describing the operation having an effect on the modeled reputation and the second one gives the name of the additional module (reputation) for the function defined earlier, including the name of the algorithm which is used for calculation of the value of the reputation of this function. Next the details concerning the earlier defined functions are described by the `primitive` operator. Here according to the `data*` operator, the `post` function is calculated based on the algorithm, whose name is *alg1*, which is defined in the module *reputation*.

6.3 Modules

Here a new structure is introduced called a module, used for describing details for different analysis modules from the base QoP-ML analysis. The structure for the reputation analysis is described in the approach under consideration. In the QoP-ML approach the security metrics structure is based only on static values defined as the primitive structure. The main feature of the module's structure is representing the results in the dynamic way. Thus the algorithms defining mathematics operations are used for estimation of the results defined in this structure.

In the approach presented, a system can be modeled which is based not only on a static reputation algorithm but can also be represented as an adaptive reputation system. It means that the reputation algorithms can be changed to be used in any system context. In order to model adaptive reputation systems one can define new control operators in the security metrics structure in the QoP-ML. The declaration and then the description of this structure will be presented as an example in next part of this section.

```
1  modules {
2      reputation {
3      # rep=0
4          alg1(par1, par2, par3, par4, par5){
5              if(rep<=100){
6                  extra = (par4 * par5)/2;
7                  rep = rep + (par1 * par2 * par3) + extra;
8                      }
9              if(rep>100 || rep <200){
10                 extra = (par4 * par5)/2;
11                 rep = rep + par1 + par2 + par3 + extra;
12                     }
13             else{
14                 rep = rep + (par1 + par2 + par3 + par4 + par5)/5
15                     }
16         }
17     }
18 }
```

Listing 6.3: The modules structure with reputation parameters for the QoP-ML.

The operator *modules* start the *modules* structure which is enclosed in curly brackets. Different types of modules can be defined inside the body of the module's structure. Here the exemplary reputation module description is presented. As in the case study of the module's structure, the curly brackets enclose the body of the reputation module. The initial values of variables can be defined in the specific modules being precoded by the# operator. Then the algorithm estimating the reputation value is defined alg1(par1, par2, par3, par4, par5). There is no restriction for the name of the algorithm and here it is alg1. The round brackets include the definition of the algorithm parameters. Their values are defined in the QoP-ML protocol modeling in the specific function taken into account during reputation modeling. The arithmetic operations defining the algorithm of reputation value calculation are included in the body of the alg1 algorithm. Condition statements can be used in the modules structure. The example includes three possible calculations which are changed depending on the current value of *rep* variable. In the case study the *rep* variable is lower or equal to 100 (rep<=100), the first conditional statement is true, and it is possible to execute the relevant algorithm. In the case it is higher than 100 and lower than 200 (rep>100 || rep <200), the second conditional statement is true. The else structure is executed in other cases. Other operators which are the same as in the language C can be applied in the modules structure. They are: true, false, &&, ||, <, >, <=, >=, +, -, *, /, ==, !=.

6.4 Case study – Average reputation system

In this section, the case study of modeling the reputations systems which implements the average reputation system in the QoP-ML is presented. An example can be found in [91]. The average system can be used for an auction system where we have three main roles: the auction server, seller, and transactions reviewer are involved in the reputation systems. The server which is the platform enables the transactions and the rates marked by the transaction reviewers are used for evaluation of the seller's reputation. All ratings (average system) for an agent are calculated as the average of all ratings the agent has received. This average value is the global reputation of this agent. The idea of this metric is that agents behave the same way for most of their lifetime. Unusual ratings have only a little weight in the computation of the final reputation. This could be used to place some bad transactions intentionally by bad agents. The possible ratings are as follows: $rate \rightarrow \{-1, 0, 1\}$. The reputation of agent (seller) *a* can be computed as:

$$r(a) = \sum_{m=1}^{N} m/N \qquad (6.1)$$

where:
$r(a)$ – the overall reputation value of the agent *a*;
m – the single rate for the transaction from the set $\{-1, 0, 1\}$;
N – the number of transactions.

In the QoP-ML it is possible to model the reputation systems and analyze them in case of resistant IT attacks and depending on the security measures used. One can imagine the situation where the rating of a seller transaction can be modified by an attacker as part of a Man in the Middle Attack [27]. It would be easy to perform that kind of attack when the rate is submitted by means of a non-encrypted channel. The TLS protocol, which first of all authenticates the auction server and encrypts the transmitted data, can be applied to defend against this attack. Another attack can be a login forgery of the user. One can imagine the situation when the transaction reviewer do not send the mark of the recent transactions but the adversary which can get the transaction reviewer password (sniffing the password, social engineering, etc.) can send the fake transaction mark instead of authorized user. That kind of attack can be prevented by using a one-time password [32] which will help to verify the mark sent by the user.

The system with an adversary with different capabilities for attack is modeled. Three scenarios are analyzed.

Scenario 1: The adversary can do a man in the middle attack (MITM).
Scenario 2: The adversary can do a login forgery attack (LF).
Scenario 3: The adversary can do man in the middle and login forgery attacks.

The transactions in the auction server can be realized by means of four security levels.

Security level 1 – no security: No security mechanisms are used; the rate of the transactions are sent as plain text and no additional user authentication methods are used.
Security level 2 – low: The one-time password is used for additional authentication of the user's mark; the mark is sent as plain text.
Security level 3 – medium: The TLS protocol is used to secure the channel so the mark is encrypted; the one-time password is not used.
Security level 4 – high: The one-time password is used for additional authentication of the user's mark and the TLS protocol is used to secure the channel so the mark is encrypted.

Three scenarios of the adversaries' differing capabilities and four security levels differing in the type of security technology applied to rate the auction transactions are presented in the case study. Agents (sellers) are assumed to have 100 transactions rated by other agents (buyers or reviewers) for all scenarios. All of these transactions are assumed to be good, and can be assessed only by honest buyers. In the next section the analysis of all possible combination of adversary capabilities and security level of the auction server will be presented. The analysis will be presented on a different number of attacks and will range from 10% to 100% of the attack which modified the same number of rates from positive rate $(+1)$ to negative rate (-1).

Table 6.1: QoP-ML's functions for reputation model – Description.

Function	Description
post(id)	posts non-modified rate of Agent transaction with identification *id*
post_mitm(id)	posts the rate which is modified by the MITM attack of Agent transaction with identification *id*
post_lf(id)	posts the rate which is modified by the LF attack of Agent transaction with identification *id*
otp(M)	creates the one-time password for the authorization of the message *M*
verotp(otp)	verifies the one-time password *otp*

6.4.1   The reputation in the QoP-ML – Protocol modeling

Five base steps can be distinguished (Figure 2.2): protocol modeling, security metrics definition, process instantiation, QoP-ML processing, and QoP evaluation (reputation evaluation is a part of QoP evaluation) in the QoP-ML. The next section will present modeling of the auction portal. The four operations: function defining, equation defining, channel defining and protocol flow description are included in the protocol modeling step. Based on the TLS protocol three steps were defined and described in Chapter 2 so here only the structure which should be added for reputation modeling is presented.

Functions
Five additional functions should be defined; the description of them is presented in the Table 6.1.

```
1  fun  post(id)[rate];
2  fun  post_mitm(id)[rate];
3  fun  post_lf(id)[rate];
4  fun  otp(M)[algorithm];
5  fun  verotp(otp);
```

Listing 6.4: The function definition for reputation modeling.

One parameter, the *rate* influencing the agent reputation value, is included in the *post, post_mitm,* and *post_lf* functions. In the *otp* function, the type of algorithm should be defined. All other functions needed for the TLS protocol can be found in Chapter 2.

Equations
The relations between functions can be described after their defining. The required equations can be found in Chapter 2. In our case study one new equation should be defined which will define the relation of the one-time password operations.

```
1  eq verotp(otp(M)) = M;
```

Listing 6.5: The equation definition for reputation modeling.

Channels

The example presents six asymmetric channels.

```
1  channels {
2    channel ch1, ch2, ch3, ch4, ch5, ch6 (*);
3  }
```

Listing 6.6: The channel definition for reputation modeling.

Protocol flow

Abstracting the protocol flow is the last and most important operation in the modeling process. Three scenarios of sending the ratings about the transactions made in the auction are analyzed in the case study. The TLS client (the agent reviewing the transaction) is modeled in Listing 6.7, whereas the TLS server (auction portal) is modeled in Listing 6.8.

```
1   host Client (rr)(*)
2   {
3    process C(ch1,ch2,ch3,ch4,ch5,ch6)
4    {
5     ID1 = id();
6     V1 = Vlist();
7     C1 = Clist();
8     Com1 = Comlist();
9     N1 = nonce()[256,Linux PRNG];
10    M1 = (ID1, V1, C1, Com1, N1);
11    out(ch1:M1);
12
13    in(ch2:Y);
14    PKScert=Y[4];
15    K1=skey()[256,Linux PRNG];
16    K1E=enc(K1,PKScert)[2048,RSA,pk];
17    ReadyEC=info(ReadyEncClient());
18    FinC=info(FinClient());
19    M3=(K1E, ReadyEC,FinC);
20    out(ch3:M3);
21
22    in(ch4:Q);
23    Status=newstate(st_active());
24
25    subprocess C_tls(*)
26    {
27     P1=post(Clinet1)[1];
28     P1E=enc(P1,K1)[256,AES,CBC];
```

```
29    P1all=hmac(P1E)[SHA1,1];
30    M5=(P1E,P1all);
31    out(ch5:M5);
32    Status=newstate(st_closed());
33    }
34
35    subprocess  C_none(*)
36    {
37     P1mod=post(Clinet1)[1];
38     M5=(P1mod);
39     out(ch6:M5);
40     Status=newstate(st_closed());
41    }
42
43    subprocess  C_otp(*)
44    {
45     P1mod2=post(Clinet1)[1];
46     P1otp=otp(P1mod2)[hash_chain];
47     M5=(P1mod2,P1otp);
48     out(ch6:M5);
49     Status=newstate(st_closed());
50    }
51
52    subprocess  C_tls_otp(*)
53    {
54     P1=post(Clinet1)[1];
55     P1otp=otp(P1)[hash_chain];
56     P1E=enc(P1otp,K1)[256,AES,CBC];
57     P1all=hmac(P1E)[SHA1,1];
58     M5=(P1E,P1all);
59     out(ch5:M5);
60     Status=newstate(st_closed());
61    }
62
63   subprocess  C_mitm_attack(*)
64    {
65     P1mitm=post_mitm(Clinet1)[-1];
66     M5=(P1mitm);
67     out(ch5:M5);
68     Status=newstate(st_closed());
69    }
70
71   subprocess  C_lf_attack(*)
72    {
73     P1lf=post_lf(Clinet1)[-1];
74     M5=(P1lf);
75     out(ch6:M5);
76     Status=newstate(st_closed());
77    }
78
79   }
80  }
```

Listing 6.7: The client of the TLS protocol modeled in the QoP-ML (reviewer)

In Listing 6.7 one can see a model of the auction client who will send the mark of the transaction *host Client*. The *host Client* includes one main process (*process C*) which has six subprocesses. These subprocesses are responsible for sending the post with the mark of the transaction. The subprocess *C_tls* encrypts the given mark as the result of a TLS protocol. The subprocess *C_none* just sends the post without any security operations. The subprocess *C_otp* uses a one-time password for additional authorization of the post. The subprocess *C_tls_otp* uses simultaneously a TLS protocol and a one-time password as the security mechanisms. The subprocess *C_mitm_attack* simulates the man in the middle attack for the posted transaction rates and the subprocess *C_lf_attack* simulates a login forgery attack.

```
 1 host Server (rr)(*)
 2 {
 3   # S = id();
 4   # CA = id();
 5   # SKS=sk(S)[2048,RSA];
 6   # PKS=pk(SKS)[2048,RSA];
 7   # T1=date();
 8   # PKScert=cert(PKS,S,T1,CA)[2048,RSA];
 9
10   process S(ch1,ch2,ch3,ch4,ch5,ch6)
11   {
12   while(true){
13     in(ch1:X);
14     V1ok=set(X[1]);
15     C1ok=set(X[2]);
16     Com1ok=set(X[3]);
17     N2=nonce()[256,Linux PRNG];
18     DoneS=info(Done());
19     M2=(V1ok,C1ok,Com1ok,N2,PKScert,DoneS);
20     out(ch2:M2);
21
22     in(ch3:Y);
23     ReadyES=info(ReadyEncServer());
24     FinS=info(FinServer());
25     M4=(ReadyES, FinS);
26     out(ch4:M4);
27
28     Status=newstate(st_active());
29
30     subprocess S_tls(*)
31     {
32       in(ch5:Z);
33       K1E=Y[0];
34       P1E=Z[0];
35       P1all=Z[1];
36       K1=dec(K1E,SKS)[2048,RSA,sk];
37       P1Ebis=hmac(P1E)[SHA1,1];
38       Vres=ver(P1all,P1Ebis);
39       P1=dec(P1E,K1)[256,AES,CBC];
40     }
41
42     subprocess S_none(*)
43     {
```

```
44    in(ch6:Z);
45    P1mod=Z[0];
46    }
47
48    subprocess  S_otp(*)
49    {
50    in(ch6:Z);
51    P1mod2=Z[0];
52    P1otp=Z[1];
53    M=verotp(P1otp);
54    }
55
56  subprocess  S_tls_otp(*)
57    {
58    in(ch5:Z);
59    K1E=Y[0];
60    P1E=Z[0];
61    P1all=Z[1];
62    K1=dec(K1E,SKS)[2048,RSA,sk];
63    P1Ebis=hmac(P1E)[SHA1,1];
64    Vres=ver(P1all,P1Ebis);
65    P1=dec(P1E,K1)[256,AES,CBC];
66    M=verotp(P1otp);
67    }
68
69  subprocess  S_mitm_attack(*)
70    {
71    in(ch5:Z);
72    P1mod=Z[0];
73    }
74
75  subprocess  S_lf_attack(*)
76    {
77    in(ch6:Z);
78    P1mod=Z[0];
79    }
80
81    Status=newstate(st_closed());
82    }
83  }
84 }
```

Listing 6.8: The server of TLS protocol modeled in the QoP-ML (auction portal)

In Listing 6.8 one can see the model of an auction server (*host Server*) who orga-
nizes and calculates the mark of the hosted transactions. The auction is organized in
the client-server architecture so all the processes modeled for the client have modeled
the server site. The *host Server* includes one main process (*process S*) which has six
subprocesses. The responsibility of these six subprocesses refers to the names which
are similar to those described for the *host Client*.

6.4.2   Security metrics definition

In the process of protocol modeling, the security metrics for all functions related to each security attribute to be tested have to be defined by the designer. Here the same security metrics for the TLS protocol as those in Chapter 2 are used. However, the addition of functionality enabling the analysis of the reputation system combined with the technical system analysis is the main contribution. Based on the structure defined in the previous section, the security metrics for the reputation analysis is defined in Listing 6.9. Three algorithms are indicated for three ways of posting the marks of the transactions. The rate can be submitted without modification, then the *post* function will be used and algorithm *alg1* will be used. The rate can modified as the result of a man in the middle attack (*post_mitm* function); then the algorithm *alg2* will be used. Finally, the rate can be modified as the result of the login forgery attack (*post_lf* function); then the algorithm *alg3* will be used.

```
 1  metrics
 2  {
 3    data*()
 4      {
 5        primhead [function][algorithm]
 6        primitive [post][alg1]
 7        primitive [post_mitm][alg2]
 8        primitive [post_lf][alg3]
 9      }
10  }
```

Listing 6.9: The metrics for the reputation analysis.

6.4.3   Reputation module

The reputation module is the next structure to be modeled. Here the set of algorithms is modeled to evaluate the reputation of the auction according to the number and types of security attacks on the reputation system (Listing 6.10).

```
 1  modules {
 2    reputation {
 3    # rep=1
 4          algorithm alg1 (rate) {
 5            rate = 1;
 6            rep = (rep + rate) / 2;
 7          }
 8
 9          algorithm alg2 (rate) {
10            if (used(P1E)) {
11              rate = 1;
12            }
13            rep = (rep + rate) / 2;
14          }
15
```

```
16      algorithm alg3 (rate) {
17          if (used(P1otp)) {
18          rate = 1;
19          }
20      rep = (rep + rate) / 2;
21      }
22
23  }
24 }
```

Listing 6.10: The metrics for the reputation analysis.

The average algorithm described earlier is used for calculation of the agent reputation. The rate value is described as the reputation parameter (qop parameters) of three types of the transaction rate posting functions: *post, post_mitm, post_lf*. In the model, the *post* function always give the mark 1 for the transactions but functions *post_mitm* and *post_lf* function always give the mark −1 for the transactions (as the result of a successful attack). However, in some cases, the attack can not be prepared with success because of the security mechanisms used for the protection of the transaction. The MITM attack (*post_mitm - alg2*) will be blocked when the TLS protocol is used, which takes place when the $P1E$ variable is used in the protocol flow of the analyzed scenario ($if(used(P1E))$). When this variable is defined in the scenario protocol flow, it indicates that the data was encrypted. The protocol flow in the protocol modeling step is used for defining the type of conditions used. The LF attack (*post_lf - alg3*) is blocked when the one-time password is used for authentication of the post which take place when the $P1otp$ variable is used in the protocol flow of the scenario analyzed ($if(used(P1otp))$).

6.4.4 Process instantiation

In the case study, the system with adversaries with different capabilities for attack and with different transactions' quality of protection is modeled. In **Scenario 1**, the adversary can do a man in the middle attack (MITM), in **Scenario 2**, the adversary can do a login forgery attack (LF) and in the **Scenario 3**, the adversary can do both man in the middle and login forgery attacks. Quality of protection can be realize on four levels: in **Security level 1** no security mechanisms are used, in **Security level 2** a one-time password is used for additional authentication of the user's mark, in **Security level 3** the TLS protocol is used to secure the channel so the mark is encrypted, and in **Security level 4** the one-time password is used for additional authentication of the user's mark and the TLS protocol is used to secure the channel.

The versions of the scenarios modeled can be defined in the course of the process instantiation. The example (Listing 6.11) shows three scenarios defined as versions 1,2,3, respectively. In all versions two high hierarchy processes are executed: host Client and host Server. In version 1 (Scenario 1) inside the process host Client, the two processes C are executed (function − run), the first one with the subprocess C_tls which is repeated 90 times (90) (which simulates 90 good rates sent by the Client (reviewer)) and the second one with the subprocess C_mitm_attack (MITM attack) which is repeated 10 times (10). Inside the process host Server, two processes S are executed, the first one with the subprocess S_tls and the second one with the subprocess S_mitm_attack.

In version 2 (Scenario 2) inside the process host Client, the two processes C are executed (function – run), the first one the same as in version 1 but the second one with the subprocess C_lf_attack (login forgery attack) which is repeated 10 times (10). Inside the process host Server, two processes S are executed, the first one with the subprocess S_tls and the second one with the subprocess S_lf_attack.

In the third version (Scenario 3) inside the process host Client, the three processes C are executed (function – run), the first one with the subprocess C_tls which is repeated 80 times (80) (which simulates 80 good rates sent by the Client (reviewer)), the second one with the subprocess C_mitm_attack (MITM attack) which is repeated 10 times (10) and the third one with the subprocess S_lf_attack (LF attack), which is repeated 10 times (10). Inside the process host Server, three processes S are executed, the first one with the subprocess S_tls, the second one with the subprocess S_mitm_attack and the third one with the subprocess S_lf_attack.

In Listing 6.11 the **security level 3** is enabled, because in all versions the *Client* executes the subprocess C_tls which indicates that TLS Protocols is enabled. **Security level 1** will be enabled when the *Client* executes the subprocess C_none which indicates that no security mechanisms is enabled. **Security level 2** will be enabled when the *Client* executes the subprocess C_otp which indicates that a one-time password is being used. The strongest security level (**security level 4**) will be enabled when the *Client* executes the subprocess C_tls_otp which indicates that the TLS protocols and a one-time password are being used.

Additionally, the simulations for the different number of the attacks can be calculated. In Listing 6.11 processes were executed which simulate that 10% of rates were attacked and 90% of them were not. It means that in versions 1 and 2, 10 transaction mark were modified into negative ones (-1) and 90 transaction marks are positive (1). In scenario 3, one can see importance differences, because then two types of attacks are run. In that case, 20 transaction marks were modified into negative ones (-1) and 80 transactions mark are positive (1).

```
1
2  version 1
3  {
4    run host Client (*)
5    {
6      run C(C_tls){90}[ch1,ch2,ch3,ch4,ch5,ch6]
7      run C(C_mitm_attack){10}[ch1,ch2,ch3,ch4,ch5]
8    }
9    run host Server (*)
10   {
11     run S(S_tls)
12     run S(S_mitm_attack)
13   }
14 }
15
```

```
16 version 2
17 {
18  run host Client(*)
19  {
20   run C(C_tls){90}[ch1,ch2,ch3,ch4,ch5,ch6]
21   run C(C_lf_attack){10}[ch1,ch2,ch3,ch4,ch6]
22  }
23  run host Server(*)
24  {
25   run S(S_tls)
26   run S(S_lf_attack)
27  }
28 }
29
30 version 3
31 {
32  run host Client(*)
33  {
34   run C(C_tls){80}[ch1,ch2,ch3,ch4,ch5,ch6]
35   run C(C_mitm_attack){10}[ch1,ch2,ch3,ch4,ch5]
36   run C(C_lf_attack){10}[ch1,ch2,ch3,ch4,ch6]
37  }
38  run host Server(*)
39  {
40   run S(S_tls)
41   run S(S_mitm_attack)
42   run S(S_lf_attack)
43  }
44 }
```

Listing 6.11: The protocol instantiation for reputation analysis when 10% of the rates were attacked and the process is realized on security level 3.

6.4.5   QoP and reputation evaluation

QoP evaluation, and reputation evaluation as a part of it, is the last step. The effect of the security mechanisms to ensure security attributes is examined by the QoP evaluation which is discussed in previous chapters. Here the emphasis is put on the reputation evaluation which is a new type. The QoP and reputation evaluation algorithms are implemented using the Automated Quality of Protection Analysis tool (AQoPA).

Here a reputation algorithm based on the average reputation system is analyzed. In Listing 6.11 the process instantiation for all three scenarios, security level 3, and 10% of attacks are executed. The results – for these particular parameters – the reputation level is equal to 1 for scenario 1 and is equal to 0.8 for scenarios 2 and 3. In scenario 1 only MITM attacks are performed, to which the auction system is resistant (in security level 3). The result of that is that the reputation level is not attacked and is equal to 1. In scenarios 2 and 3 the reputation level is modified and is decreased

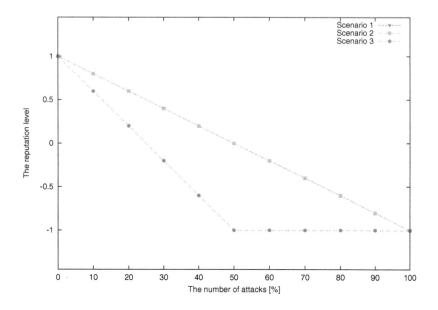

Figure 6.1: The reputation evaluation for security level 1.

to 0.8. In scenario 2, 10% of the attacks refer to login forgery, for which the transactions were not secured. In scenario 2, 20% of the marks were attacked but 10% of
them were protected by the TLS protocol, and the second 10% were not, because this
attack used to login forgery.

It is worth analyzing all defined security levels and the range of the attacks from
10% to 100%. Figure 6.1 presents the results of the three scenarios analyzed for all
range of attacks at security level 1. In **security level 1** no security modules are used
so one can see how the global reputation level of the agent can be modified by means
of IT attacks on the system. Scenarios 1 and 2 have a similar effect on the reputation
level because only one type of the attack took place. After 50% of the attacks the
reputation is decreased to neutral (0) and is decreased to a negative value (-1) when
all the transactions votes are attacked. In the scenario 3, two types of attack took
place (MITM and LF) and when no security mechanism was enabled after 50% of
the attacks, the reputation level equaled -1 (negative value).

Figure 6.2 presents the results of the three scenarios analyzed for all ranges of
attacks and security level 2. In this security level the one-time password is used for
authentication of the posted marks of the transactions. One can see that adversaries'
attacks based on login forgery (scenario 2) do not influence reputation system (positive value 1) because of security mechanisms used. In the scenario 1 the system
is still vulnerable to attacks because the adversaries do man in the middle attacks
which the one-time password module cannot protect. In the scenario 3, the system is

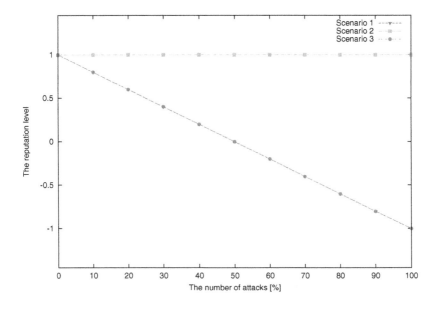

Figure 6.2: The reputation evaluation for security level 2.

partially protected, because login forgery attacks are blocked but man in the middle attacks successfully modified the transactions' marks.

Figure 6.3 presents the results of the three scenarios analyzed for all ranges of attacks and having security level 3. In this security level the TLS protocol is used for posting the marks of the transactions. One can see that adversaries' attacks based on the MITM attack (scenario 1) do not influence the reputation system (positive value 1) because of the security mechanisms used. In the scenario 2 the system is still vulnerable to the attacks because the adversaries do login forgery attacks which TLS protocol does not protect. In scenario 3, the system is partially protected, because MITM attacks are blocked but login forgery attacks do successfully modify transactions' marks.

Figure 6.4 presents the results of the three scenarios analyzed for all ranges of attacks with security level 4. In this security level both security modules are used (one-time password and the TLS protocol). In this security level all attacks are blocked and the agent's reputation level is not modified, and is equal to 1 (positive value).

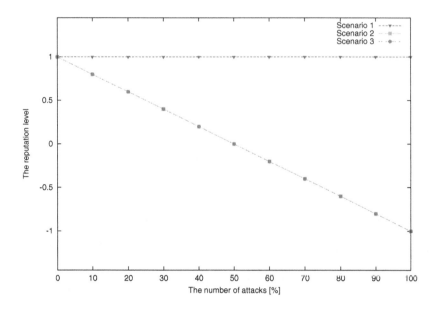

Figure 6.3: The reputation evaluation for security level 3.

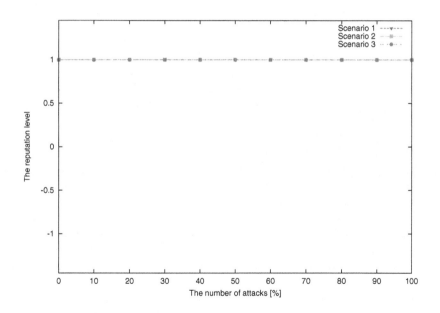

Figure 6.4: The reputation evaluation for security level 4.

Chapter 7

Security metrics – Methodology

CONTENTS

Information security is brought under explicit control by the ISO/IEC 27001 standard which is a part of the growing ISO/IEC 27000 family of standards. ISO/IEC 27001, as a formal specification, gives the requirements for establishing, implementing, maintaining and improving the Information Security Management System. A systematic examination of the information security risks considering threats, vulnerabilities, and impacts is required by this system. Suitable information security controls providing best practice recommendation on information security management are provided by the ISO/IEC 27001 using ISO/IEC 27002 which works out instructions and general principles for initiating, implementing, maintaining and improving information security management, and sets up controls related to specific requirements identification via a formal risk assessment. ISO/IEC 27002 determines the controls of various security disciplines such as operational security, application security, computing platform security, network security, and physical security.

The monitoring and verification provided correct functioning of defined controls, which is done by the *check* phase of *Act-Plan-Do-Check* Deming cycle introduced in the ISO/IEC 27001 standard. Using one of several available models can satisfy the check phase. Formal description of the processes controlling proper functioning of defined controls can be made using these models. An example of formal description of the measurement development is the detailed model presented in ISO/IEC 27004. The U.S. NIST 800 series [21, 22] presents other standards applied in this area. They respond to the requirements for the systematics techniques to obtain quantitative evidence of the system security performance. Security evidence for security engineering, security management as well as external and internal evaluation can be achieved using security metrics which have become a standard term for IT with regard to metrics depicting security level, security performance, security indicators, or security strength of the IT systems [78, 79].

With hardware and software becoming a part of more and more complex IT systems, it is more and more difficult to measure their performance. To obtain proper measurement results, one should be aware of many things taking place in the system which are invisible to the application programmer and can affect the measurement process (OS interruptions, data cache misses, hard drive accesses, unexpected activity of other applications etc.) as well as delay and obfuscate results making measurement unreliable.

Though detailed guidance on same operational aspects of security measurements is provided by the ISO/IEC 27004 and NIST standards, they are not comprehensive instructions on all relevant issues. It should be mentioned that the model in question does not contain a data profiling step, which is essential for some types of processes such as determination of consistency, uniqueness and logic of the actual content, structure and quality of data values within a dataset. Moreover, it should be kept in mind that some activities/functions largely depend on randomness. Therefore validation of the data is essential for the whole measurement process.

Data corruption or security vulnerability can be caused by incorrect data validation. The task of data validation is to check if the data is valid, sensible, reasonable, and secure before its processing.

Introduction of a new security measurement model extending the one presented in the ISO/IEC 27004 with the measurement validation methods is presented in [64] and is further discussed in this chapter. The validated measurements being robust and reproducible make performance metrics more reliable and provide key information for decision makers. Due to the verification of the gathered results, a means for monitoring, reporting, improving, and assessing the effectiveness of the implemented security controls is provided by the developed information security performance metrics.

A case study employing the new model proposed for cryptographic modules is also presented. Besides, the Crypto-Metrics Tool (CMTool) which is a benchmarking and results validation tool to test the performance of the cryptographic primitives is implemented. Of significant importance for Quality of Protection models is benchmarking of cryptographic modules as it evaluates information security of the IT Systems [44, 43, 42, 45]. Security metrics for cryptographic modules required for Quality of Protection Modeling Language (QoP-ML) are created by the CMTool based on the measurement model. It is possible to download the CMTool from the web page of the *QoP-ML* project [7].

7.1   The model

The ISO/IEC 27004 standard [82] presents the model of measurements of control objective which includes six steps: definition of controls, control objectives and implementation, elaboration of object of measurement and its attributes, base measures specification, derived measures specification, and separation of indicators and analysis of gathered measurement results. A new model for robust measurement of security control objectives based on the ISO/IEC 27001 standard is proposed. It was expanded by adding the three steps: validation of the measurement method, base measures, and derived measures validations. Figure 7.1 presents the modified model, all of whose steps are described later.

7.1.1   Step 1: Information needs

To obtain relevant security metrics, first the quantifiable performance measures producing important performance data for developing security analysis should be designed and implemented. Then suitable control objectives, controls and processes satisfying required conditions have to be implemented. Specifying control objectives, controls and processes are described in statements related to risks and supporting processes, procedures, policies, and activities connected with them. That should mitigate these risks effectively. Moreover, control objectives, controls, and processes to treat risks have to be defined. There must be good selection of control objectives, controls and processes in order to implement them so that they satisfy the requirements identified earlier.

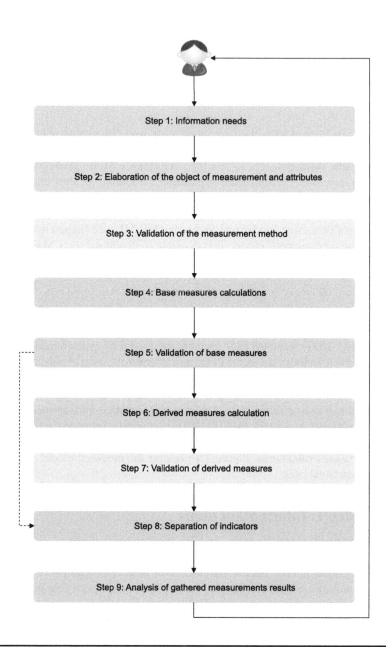

Figure 7.1: The new security measurement model with measurement validations.

7.1.2 Step 2: Elaboration of the object of measurement and attributes

As for the information security measurement model, various attributes related to the decision making process are provided by the object of measurement. When the attributes are defined, they are quantified and converted into indicators. They contribute to the assessment of the implemented processes' effectiveness as a basis for further security analysis.

7.1.3 Step 3: Validation of the measurement method

The validation of the environment including the measurement process is the measurement method validation. The factors affecting this process are, among others, the validation of the source of data, the state of the computer referring to data interfaces, quality of the measurement device, elimination of sources of external noises and disturbances, correctness of the measurement methodology and protection against attacks on data sources like: masquerade, loss of data integrity or data freshness.

7.1.4 Step 4: Base measures calculations

The base measure is the simplest one possible to gather. In order to identify it, one should keep in mind its close relation with identification of objects of measurement and their attributes.

7.1.5 Step 5: Validation of base measures

For further calculations it is necessary to classify and validate the results of measurements. First, it is necessary to decide if the measurements make a time series (if they are statically dependent and/or their statistical distributions are time dependent) or if they are a statistical sample (whether they are the results of measurements of a random variable). To make such a decision, first the measurements series should be analyzed by means of the methods belonging to the time-series theory e.g., moving average methods [14], cross-validation [14], Markov or Hidden Markov Models [75]. When the measures are the time series, they have to be decomposed to the form applicable in further calculations, e.g., as a sum of non-stationary (deterministic trend) and stationary (random fluctuations) parts. In the next step, depending on the autocorrelation function properties [28], whether the fluctuation is a stationary time-series or a statistical sample should be considered. It is also possible to use a sorting method in order to group the data into the sub-samples which will each be of the stationary character. In the case measurements are a statistical sample, its homogeneity and independence have to be verified by using the statistical homogeneity tests [58], [50]. Additionally, single (or multiple) outliers can be detected in the sample by applying e.g., the *Dixon Q test*. Derived quantities can calculated using such validated measurements.

When the base measures defined have been validated, it is possible to apply validated measurement results as the input for the statistical analysis which consists of the calculation of several defined formulas (statistical primitives) on a collected and verified series.

7.1.6   Step 6: Derived measures calculations – Optional step

The derived measure is considered to be an aggregation of two or more base measures. Input for several derived measures come from a given base measure.

7.1.7   Step 7: Validation of derived measures – Optional step

In the process of indicators definition there are taken into consideration the derived measures whose correctness and meaningfulness should be validated. The two properties: the information about the phenomenon gathered by each measure should be maximal while overlapping information estimated from the measures pairwise should be minimal have to be satisfied by derived measures. Providing sufficient information for calculation of the required indicators, it is possible to protect against cumulating measurement errors. In order to accomplish this, the methods based on the measurements mutual correlation analysis or the information theory approach [41] must be applied.

7.1.8   Step 8: Separation of indicators

An indicator can be defined as a measure providing an estimate or evaluation of defined attributes derived from an analytical model which is used for a base measure or the derived measures (if any of them are determined).

7.1.9   Step 9: Analysis of gathered measurement results

It is possible to develop the measurement results with interpreting indicators for decision criteria. For effectiveness and other defined factors the overall measurements objectives should be taken into account. Indicators in correlation with defined decision criteria provide information for improving the performance of information security programs. The results obtained can provide meaningful information (and thus be useful) only when defined control objectives will refer to the concrete organization and process for which measurements are performed. Since defining control objectives which will satisfy all the security requirements and provide decision making and guide compliancy to security standards simultaneously in complex environments is a challenging task, we can provide only general rules for determining the increase or decrease of a risk. Nevertheless, it is worth noting that the general rules should be carefully analyzed and adjusted to facilitate the relevant actions for security improvement, reflecting any changes to the organization goals and information needs. Determination of the indicator value should take into account the fact that even if the security controls are implemented, the risk of attacks can still oc-cur. Therefore, defined indicator value depicts the strength of the existing security mechanisms in mitigating the risks. As the trends of the defined measures, indicators must be within the same scale as measures, in order to easily assess if the risk is adequately controlled (they must be comparable). When all defined security controls have their indicators established, and equivalent measures are gathered and validated, one can determine the effectiveness of the security controls quite straightforwardly. If the measure obtained is equal to or below the recommended value (the indicator value), then the risk is considered adequately controlled, otherwise existing security mechanisms are not as effective as they may seem to be. However, bear in mind that for complex, often distributed environments, such estimations can be very compli-cated and besides the indicator values should include also the thresholds, targets, or patterns (as stated in 27000 series – *decision criteria*) used to determine the need for action or further investigation.

7.2 Case study – Cryptographic modules

Here the case study of the proposed method to generate robust measurements in the complex environments is presented. The benchmarking of the cryptographic modules is chosen. The explanation of obtaining, verifying and transforming relevant security attributes into indicators (which are the most important components for the decision making process) is given below.

7.2.1 Step 1: Information needs

Security and efficient performance are the two most relevant information needs in benchmarking of cryptographic protocols. They are also of significant importance in the analysis of the performance of cryptographic primitives. Selection of a crypto-graphic protocol with minimum machine workload adjusting possible is the strongest security mechanism and the main objective here. A maximum required level of secu-rity with minimum machine workload is the purpose of the measurement construct. The stability of the machine tested or the performance of its basic tasks can not be affected by the security mechanisms. Checking the performance and speed of the machine during the cryptographic operations is done by the measurement construct by means of cryptographic algorithms with different input parameters – key length, mode of operation, the length of the input data. The second principle to be accom-plished by the presented model is automation of creating security metrics for the QoP-ML Language for chosen cryptographic primitives. Gathering the QoP-ML se-curity metrics should consider many different attributes. It is necessary to calculate the benchmarks individually, for creating metrics for each host tested, and to pro-duce meaningful results their hardware and software configuration should be taken into account.

The control objectives defined are used for managing the overall system workload to obtain a required level of performance and to prevent an excessive increase in the system load. Selection of a proper cryptographic algorithm is being considered. Security within the organization together with proper performance, comfortable work, availability and stability of the tested machine should be actively supported by the cryptographic primitive chosen.

7.2.2 Step 2: Elaboration of the object of measurement and attributes

Based on the model presented, a central processing unit (CPU) is considered to be the uppermost object of measurement. Five attribute (base measures) obtained after the measurement process are identified.

1. **CPU time**: a unit of measurement indicating the amount of time used for a central processing unit.

2. **Wall time** (also referred as real time or wall clock time): a unit of measurement which indicates the actual time that a program takes to run or to execute its assigned tasks, refers to elapsed time as determined by a wall clock.

3. **Speed**: a unit of measurement indicating the amount of data [in megabytes] which is processed within one second.

4. **Number of cycles per byte**: a unit of measurement which indicates the number of clock cycles a microprocessor will perform per byte.

5. **Calls per second**: a unit of measurement which indicates the number of calls for the chosen cryptographic operation within a given time interval (here one second).

7.2.3 Step 3: Validation of the measurement method

Hardware and software are very important for preparation of security metrics for cryptographic modules. A few things should be considered in order to minimize the impact of the overall system performance and to get the most reliable, accurate, and meaningful results before actual measurement starts.

The delays resulting from accessing the data which are far from the CPU constitute a vital problem. It can be overcome be removing all effects of transactions between the memory to data cache and that to the instruction cache. "CPU warmings" is the technique which can be applied. The CPU cache is believed to be a good method for warming-up the CPU cache first and performing suitable measurements later because of quick access to it and possibility of storing the most frequently or recently used data.

Another problem concerns the fact that a large number of interactions is needed for most performance measurements caused by the processing speed and the troubles connected with obtaining micro and milliseconds resolutions. Long enough time is necessary for the benchmark to run to provide a set of samples significant from a statistical point of view. Side effects are produced because of too few iterations, inaccurate, non-reproducible timing, or because the machine is under load.

The last but not least problem is turning off all networking and stopping all software programs that might run periodically (even those running in the background) because the overall system performance is affected by them. It is important to remember that the efficiency of the cryptographic algorithm is measured but the not performance of a virus checker or a music player.

7.2.4 Step 4: Base measures specification

Five different attributes (base measures) are introduced and the defined measures are calculated in the presented model in the second step.

7.2.5 Step 5: Validation of base measures

The measurement results, being the input for decision making, have to be validated before further analysis. In the first stage, one of the time-series methods mentioned should be used to determine if the results are the time series (then coefficient of variation, CV, known also as the *unitized risk* or *the variation coefficient* [85]). Then the value of the *coefficient of variation* calculated (which is the ratio of the standard deviation to the mean) is used for the validation. Thus if the CV value determined is greater than 10%, the data are considered non-stationary. Otherwise, the *Dixon's Q test* can be applied and the final statistical calculations can be done for the stationary series. The fifth step will be described in further detail.

Pre-requirements. Some measurements should be made before validation. Step one includes the choice of the cryptographic primitive to measure its performance (e.g., measure the wall time [performance attribute] of AES encryption in CBC mode [cryptographic primitive]), run n tests (where $n \geq 3$) with k iterations per each (where $k \geq 1000$), with m byte length input (where $m \geq 1$); collect measurement results, $X = \{x_1, x_2, ..., x_n\}$, and apply *the validation process* as follows.

1. Check for the stationarity of the measurement results gathered

    (a) Let $\bar{x}$ be the sum of all the x_i within the subset X divided by the total number of data points, n

    (b) Let δ be the standard deviation calculated using of the values from the X set

    (c) Let *CV* be the *coefficient of variation*, given by $CV = \frac{\delta}{\bar{x}} * 100$

    (d) Decide if the measurement results are stationary or not, that is, if the

Table 7.1: Formulas for calculating the experimental Q-value.

	Q_{exp_1}	Q_{exp_n}
$3 \leqslant n \leqslant 7$	$\frac{x_2-x_1}{x_n-x_1}$	$\frac{x_n-x_{n-1}}{x_n-x_1}$
$8 \leqslant n \leqslant 10$	$\frac{x_2-x_1}{x_{n-1}-x_1}$	$\frac{x_n-x_{n-1}}{x_n-x_2}$
$11 \leqslant n \leqslant 13$	$\frac{x_3-x_1}{x_{n-1}-x_1}$	$\frac{x_n-x_{n-2}}{x_n-x_2}$
$n \geqslant 14$	$\frac{x_3-x_1}{x_{n-2}-x_1}$	$\frac{x_n-x_{n-2}}{x_n-x_3}$

coefficient of variation, CV, is greater than 10% (meaning data are non-stationary) or smaller than 10% (supplying an assumption of the stationarity of the series)

2. If the data gathered are stationary, one can now test for its homogeneity by applying the *Dixon's Q test* as follows (algorithm A.22).

   (a) Get measurement results from the second validation step; let x_i be the measurement result from the *ith*-test (where $i = 1,...,n$), and arrange them in the ascending order: $x_1 < x_2 < ... < x_n$.

   (b) On the basis of the measurement results set size, n, calculate Q_{exp_1} and Q_{exp_n} (algorithms A.17 and A.18). In Table 7.1 the formulas for calculating the experimental Q-value, the difference of the suspect value from its nearest one divided by the range of the values are presented.

   (c) Compare Q_{exp_1} and Q_{exp_n} with the critical value, Q_{critic}. If $Q_{exp_1} > Q_{critic}$ (or $Q_{exp_n} > Q_{critic}$), then the suspect value can be rejected and one will reject the *null hypothesis*, (H_0), and consider the *alternative* one – (H_1) – the measurement results do not belong to the same population. However, when $Q_{exp_1} < Q_{critic}$ (or $Q_{exp_n} < Q_{critic}$), then the *null hypothesis* that there is no significant difference between the suspect value and the other values in the data set is accepted (algorithms A.19 and A.20). Also, the suspect value is retained for further analysis, meaning there are hardly any measurement errors. The critical value should correspond to the confidence level that one decided to run the test with. The value of Q_{critic} for the appropriate confidence level can be obtained from [26].

   (d) After the *Dixon's Q test* is completed, one can finally use the measurement results for the estimation of indicators.

3. Non-stationary data, being unpredictable, cannot be modeled or statistically analyzed to provide meaningful results. Using a non-stationary time series the results can be spurious as they may indicate a relationship between two variable of which one does not exist. When the data are indicated in the first stage as non-stationary by the validation process, they should be transformed into the stationary series. Obtaining stationary strictly depends on the type of analysis process that produced the measurement results collected. Applying the

correct transformation results from better understanding of the type of the non-stationary series. Careful examination of the data gathered enables application of the most suitable transformation techniques. The *Dixon's Q test* (step 2) can be applied for identification and rejection of possible outlier values from the measurements results collection gathered after the data conversion into the stationary set.

4. Finally the statistical analysis can be done after the validation process. Mean, mode, median, variance, standard deviation, skewness and kurtosis values can be calculated after defining well known statistical formulas and using the obtained and verified results.

7.2.6 Step 6 and 7: Derived measures specification and validation

In this case study the main measures used for creating final indicators are the base measures. However, the derived measures are not assessed.

7.2.7 Step 8: Separation of indicators

The attributes measured are used for estimation of step indicators which proceeds based on the defined analytical model or formulas being accurate for specific control objectives determined in the first step (*The information needs* step). The condition for defining such formulas is that control objectives concern concrete organization and the process being measured.

7.2.8 Step 9: Analysis of measurement results gathered

The information about how to improve the performance of information security programs is provided by indicators along with defined decision criteria. Similar to the eight steps, here the condition is that the control objective has to deal with organization and process subjected, as specific organizations and processes are not dealt with.

7.3 Test of cryptographic primitives

The two algorithms: RC4 with 256-bit key and HMAC based on the SHA1 were taken to test the security measurement model. There were performed $n = 10$ tests, $k = 10000$ iterations per each (which gives $10000 * 10 = 100000$ operations in total). As the operation was chosen the encryption of the input message with the length of $m = 512$ bytes. We also tested the performance of the RSA key generation ($n = 10$ tests, $k = 50$ iterations per each with the *keylength* = 4096). The tests were performed

Table 7.2: Calculated statistical primitives for each of defined base measures of the performance of RC4 with 256-bit key. These statistical primitives were calculated with the use of the raw and validated measurement results.

base measure \ statistical primitive	mean		standard deviation		variance		median	
	raw	validated	raw	validated	raw	validated	raw	validated
Cycles per byte [#]	2.969	2.967	0.010	0.006	0.000000	0.000000	2.967	2.965
Wall time [ms]	0.0012699400	0.0012699400	0.0000048405	0.0000048405	0.000000	0.000000	0.0012681500	0.0012677000
CPU time [ms]	0.0012689300	0.0012677111	0.0000046596	0.0000030443	0.000000	0.000000	0.000120	0.000887
Speed [MB/s]	763.609	765.491	6.992	4.348	48.887	18.903	767.342	768.447
Operations per second [#]	781936	783863	7160	4452	51261781	19821247	785758	786890

Table 7.3: Calculated statistical primitives for each of defined base measures of the performance of HMAC-SHA1. These statistical primitives were calculated with the use of the raw and validated measurement results.

base measure \ statistical primitive	mean		standard deviation		variance		median	
	raw	validated	raw	validated	raw	validated	raw	validated
Cycles per byte [#]	5.870	5.858	0.001	0.000	0.038	0.013	5.861	5.857
Wall time [ms]	0.0025052900	0.0025042556	0.0000043318	0.0000031858	0.000000	0.000000	0.0025047500	0.0025038000
CPU time [ms]	0.0025092800	0.0025092800	0.0000070407	0.0000070407	0.000000	0.000000	0.0025085000	0.0025085000
Speed [MB/s]	385.428	386.478	3.989	2.580	15.915	6.654	386.117	387.318
Operations per second [#]	394678	395754	4085	2642	16687781	6977606	395384	396614

on an Intel(R) Core(TM) i7-3930K CPU @ 3.20GHz processor under Linux Linux Mint 13 Maya 3.2.0-23-generic 32 bit OS with OpenSSL 1.0.1 14 Mar 2012 as the cryptographic library for AES and RSA encryption, and on Intel(R) Core(TM) i7-3630QM CPU @ 2.40GHz processor under Linux Ubuntu 13.10 3.11.0-15-generic 64 bit OS with OpenSSL 1.0.1e 11 Feb 2013 as cryptographic library for RSA key generation. We ran the validation process with the confidence level, $CL = 80$ (needed for *Dixon's Q test*).

The validation process has to be carried out after the measurement results collection: in the first phase the coefficient of variation is calculated. After separating measurements results into stationary and non-stationary sets, further statistical analysis can be made. The basis for such division is the determined CV value.

The data regarded as stationary can be tested using the *Dixon's Q test* with respect to their homogeneity and independence. In the case of a non-stationary series first the measurement results obtained should be transformed into stationary sets.

It is possible to calculate statistical primitives for the indicators separation when the measurement results obtained are verified and free of random gross errors. Comparison of chosen statistical primitive values obtained for raw data and validated results shows the significance of the validation process for gathering robust measurements results (Tables 7.2, 7.3).

It is possible to assess the importance of the validation process in obtaining reproducible measurement results from the analysis of the standard deviation values (the measure showing the extent of dispersion from the average). The lower the standard deviation the more data points are very close to the expected value, and in the case of a higher standard deviation, more data points are distributed over a larger range of values. For comparison the raw and validated standard deviation values of the speed base measure for RC4 with 256-bit key can be taken into account. Before applying the validation process the raw standard deviation value for speed was 6.992 (Table 7.2). After the *Dixon's Q test* it decreased to 4.348. This significant change leads to the assumption that the validation process is vital for collecting correct and reproducible results. Moreover, as follows from the base measure called cycles per byte obtained for RSA with 4096-bit key, the validation process does not affect the original data i.e., it does not distort the collected series when no significant difference is observed in the measurements obtained (7.3). Significant improvement of the validation methods suggested is found while considering the speed base measure HMAC-SHA1 generation. The raw standard deviation value for speed was 3.989 before the use of the validation process. Then it dropped to 2.580 when applying the *Dixon's Q test.*

Chapter 8

Tool support

CONTENTS

8.1 AQoPA – Automatic quality of protection analysis tool

One of the most challenging issues for the QoP models is performing a multilevel evaluation for complex and distributed systems. The manual analysis of such systems is almost impossible to perform. The analysis of any type of the security protocol is difficult when the experts do not use automated tools. In literature, we can indicate programs which helped the experts analyze the protocols. We can indicate the AVISPA tool [15, 88] or ProVerif [18, 49] application, which verifies security properties for cryptographic protocols. From the Quality of Protection analysis point of view, AVISPA and ProVerif have two limitations. The first one refers to the types of the function which can be modeled; one can model only cryptographic primitives and cryptographic algorithms. The full QoP analysis must refer to all security factors which affect overall system security. The second limitation is that these languages do not provide the structure for evaluation of the security factors' performance. In the literature one can indicate the tool for QoP analysis which is modeled on the UMLsec [39]. This tool can be used for automated analysis of simple models but when we would like to analyze the scenarios when thousands of hosts take part in the protocol, then the analysis is too complex and cannot be done properly.

In this section, the Automated Quality of Protection Analysis tool for the QoP-ML models (AQoPA) is presented. The AQoPA performs the automatic evaluation of QoP-ML models which were created in the Quality of Protection Modeling Language. One of the main contributions of the tool is to analyze complex models which may consist of thousands of hosts representing a wide area network which are actors in the cryptographic protocol or a complex IT system. The full description of the AQoPA will be presented in the next sections. The AQoPA tool can be downloaded from the official web page of the Quality of Protection Modeling Language Project [7].

The data flow of AQoPA is presented in Figure 8.1. The figure presents four successive steps: step 1 – model creation, step 2 – security metrics definition, step 3 – scenarios definition, and step 4 – simulation. These steps refer to the methodology of creating QoP-ML models defined in Chapter 2 where the details about syntax and semantics can be found.

8.1.1 Step 1 – Model creation

The model creation stage is the first stage which must be performed using the AQoPA tool. The goal of this stage is to create the QoP-ML model that will be evaluated in the analysis process. The stage is divided into 4 phases presented in Figure 8.2. Initially the designer has to define functions (phase 1), function equations (phase 2), and channels (phase 3). Later he can use them to create protocol flow (phase 4).

Protocol flow is defined for hosts because they are the highest level elements of the analysis. Hosts contain processes, and processes can contain subprocesses. Each process and subprocess contains an instructions list.

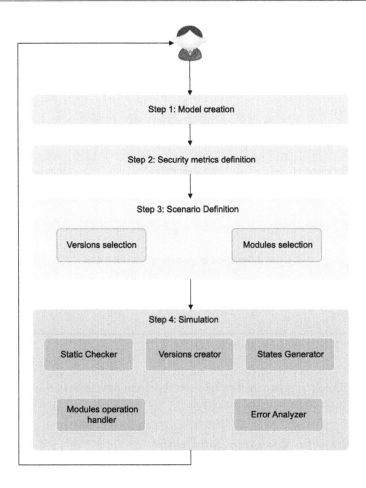

Figure 8.1: AQoPA data flow.

8.1.2 Step 2 – Security metrics definition

The second stage is the security metrics definition stage which is divided into 4 phases. In the first phase, the designer has to gather metrics and configurations of devices analyzed (servers, sensors, etc.). In the second phase the designer has to select a subset of metrics for the functions that are used in the protocol flow created in the first stage.

The aim of the last two phases is to group selected metrics in sets and assign them to hosts. The designer can model different devices; therefore, the metrics for the same functions may have different values. For example, the encryption operations are many times faster on high-performance servers than on the wireless sensor's nodes.

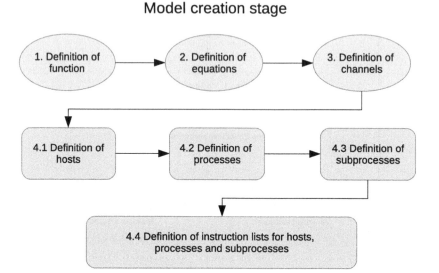

Figure 8.2: Model creation stage in AQoPA.

The designer has to group metrics into sets representing one device and assign these sets to the hosts created in the first stage.

8.1.3 Step 3 – Scenario definition

The aim of the third stage is to define the scenarios of the analysis process. The protocol flow is already created and the designer has to define versions that he would like to evaluate.

Version selection

Versions represent different variants of the protocol evaluated. Versions include a list of hosts executed, their processes and the subprocesses that will be included in independent evaluations. The designer does not have to choose all processes from the host, but any subset that will create the target protocol flow. The differences in versions may come from using different devices or security mechanisms resulting in different metrics or from different protocol flows (i.e., including additional processes or subprocesses in the version that implement an additional security mechanism). Versions allow one to evaluate complex models with a large number of hosts, by using repetition. The designer can repeat hosts and processes. At the end of the analysis, the designer obtains results for all evaluations and can compare them.

Module selection

Besides versions, the designer must select the modules that he would like to use in the analysis process. The AQoPA is module based, which means that the designer can easily add modules to the analysis process. The core of AQoPA is responsible for generating the next states according to the protocol flow. The additional operations that bring the results of the analysis are executed in modules.

8.1.4   Step 4 – Simulation

The simulation stage is the core stage of the AQoPA architecture. The analysis process is realized by this stage and proceeds automatically without the user's interaction.

Static Checker

First, the model provided is passed to the Static Checker, which is responsible for the syntax validation of the model. Any syntax error is passed to the Error Analyzer.

Version creator

When the model has been validated by the Static Checker, it is passed to the Versions creator. The task of this component is to create an independent analysis process for each version selected in the Scenarios Definition stage. Creating versions involves the modification of protocol flow according to the list of executed hosts, processes and subprocesses in a particular version. As a result, the AQoPA obtains as many protocol flows as the versions that were selected. Each modified protocol flow is passed to the States Generator component and is analyzed independently.

States Generator

In the States Generator component the AQoPA generates successive states of evaluated hosts, executing their instructions. This process is repeated until all the hosts are finished or an error occurs. Each process of next state generation includes the execution of the instruction that was modeled in the QoP-ML.

This component is also responsible for the detection of QoP-ML model errors. These errors may result from a designer's mistake during modeling of the system (or protocol) or from the limitations due to the metrics (i.e., using sensors – devices with limited resources). These errors may lead to the situation when a variable is used before assignment, to a deadlock in communication, or to ambiguity of equations. This component detects these kinds of problems and passes them to the Error Analyzer, which outputs the information to the user.

QoP-ML introduces equations that are used to reduce complex function calls (nested function calls in parameters). Syntax validation checks all equations according to the syntax rules, finds and reports contradictory equations, and checks whether one equation contains the other one. The States Generator component finds ambiguity during the reduction process. All the above situations pass an error to the Error Analyzer.

Modules operation handler
Modules selected in the Scenarios Definition stage take part in the process of generating the next state of protocol. Execution of all instructions is passed to the modules so that they can retrieve information about the current state and prepare the results. Additionally, modules can change the default instructions flow.

Error Analyzer
The Error Analyzer is the last component of the simulation stage. It outputs the information about the error received from the Static Checker or the States Generator. When the analysis finishes successfully, the Error Analyzer creates a results report.

8.2   SMETool – Security mechanisms evaluation tool

The *SMETool* is an automatic tool designed and implemented according to the methodology presented in Chapter 3. It is used for the quality of protection evaluation of security mechanisms. The *SMETool* can be used in user-friendly GUI mode. The tool and user manual can be downloaded from the web page [7].

8.2.1   Data flow model

In this section, the data flow of the *SMEtool* is presented. The general data flow of *SMETool* modules, their relationships, and a more specific model of the data flow are presented in Figure 8.3.

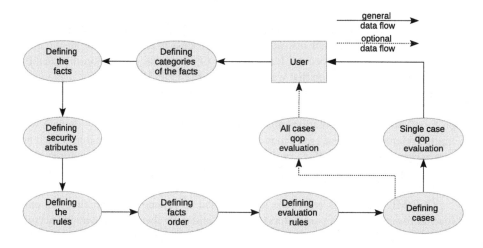

Figure 8.3: General *SMETool* data flow.

Defining categories of the facts

In the first stage, the categories of the facts should be defined. The categories help us to sort all the facts which will be defined in the next step. For example, one can create symmetric ciphers, asymmetric ciphers, key length, etc.

Defining the facts

After creating facts' categories one can define facts within these categories. The facts are the main elements in the model because they refer to the specific security mechanisms or security configuration. The facts could be AES algorithm (in symmetric cipher category), 256 bit (in key length category), etc.

Defining security attributes

The facts influence the fulfilment of different security attributes (confidentiality, integrity, availability, authorization, anonymity, etc.). In this step, the security attributes must be defined.

Defining the rules

When the facts are defined, the rules between them should be defined. The rules represents relations between various facts.

Defining the facts' order

After rules definition, the facts' order must be defined. Structure is necessary for the cases with no directly defined scenarios.

Defining the evaluation rules

The evaluation rules define the impact of the facts on the fulfilment of security attributes. In this step, evaluation rules must be defined for all previously defined security attributes.

Defining cases

The SMETool prepares the qop evaluation of specific cases based on the knowledge (model) created in the previous steps. In this step, one has to defined the configurations of the cryptographic protocols analyzed or the wide security system.

QoP Evaluation of security mechanisms

In the last step, the quality of protection evaluation of defined cases is prepared. The evaluation can be performed on a single case and then the quantified results will be obtained, or an evaluation can be performed for all defined cases and then besides quantified results the qualitative interpretation will be estimated.

8.3   Crypto-metrics tool (CMTool)

The *CMTool* is an automatic tool designed and implemented according to the methodology presented in Chapter 7. It is used for testing the performance of the

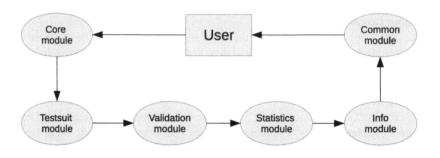

Figure 8.4: General *SMETool* data flow.

cryptographic primitives and validating measurement results obtained using the statistical approaches defined. The *CMTool* can be used in two modes: console and user-friendly GUI mode. The console version of *CMTool* is written in C, the *CMTool* GUI is written and built with C++/Qt 5.0.1 (the GUI version uses base functions from the console version, those written in C). The tool and user manual can be downloaded from the web page [7].

8.3.1 Data flow

In this section, the architecture of the *CMTool* and model of the data flow during the measurement process is presented. The general architecture of *CMTool* modules, their relationships, and a more specific model of the data flow are presented in Figure 8.4. *CMTool* contains six modules: *Core*, *Test suite*, *Validations*, *Statistics*, *Info* and *Common*.

Core module
One of the most important modules is the module named *core*. The *core* module contains functions used for measuring cryptographic algorithms' performance. Functions defined in the *core* module are able to measure five performance attributes (base measures): wall-clock time (also known as a wall time), CPU time, speed, amount of cycles per byte, and the number of function calls per second. The module provides a self-explained and easy-to-use API so one can use the exact same function name to measure for instance, wall time, regardless of the operating system.

Test suite
This is another crucial part of *CMTool*. It uses the *core* module for obtaining base measures and contains tests needed for the analysis of cryptographic algorithms' performance. The *test suite* module is divided into several source files, where each of them is capable of measuring different cryptographic primitives (hash functions, hmacs, digital signatures, stream ciphers, block ciphers in CBC, CFB, CTR, ECB, IGE mode as well as asymmetric ciphers).

Validations

The aim of the *validations* module is to implement the validation process described in the proposed model. The *validations* module takes as an input raw measurement results collected with the use of the *test suite* module and applies chosen validation methods to them. After the validation phase is completed, verified results may serve as an input for the statistical analysis.

Statistics

Last but not least significant of the four main modules is the *statistics* module. The *statistics* module is responsible for the statistical analysis of measurement results obtained. It contains seven functions used for calculating statistical formulas on an input data sample (which basically is a data set of the validated benchmarking results). Each of the functions defined is accountable for computing different statistical values (mean, variance, standard deviation, median, modal value, skewness and kurtosis). The *statistics* module provides the possibility of calculating defined statistical primitives on validated as well as on raw measurement results. Such analysis helps understand how important the validation process is for gathering robust measurement results.

Info

This module provides information about the hardware (CPU model and architecture, total amount of RAM) and software (operating system name, version and mode (32- or 64- bit)) of the machine on which *CMTool* was run.

Common

Common defines functions responsible for final results representation. Methods declared in *prettyprint.h* are able to print them as HTML pages, XML files, and also export them as QoP-ML security metrics.

8.3.2   Data flow model

This subsection presents a model of the data flow during the measurement process; the flow is presented in the Figure 8.4. Irrespective of the tested cryptographic primitive *CMTool's* data collection process is always the same. The first step is CPU cache-warming, which is run by default for one second. (Keep in mind that CPU warming by the mean of running some number of iterations before the actual test, is not taken into consideration when obtaining base measures. However, it has an impact on the total duration time of the measurement process).

In the very first stage of the measurement process the user is obliged to provide input parameters (number of tests, number of iterations in each of them as well as a list of cryptographic algorithms, the type of measured operation (encryption/decryption or signing/verifying, respectively) and the size of the input for cryptographic primitive tested, in bytes). The application also takes as an input an argument needed for the validation process: value of the confidence level, we have decided to run the test, and verifies it (the application supports six given *confidence levels*: $80\%, 90\%, 95\%, 96\%, 98\%, 99\%$).

If the verification process fails, the measurement will not proceed and results will not be obtained. Otherwise the application flow goes directly into the measurement phase. It is one of the two most important stages of *CMTool's* measurement process. Application tests choose cryptographic primitives one by one. Before every test it runs a *warm-up phase* and does appropriate measurements afterwards. The first of the four tests checks the wall-time of cryptographic operations. The second obtains the amount of time for which a CPU was used for processing, while the third test evaluates the speed of the operation tested in megabytes per second. The last test gives information about the number of clock cycles a microprocessor performed per byte of data processed in a cryptographic algorithm.

The base measure collection is followed by the second most important stage – the validation process. The validation process consists of calculating the *variation coefficient* and *Dixon's Q test*. Measurement results validated next become the input for the statistical analysis, which is in fact a set of mathematical formulas and the last stage defined in the proposed model. Validation of the collected measurement results helps in obtaining more reliable, statistical indicators free of random errors.

When the statistical analysis is completed, the final results are presented. The *CMTool* saves them as HTML web pages (documentation in **.html* format), XML files and also exports security metrics which can be used as input for further security analysis as QoP-ML.

Chapter 9

Functionality and usability of QoP-ML

CONTENTS

9.1 Security modeling framework

Systematic approaches can be applied for distinct security modeling system evaluation. Thus the SEQUAL framework and formulated systematic were chosen in [61].

The commonly applied SEQUAL framework is a semiotics-based reference model used for determination of physical, empirical, syntactical, semantic, perceived semantic, pragmatic, social, and knowledge qualities. It discusses modeling goals, ways of achieving them, aspects regarding the domain, alignment with the model and modeling language principles. It also deals with model creation as a correspondence between explicit knowledge of its interpreters.

As SEQUAL is a rich, completed framework, the authors in [61] used abstract concepts and simplified a set of systematic steps. Their main focus was semantics, pragmatics and syntax qualities. Thus a group of qualitative properties with their quantitative measures was distinguished. This methodology is discussed here in the context of evaluation of quality of the security model prepared with QoP-ML. The first view of the methodology and assessment of functionality and usability of QoP-ML arc discussed in [62] and further discussed in this chapter.

9.1.1 Semantic quality

Semantic quality can be defined as the degree of the correspondence between the model and the domain being modeled. Taking semantic quality into account, five qualitative properties are proposed: *semantic completeness, semantic correctness, traceability, annotation* and *modifiability*.

Semantic completeness deals with the problem of including all of the important aspects in the model. Based on it, there is a proposed percentage of the domain coverage measure which is presented as the ratio of the number of concepts in the model, and also the total number of concepts.

With respect to semantic correctness, the measure of semantic correctness is introduced, a percentage of security related statements which corresponds to the number of security modeling elements in the model compared to the total number of modeling statements.

Traceability is a measure which is calculated by counting links traced to the model origin.

An important role in the modeling process is played by annotations because they include security aspects. So a number of annotation elements were proposed as the count of explanatory notes.

Modifiability is obtained evaluating the time spent on modification measures including the time needed to customize the security system.

9.1.2 Syntactic quality

The relationship between the model and the modeling language is synthetic quality, which is characterized by two relevant measures: *syntactic validity* and *syntactic completeness*.

Evaluation of the model syntactic validity includes examination of the number of syntactically incomplete statements. The degree of the model's grammatical correctness is defined by the above mentioned measure. It follows that the lower the value, the better-adjusted the syntactic validity is. When all available grammar structures of the language are involved in the model, this is refereed to as syntactic completeness. The number of syntactically incomplete statements can be estimated by means of profound analysis of the modeling language syntax, similar to the syntactic validity.

9.1.3 Pragmatic quality

Pragmatic quality is aimed at the actors' interpretation of the model and how much they know about crucial aspects with respect to the system's usefulness and applicability. Such quantitative measures as *time spent to understand, cross-referencing, organization* and *technology capable to execute the model* are taken into consideration. The time needed to understand a model prepared by stakeholders is determined by understanding and time spent on understanding. This quality can be estimated based on the time necessary for model abstraction.

The internal structure of the model is estimated based on cross-referencing and organization. Estimation of the number of relationships between model concepts is based on the number of cross reference links. Good organization of the model is indicated by the large value of the organization measure, which is easy to find. The executability measure value is reflected by the presence of automated tools which are able to execute the model. Non-manual tools are important for complex environment modeling because they can transform the model into a running application.

9.1.4 Methodology extensions

AS follows from the analysis of methodology presented in [61] and discussed earlier, there is a large demand for objective measures in order to enhance the user's understanding of the model in a systematic and standardized way. The qualities presented are based largely on empirical experience and subjective opinions. In the approach presented here, the emphasis is put on an estimation of understandability in a technical context taking into account the role of automated tools. Based on the above, in [62] the pragmatic quality called technical understandability is proposed as an additional measure. It is assumed that the model is fully understood when the user can execute it and experience its changing nature as well as understand the syntax and semantics of the model creating system. At the same time one should be familiar with its graphical representation. Distinctions should be made between understood and understandable. Syntax, semantics, and graphical features constitute technical understandability. According to the framework, when the user is able to validate relevant model elements with automated tools (changes in the model, verification of modification correctness), he or she understands the model in a technical way. Two aspects should be considered. It should be defined whether the actor understands the model and then the level of understandability should be investigated. If technical understandability is stated, then its sub-measures, that is, syntax understandability, semantics understandabilities, and graphical editability, should be examined. Higher values indicate better understandability.

The validity of grammatical constructs in the model constitutes syntax understandability, which can be evaluated by checking the correctness of model elements by means of automated tools (syntax error analysis only). The submeasure can be calculated as the ratio of valid grammar constructs and the total number of syntax elements usage times a hundred percent. Higher value (over 70%) of this property is the evidence that it is quite simple to understand and learn the proposed syntax. This can be illustrated by the following example. After making some modifications, the user needs to verify the usage using the automated tools if the changes are syntactically correct. This is a systematic, formalized way of testing the syntax validity and thus syntax understandability.

Semantics understandability consists in checking if all grammar constructs are used in an appropriate context. To obtain reliable results, semantics comprehension must be verified automatically.

Graphical editability is defined as the graphical representation of the model including its flexibility and ability to personalize the elements of the model in order to understand better. A group of submeasures can be distinguished: *model layout customizability*, *fonts/colors/shapes customizability*, *customizability of the connections between model elements*. They are highly evaluated if all (or almost all) graphical elements of the model are fully customizable, medium – more than 70% of the parts and low – below 70% are customizable. Comprehension is regarded as empirical quality, so understanding of the modeled abstraction can be achieved through graphical editability.

9.2   Assessment of PL/SQL, secureUML and UMLsec

9.2.1   PL/SQL security model

The programming language which can be used by developers is PL/SQL (Procedural Language/Structured Query Language) [29] which is an Oracle Corporation's procedural language extension for SQL. SQL alone can not be used when conditional, iterative, and sequential statements are needed, because it is a limited language. In order to overcome these drawbacks PL/SQL was introduced which includes all features of other programming languages (loops and if/then/else statements).

The research results [61] indicate that security in PL/SQL can be problematic and insufficient in general modeling. Based on the semantics quality as a compatibility between a model and its semantics domain, it can be seen that the model does not include all the features it should. Moreover, a low value of percentage security related statements indicates that data separation from the security concerns is not well supported by PL/SQL. Other factors against modeling security are the lack of annotation elements and the length of time needed to update the model. Modification of the PL/SQL model requires a technical knowledge and understanding of the syntax. The security model created with a programmable language provides high syntactic validity and syntactic completeness. The model possesses satisfactory ability to be expressed with available grammar constructs and syntax. As regards examination of the correspondence between a model and its interpretation with respect to understandability, organization, cross-referencing, and executability, the number of explanations measure is the largest disadvantage of the PL/SQL security model. The high value of the measure may be an indicator that the model prepared with PL/SQL is not easy to understand when the knowledge of the PL/SQL language is not sufficient. PL/SQL might not be the best solution for complex security models for multilevel analysis to secure an adequate level of protection when the user does not know PL/SQL (or other programming languages).

9.2.2   SecureUML model

A model-driven security approach is represented by SecureUML [56, 17] derived from UML, which is a general purpose modeling language. It shows security models as UML diagrams developed using stereotypes, constraints, and tagged values. The SecureUML based model can be developed into an executable application after translation into PL/SQL by means of automated tools first, and compilation afterwards. As regards other pragmatic measures, the SecureUML based model exhibits great understanding and intuitiveness so it can be easily modified by anyone knowing UML modeling. This model is also highly evaluated as regards a number of elements for model organization and a number of cross-reference links, as it is supported by automated tools which simplify the modeling process. Moreover, it is highly evaluated for the semantic quality. The UML based model is semantically complete, reveals a semantic correctness, and is fully modifiable. It is characterized by syntactic invalidity, that is, not every grammatical expression used for model preparation is a part of the modeling language and this may be awkward.

9.2.3   UMLsec model

High-quality security-critical systems can be developed using the UMLSec – UML extension mechanisms [39]. UMLSec, which is a lightweight UML dialect, introduces elements needed for a proper security modeling. These are stereotypes, along with tags and constraints.

Semantic completeness of the security model prepared with UMLSec was proved to be at a high level (about 86%) in [61], taking its semantic quality into account. Such measures as traceability, annotation, and modifiability are similar to those in the SecureUML model. On the other hand, the value of the semantic correctness measure indicates that not every security aspect to be developed appropriately is represented by the model. As regards the syntactic quality the UMLSec model was evaluated as syntactically valid and complete by the methodology introduced. However, such evaluation may be wrong, as it was performed without automated tools and it should be carefully revised. Finally, the pragmatic quality of the security model created with UMLSec resembles that of SecureUMLs but there are no automated tools able to transform the model into the programming language code.

Security-relevant aspects can be expressed correctly applying UMLSec integrating security related information in UML specification. A disadvantage of this method is the inability of UMLsecs model execution as well as a low semantic correctness measure value due to the presence of the grammar constructs required in the model.

9.3 Case study – RBAC in QoP-ML

Based on the meeting scheduling system discussed in [61], an RBAC security model was created in QoP-ML, and evaluated with the methodology presented in [61]. These results and those obtained by other researchers are compared in [61].

9.3.1 RBAC security model prepared in QoP-ML

While modeling the RBAC model, QoP-MLs functions, equations, channel processes, and hosts were defined. Here, all the elements for creation of the security model will be presented and discussed.

The RBAC model regarded as ideal for security systems modeling is presented in [61]. It distinguished three types of user permission: *User*, *SuperUser*, and *Admin*.

The functions determined using the QoP-ML referring to the meeting scheduling system are presented below. They show the *User* role and its permissions.

```
 1
 2 functions {
 3  fun SelectData(id);
 4  fun InsertData(meeting);
 5  fun CheckCorrectness(meeting);
 6  fun UpdateData(meeting);
 7  fun DeleteData(id);
 8  fun GetRole();
 9  fun GetUserID();
10  fun Authorized(role);
11  fun GetMeetingID(meeting) ;
12  fun organize(startTime, endTime, location, ownerID);
13  fun owns(userID, meetingID);
14  fun editable(meetingID);
15  fun wait()[Time: seconds];
16 }
```

Listing 9.1: The functions definition for RBAC. label

Along with *functions equational rules* are declared.

```
1 equations {
2  eq CheckCorrectness(meeting) = true;
3  eq Authorized(role) = true;
4  eq owns(userID, meetingID) = true;
5  eq editable(meetingID) = true;
6 }
```

Listing 9.2: The equations definition for RBAC. label

Table 9.1: QoP-ML's functions for RBAC model.

Function	Parameters	Description
fun SelectData(id);	id	selects information about the meeting with a given id
fun InsertData(meeting);	meeting	inserts information about the new meeting into the meeting resource pool, gives the meeting its unique id
fun CheckCorrectness(meeting);	meeting	checks if given the meeting information are correct
fun UpdateData(meeting);	meeting	updates information about the given meeting
fun DeleteData(id);	id	deletes information about the meeting with a a given id
fun GetRole();	-	gets the role [user/superuser/admin] of the currently logged in user
fun GetUserID();	-	gets the id [user/superuser/admin] of the currently logged in user
fun Authorized(role);	role	checks if user with a given role is authorized to select/add meetings
fun GetMeetingID(meeting);	meeting	gets unique id of the given meeting
fun owns(userID, meetingID);	userID, meetingID	checks if a given user owns a given meeting id
fun organize(startTime, endTime, location, ownerID);	startTime, endTime, location, ownerID	creates a meeting with given parameters
fun editable(meetingID);	meetingID	checks if the meeting with a given ID can be edited
fun wait()[Time: seconds]	seconds	does nothing; waits for a given number of seconds

Table 9.1 summarizes fundamental QoP-MLs *User* operations and presents their short descriptions.

In order to reach communication between running processes, QoP-MLs channel must be defined.

```
1
2 channels {
3     channel ch1(*);
4 }
```

Listing 9.3: The channels definition for RBAC. label

This method includes the operations which can be performed by the *User*. While modeling RBAC and using a meeting scheduling system, *User* has the possibility to select and insert information about the meeting. Possessing the meeting, in case of need, she/he can update or delete it.

In defining, processes can be grouped into host named *User*. It expresses the *User* role in RBAC model.

```
1 hosts
2 {
3   host User(rr)(*){
4
5     process Main(*){
6
7       subprocess Select(*){
8         role = GetRole();
9         if(Authorized(role) == true){
```

```
10        in(ch1:id);
11        meeting = SelectData(id);
12      }
13    }
14
15    subprocess Insert(*){
16     role = GetRole();
17     if(Authorized(role) == true){
18      userID = GetUserID();
19      in (ch1 : input);
20      startTime = input[0];
21      endTime = input[1];
22      location = input[2];
23      meeting = organize(startTime, endTime, location, userID);
24      if (CheckCorrectness(meeting) == true){
25        InsertData(meeting);
26      }
27     }
28    }
29
30    subprocess Delete(*){
31     role = GetRole();
32     userID = GetUserID();
33     if(Authorized(role) == true){
34      in (ch1 : input);
35      meetingID = input[0];
36      if(owns (userID, meetingID) == true){
37        DeleteMeeting(meetingID);
38      }
39     }
40    }
41
42     subprocess Update(*){
43      role = GetRole();
44      if(Authorized(role) == true){
45       userID = GetUserID();
46       in (ch1 : input1);
47       meetingID = input1[0];
48       if(owns (userID, meetingID) == true){
49        if(editable() == true){
50         in (ch1 : input2);
51         startTime = input2[0];
52         endTime = input2[1];
53         location = input2[2];
54         newMeeting = organize (startTime, endTime, location, ←
               userID);
55         if(CheckCorrectness(newMeeting) == true){
56          UpdateData(newMeeting);
57         }
58        }
59       }
60      }
61     }
62    }
63
64 }
65
```

```
66 host STDIN(rr)(*){
67   process Main(*){
68     subprocess GetID(){
69       wait()[100];
70       id = GetMeetingID();
71       out(ch1:id);
72     }
73   }
74 }
75 }
```

Listing 9.4: The processes definition for RBAC. label

9.3.2 Assessment of the QoP-ML's security model

Here the results of the QoP-ML security abstraction evaluation are presented. Semantic, syntactic, and pragmatic qualities of the security model created with QoP-ML are discussed. The results of the semantic quality analysis, in which every measure from the semantic quality set, are examined step by step and presented in Table 9.3.

Percentage of the RBAC domain coverage Being a largely extensible modeling language, QoP-ML is simple enough to completely cover the RBAC domain. It affects the percentage of the RBAC domain coverage measure which reaches the value of 100%. Using the security model sample presented, all seven RBAC concepts were covered (Table 9.2).

Percentage of security related statements Apart from the constructs connected with security aspects, the model included some actions referring to the business logic (*select_data*, *insert_data* and so on). Though the data and security concerns should be considered separately in security modeling, business logic should also be taken into account. In the model under consideration, each business action needs earlier defined security methods. In the simplest scenario analyzed (where functions for *User* role are defined, and the data is selected by the *User*), the high value of semantic correctness indicates that the actions were security related operations (directly or indirectly).

Number of traced links As no explanation was found for inclusion of such security analysis solutions in the model, the value of 0 was given to the number of links measure traced.

Number of annotation elements Being like a programming language, QoP-ML gives a set of valuable features not directly available in other modeling languages. Thus it makes it possible for developers to place comments considered as a kind of annotations everywhere in the model.

Time spent to modify There was identified the measure: time spent to modify which is 10 minutes long. This is meant for fluent designers who have a knowledge

Table 9.2: QoP-ML's correspondence to the RBAC domain.

RBAC concept	QoP-MLs RBAC domain coverage
users can be assigned to roles	if user is assigned to the specific role, he/she has permissions given to this specific role, functions like authorized have the ability of authorizing the user
permissions are assigned to roles	if user is assigned to a given role she/he has permissions defined for the specific role functions like authorized have the ability of authorizing the user
users acquire permissions	when user is given a role, she/he acquires permissions too
the same user can be assigned to many roles	in our example model, users are distinguished by their unique ids - it is fairly straightforward to manage roles and users in such case
single role can have many users	same as above
single permission can be assigned to many roles	modeling security with QoP-ML one has enormous flexibility - declaring functions and equational rules, one can decide which permissions assign to which roles
single role can be assigned to many permissions	same as above

Table 9.3: Semantic quality of compared security models.

Qualitative property	Measure	QoP-ML security model	PL/SQL security model	SecureUML security model	UMLsec security model
Semantic completeness	Percentage of the RBAC domain coverage	100%	42.86%	71.43%(100%)	85.71%
Semantic correctness	Percentage of security related statements	100%	7.69%	100%	33%
Traceability	Number of traced links	0	0	0	0
Annotation	Number of annotation elements	fully annotated	0	5	1
Modifiability	Time spent to modify	about 10 minutes (or not known)	not known	5 − 10 minutes	5 − 10 minutes

of at least one programming language. For stakeholders, the time can be even longer as the measure value largely depends on the developer's skills.

We assessed the *syntactic* quality of the QoP-MLs security model through *syntactic completeness* and *syntactic validity* measures [Table 9.4].

Syntactic completeness and validity Being much like the general programming language in its essence, QoP-ML gains high scores in *syntactic* quality evaluation. After profound investigation of the language syntax, we state that security model prepared with QoP-ML is syntactically valid and complete. All the grammar constructs and structures used in the modeling process are the part of the language, resulting in the low value of the *syntactic completeness* measure (which is the desirable value of this measure).

Aside from *semantic* and *syntactic* qualities, we evaluated a set of *pragmatic* measures in terms of the QoP-MLs security model.

Table 9.4: Syntactic quality of compared security models.

Qualitative property	Measure	QoP-ML security model	PL/SQL security model	SecureUML security model	UMLsec security model
Syntactic completeness	Number of syntactically incomplete statements	0	0	0	0
Syntactic validity	Number of syntactically invalid statements	0	0	1	0

Table 9.5: Pragmatic quality of compared security models.

Qualitative property	Measure	QoP-ML security model	PL/SQL security model	SecureUML security model	UMLsec security model
Understandability	Number of explanations	5−10 minutes	more than 45 minutes	10−15 minutes	10−15 minutes
Organization	Number of elements for model organization	5	2	4	4
Cross referencing	Number of cross-reference links	plenty	1	3	3
Executability	Tools to execute the model	Yes (AQoPA)	Yes	Yes	No

Number of explanations *Understandability*, in its intent, is similar to the *time spent to modify* measure from the *semantic* group of measures. It focuses on aspects that can be measured with subjective opinions. The relationship between the model and its recipients is expressed by pragmatic quality but measuring and evaluating the model on such a basis is problematic because it can be viewed by both engineers and stakeholders. However, the QoP-MLs model is considered understable, as it is prepared in a consistent and logical language.

Number of elements for model organization The model created based on QoP-MLs is considered to be well organized because it is divided into logical modules. Thus required information can be easily found and crucial logical relationships among associated facts are found without difficulties. Such organizational elements as *functions*, *equations*, *processes*, *hosts*, *channels*, *versions* etc., can be mentioned.

Number of cross-reference links The internal structure of the model can be presented by number of cross-reference links. Despite not containing direct reference links, the QoP-ML's model is cross-referenced by its structure. It is possible for individual modules to cooperate with each other: *hosts* contain *processes*, *processes* are made of *subprocesses* which can execute *functions* with the help of defined *equations*.

Tools to execute the model The model can be executed based on the QoP-ML's executability. The automated Quality of Protection Analysis Tool (AQoPA) is a powerful tool in the QoP-ML. It can run models created in QoP-ML.
Besides evaluating *pragmatic* measures introduced in [61] it is worth introducing new properties. The *syntax understandability*, *semantics understandability* and *graphical editability* with respect to models prepared in QoP-ML, PL/SQL, UMLsec and SecureUML were analyzed.

Table 9.6: Evaluation of the extended pragmatic measures.

Qualitative property	Measure	QoP-ML security model	PL/SQL security model	SecureUML security model	UMLsec security model
Technical understandability	Syntax understandability	93%	70%	95%	97%
	Semantics understandability	98%	70%	80%	85%
	Graphical editability	No	No	Yes	Yes

Technical understandability scores high for UMLsec, and SecureUML as well as for QoP-ML and PL/SQL. Although, considering QoP-ML and PL/SQL models it is not possible to evaluate the *graphical editability* property. However, a lack of *graphical editability* results from the nature of these languages, and cannot and should not be considered a limitation or a drawback of the given modeling languages, since this measure is simply not applicable to the general programming languages like QoP-ML or PL/SQL. Thus, as stated in the methodology extension [62], we can estimate *model layout customizability, fonts/colors/shapes customizability*, and *customizability of the connections between model elements* only for the UMLsec and SecureUML security models.

Syntax understandability for the model created with QoP-ML was estimated to be 93% which shows that only 7 of 100 QoP-ML's statements, prepared by a developer knowing at least one programming language, were found invalid by AQoPA. QoP-ML possesses high intuitiveness compared to the PL/SQLsmodels. The best understandability is expressed by SecureUML and UMLsec as the graphical modeling language.

For the developer having knowledge of basic concepts, grammar structure, and the basic principles of modeling, it is easy to understand QoP-ML semantics. As regards semantic comprehension of varous security models, QoP-ML's is the best-semantically understood.

Tools used for analysis and creation of a model largely affect the values of model layout customizability, fonts, colors, shape customizability, and customizability of the connections between model elements. These measures were estimated based on the approach presented in [61]. Using powerful tools, graphical editability properties were highly estimated for SecureUML and UMLSec models.

9.3.3   Comparison of security models in terms of QoP-ML

The results from comparison of various security models are given in Table 9.7. Varied measures were determined following the methodology presented in [61]. Based on the comparison of QoP-ML's and PL/SQL models, it was found that another seven qualitative properties, *percentage of the RBAC domain coverage, percentage of security related statements, number of annotation elements, time spent to modify, number of explanations, number of elements for model organization*, and *number of cross-reference links* are more suitable for QoP-ML's model. Equal values were evaluated

Table 9.7: Comparison of PL/SQL, SecureUML, UMLsec and QoP-ML security models.

Model A created in	Model B created in	Model A is better in	Two models score equal in	Model B is better in
QoP-ML	PL/SQL	*percentage of the RBAC domain coverage, percentage of security related statements, number of annotation elements, time spent to modify, number of explanations, number of elements for model organization, number of cross-reference links, syntax understandability, semantics understandability*	*number of traced links, number of syntactically incomplete statements, number of syntactically invalid statements, tools to execute the model, graphical understandability*	-
QoP-ML	SecureUML	*percentage of the RBAC domain coverage, percentage of security related statements, number of annotation elements, number of syntactically invalid statements, number of cross-reference links, semantics understandability*	*number of traced links, number of syntactically incomplete statements, number of explanations, tools to execute the model, time spent to modify*	*syntax understandability, graphical understandability*
QoP-ML	UMLsec	*percentage of the RBAC domain coverage, percentage of security related statements, number of annotation elements, number of elements for model organization, number of cross-reference links,, tools to execute the model, semantics understandability*	*time spent to modify, number of syntactically incomplete statements, number of syntactically invalid statements, number of explanations,*	*syntax understandability, graphical understandability*

for the *number of traced links, number of syntactically incomplete statements, number of syntactically invalid statements, and the tools to execute the model* measures. As follows from the investigations of the QoP-ML's and SecureUML's models, the model made in QoP-ML is evaluated more highly. The same is found for the QoP-ML's and UMLsec's models.

The model obtained in the implementation stage with PL/SQL in [61] proved to be less powerful than that created with QoP-ML. As follows from comparison, the PL/SQL's model is more challenging as regards modification than QoP-ML's. It does not have a satisfactory number of security related elements and is not annotated enough.

When the models designed in the system development stage are compared with the QoP-ML one, it is obvious that the QoP-ML's model is much better than UMLsec's. This is because the model created with QoP-ML can be executed with AQoPA, but no outcome total is offered by UMLsec. In the case of SecureUML's model a serious disadvantage was found, namely, that it can contain syntactically invalid statements which does not concern QoP-ML modeling.

9.4 Summary

The security model made in QoP-ML was estimated and compared with other modeling systems by means of methodology presented in [61] and originating from the SEQUAL framework. The quality analysis of the RBAC model obtained using quality of protection modeling language was made. Various models such as PL/SQL's, SecureUML's UMLsec's were compared with the QoP-ML model.

The methodology proposed in [61] and the results obtained using it should be carefully examined. As follows from the investigations, some proposed measures are based on inner experience rather than on facts, as their results depend on subjective options. Taking the above into account, an extension to the pragmatic quality with its qualitative and quantitative measures was proposed. The analysis showed flexibility of protection modeling language quality and importance of multilevel analysis in modeling security systems. At the beginning understanding the model created with QoP-ML seems to be more difficult than the one obtained using graphical methods but the power of the language is unquestionable.

Appendix

CONTENTS

A.1   BNF of QoP-ML

The following list defines the grammar of the QoP-ML in Backus-Naur Form [16] with the following additions.

■ Optional parts are included in square brackets: [...].

■ Curly brackets { ... } indicate zero or more repetitions of the included fragment.

```
<qopml_model>         ::= <model_spec> <metrics_spec> <version_spec>

<model_spec>          ::= <model_module> { <model_module> }
<version_spec>        ::= <version_module>
<metrics_spec>        ::= <metrics_module>

<name>        ::= <letter> { <letter> | <digit> }

<text>        ::= { <letter> | <digit> | "-" | " " }

<qualified_name> ::= <name> "." <valuei> { "." <valuei> }

<comma_separated_names> ::= <name> { "," <name> }

<letter>      ::= "a" | "b" | "c" | "d" | "e" | "f" | "g" |
                  "h" | "i" | "j" | "k" | "l" | "m" | "n" |
                  "o" | "p" | "q" | "r" | "s" | "t" | "u" |
                  "v" | "w" | "x" | "y" | "z" | "A" | "B" |
                  "C" | "D" | "E" | "F" | "G" | "H" | "I" |
                  "J" | "K" | "L" | "M" | "N" | "O" | "P" |
                  "Q" | "R" | "S" | "T"| "U" | "V" | "W" |
                  "X" | "Y" | "Z" |"_"

<digit>       ::= "0" | "1" | "2" | "3" | "4" | "5" | "6" |
                  "7" | "8" | "9"

<value>       ::= <digit> { <digit> } [ "." { <digit> } ]

<valuei>      ::= <digit> { <digit> }

<model_module>  ::= <fun_module> | <host_module> | <channel_module> |
                    <eq_module> | <algorithm_module> | <communication_module> |
                    <modules_module>

<fun_module> ::= "functions" "{" <fun_list> "}"

<fun_list>   ::= <fun> ";" { <fun> ";" }

<fun>        ::= "fun" <name> <fun_params> [ <fun_qopparams> ] [ <fun_comment> ]

<fun_params> ::= <fun_params_empty> | <fun_params_nonempty>

<fun_params_empty> ::= "(" ")"

<fun_params_nonempty> ::= "(" <comma_separated_names> ")"

<fun_qopparams>  ::= "[" <fun_qopparam> { ";" <fun_qopparam>} "]"

<fun_qopparam>   ::= <name> ":" <comma_separated_names>
```

```
<fun_comment> ::= "(" <text> ")"

<host_module> ::= "hosts" "{" <host> { <host> } "}"

<host>           ::= "host" <name> "(" <host_scheduling> ")" "(" <host_channels> ")" "{"
                     [ <host_predefined_vars> ] <host_body> "}"

<host_scheduling> ::= "fifo" | "rr"

<host_channels> ::= "" | <comma_separated_names> | "*"

<host_predefined_vars> ::= "#" <instruction_assignment>
                           { "#" <instruction_assignment> }

<host_body>     ::= <host_process> { <host_process> }

<host_process> ::= "process" <name> "(" <host_channels> ")"
                   "{" <instruction> { <instruction> } "}" [ ";" ]

<instruction> ::= <instruction_assignment> |
                  <instruction_subprocess> |
                  <instruction_communication> |
                  <instruction_while> | <instruction_if> |
                  <instruction_special_command> |
                  <instruction_call_function>

<instruction_subprocess> ::= "subprocess" <name> "(" <host_channels> ")"
                             "{" <instruction> { <instruction> } "}" [ ";" ]

<instruction_assignment> ::= <name> "=" <expression_simple> ";"

<instruction_communication> ::= <instruction_communication_in> |
                                <instruction_communication_out>

<instruction_communication_in> ::= "in" "(" <name> ":" <name> [ ":" "|"
                                   <instruction_in_filter>
                                   { "," <instruction_in_filter> } "|" ] ")" ";"

<instruction_in_filter> ::= "*" | <name> | <expression_call_function>

<instruction_communication_out> ::= "out" "(" <name> ":" <name> ")" ";"

<instruction_while> ::= "while" "(" <expression_conditional> ")" "{"
                        <instruction> { <instruction> } "}" [ ";" ]

<instruction_if> ::= "if" "(" <expression_conditional> ")" "{" <instruction>
                     { <instruction> } "}" [ "else" "{" <instruction>
                     { <instruction> } "}" ] [ ";" ]

<instruction_special_command> ::= "continue" | "end" | "stop" | "break" ";"

<instruction_call_function> ::= <expression_call_function> ";"

<expression_conditional> ::= <expression_comparison> | <expression_bool>

<expression_comparison> ::= <expression_equal>
| <expression_nonequal>

<expression_equal> ::= <expression_simple> "==" <expression_simple>
```

```
<expression_nonequal> ::= <expression_simple> "!=" <expression_simple>

<expression_bool> ::= "true" | "false"

<expression_tuple> ::= "(" [ <expression_simple>
                           { "," <expression_simple> } ] ")"

<expression_tuple_element> ::= <name> "[" <valuei> "]"

<expression_call_function> ::= <expression_call_generic_function>
| <expression_call_id_function>
| <expression_call_routing_next_function>

<expression_call_generic_function> ::= <name> "(" [ <expression_simple>
                                       { "," <expression_simple> } ] ")"
                                       [ "[" <text> { "," <text> } "]" ]

<expression_call_id_function> ::= "id" "(" [ <name> | <qualified_name> ] ")"

<expression_call_routing_next_function> ::= "routing_next"
                                            "(" <name> "," <name> |
                                            <expression_call_function> |
                                            <expression_tuple_element> ")"

<expression_simple> ::= <expression_call_function>
| <expression_tuple_element>
| <expression_tuple>
| <name>
| <expression_bool>


<channel_module> ::= "channels" "{" <channel> { <channel> } "}"

<channel> ::= "channel" <comma_separated_names> "(" <channel_buffer> ")"
              [ "[" <name> "]" ] ";"

<channel_buffer> ::= <valuei> | "*"


<eq_module> ::= "equations" "{" { <eq> } "}"

<eq> ::= "eq" <eq_complex_expression> "=" <eq_simple_expression> ";"

<eq_complex_expression> ::= <name> "(" [ <eq_expression>
                            { "," <eq_expression> } ] ")"

<eq_simple_expression> ::= <name> | <expression_bool>

<eq_expression> ::= <eq_complex_expression>
| <eq_simple_expression>


<algorithm_module> ::= "algorithms" "{" <algorithm> { <algorithm> } "}"

<algorithm> ::= "alg" <name> "(" <name> ")" "{" <alg_instruction>
                { <alg_instruction> } "}"

<alg_instruction> ::= <alg_instruction_assignment>
| <alg_instruction_return>
```

```
| <alg_instruction_if>
| <alg_instruction_while>

<alg_instruction_assignment> ::= <name> "=" <alg_expression> ";"

<alg_instruction_return> ::= "return" <alg_expression> ";"

<alg_instruction_if> ::= "if" "(" <alg_expression_conditional> ")"
                         "{" <alg_instruction> { <alg_instruction> } "}"
                 [ "else" "{" <alg_instruction> { <alg_instruction> }  "}" ]

<alg_instruction_while> ::= "while" "(" <alg_expression_conditional> ")"
                            "{" <alg_instruction> { <alg_instruction> } "}"

<alg_expression> ::= <name>
| <value>
| <alg_expression_neg>
| <alg_expression_paran>
| <alg_expression_plus>
| <alg_expression_minus>
| <alg_expression_multiply>
| <alg_expression_divide>
| <alg_expression_function_size>
| <alg_expression_function_quality>

<alg_expression_neg> ::= "-" <alg_expression>

<alg_expression_paran> ::= "(" <alg_expression> ")"

<alg_expression_plus> ::= <alg_expression> "+" <alg_expression>

<alg_expression_minus> ::= <alg_expression> "-" <alg_expression>

<alg_expression_divide> ::= <alg_expression> "/" <alg_expression>

<alg_expression_multiply> ::= <alg_expression> "*" <alg_expression>

<alg_expression_function_size> ::= "size" "(" <name> [ "[" <valuei> "]" ] ")"

<alg_expression_function_quality> ::= "quality" "(" ")"

<alg_expression_conditional> ::= <alg_expression_conditional_equal>
                               | <alg_expression_conditional_nonequal>
                               |<alg_expression_conditional_greater>
                               | <alg_expression_conditional_greater_equal>
                               | <alg_expression_conditional_lower>
                               | <alg_expression_conditional_lower_equal>
                               | <alg_expression_conditional_and>
                               | <alg_expression_conditional_or>
                               | <alg_expression_conditional_paran>

<alg_expression_conditional_equal> ::= <alg_expression> "==" <alg_expression>

<alg_expression_conditional_nonequal> ::= <alg_expression> "!=" <alg_expression>

<alg_expression_conditional_greater> ::= <alg_expression> ">" <alg_expression>

<alg_expression_conditional_greater_equal> ::= <alg_expression> ">="
                                               <alg_expression>
```

```
<alg_expression_conditional_lower> ::= <alg_expression> "<" <alg_expression>

<alg_expression_conditional_lower_equal> ::= <alg_expression>
                                             "<=" <alg_expression>

<alg_expression_conditional_and> ::= <alg_expression_conditional> "&&"
                                     <alg_expression_conditional>

<alg_expression_conditional_or> ::= <alg_expression_conditional> "||"
                                    <alg_expression_conditional>

<alg_expression_conditional_paran> ::= "(" <alg_expression_conditional> ")"


<communication_module> ::= "communication" "{" <medium> { <medium> } "}"

<medium> ::= "medium" "[" <name> "]" "{" <medium_elements> "}"

<medium_elements> ::= <medium_default_parameter> ";"
                      { <medium_default_parameter> ";" } <medium_topology>

<medium_default_parameter> ::= <medium_default_q>
                               | <medium_default_sending_current>
                               | <medium_default_receiving_current>
                               | <medium_default_listening_current>

<medium_default_q> ::= "default_q" "=" <value>

<medium_default_sending_current> ::= "default_sending_current" "="
                                     <communication_current_value>

<medium_default_receiving_current> ::= "default_receiving_current" "="
                                       <communication_current_value>

<medium_default_listening_current> ::= "default_listening_current" "="
                                       <communication_current_value>

<communication_current_value> ::= <communication_current_metric>
   | <communication_current_algorithm>

<communication_current_metric> ::= <value> "mA"

<communication_current_algorithm> ::= <name> [ "[" "mA" "]" ]

<medium_topology> ::= "topology" "{" <topology_rule> { <topology_rule> } "}"

<topology_rule> ::= <topology_rule_simple> | <topology_rule_broadcast>

<topology_rule_simple> ::= <name> <topology_arrow> <name> [ ":"
                           <topology_rule_simple_parameter>
                           { "," <topology_rule_simple_parameter> } ] ";"

<topology_rule_simple_parameter> ::= <topology_rule_parameter_q>
                                     | <topology_rule_broadcast_parameter>

<topology_rule_broadcast> ::= <name> "->" "*" ":"
                              <topology_rule_broadcast_parameter>
                              { "," <topology_rule_broadcast_parameter> } ";"

<topology_arrow> ::= "->" | "<-" | "<->"
```

```
<topology_rule_broadcast_parameter> ::= <topology_rule_sending_parameter>|
                                         <topology_rule_receiving_parameter>
                                       | <topology_rule_listening_parameter>

<topology_rule_sending_parameter> ::= "sending_current" "="
                                      <communication_current_value>

<topology_rule_receiving_parameter> ::= "receiving_current" "="
                                        <communication_current_value>

<topology_rule_listening_parameter> ::= "listening_current" "="
                                        <communication_current_value>

<topology_rule_parameter_q> ::= "q" "=" <value>


<modules_module> ::= "modules" "{" { <module_specification> } "}"

<module_specification> ::= <module_reputation>


<module_reputation> ::= "reputation" "{" <reputation_init_var>
                        { <reputation_init_var> } <reputation_alg>
                        { <reputation_alg> } "}"

<reputation_init_var> ::= "#" <name> "=" <value> ";"

<reputation_alg> ::= "algorithm" <name> "(" <comma_separated_names> ")"
                     "{" <reputation_instruction> { <reputation_instruction> } "}"

<reputation_instruction> ::= <reputation_instruction_assignment>
| <reputation_instruction_conditional>

<reputation_instruction_assignment> ::= <name> "=" <reputation_expression> ";"

<reputation_instruction_conditional> ::= "if"
                                "(" <reputation_expression_conditional> ")"
                     "{" <reputation_instruction> { <reputation_instruction> } "}"
[ "else" "{" <reputation_instruction> { <reputation_instruction> } "}" ] [ ";" ]

<reputation_expression> ::= <value>
                            | <name>
                            | <reputation_expression_neg>
                            | <reputation_expression_plus>
                            | <reputation_expression_minus>
                            | <reputation_expression_multiply>
                            | <reputation_expression_divide>
                            | <reputation_expression_paran>

<reputation_expression_neg> := "-" <reputation_expression>

<reputation_expression_plus> ::= <reputation_expression> "+"
                                 <reputation_expression>

<reputation_expression_minus> ::= <reputation_expression> "-"
                                  <reputation_expression>

<reputation_expression_multiply> ::= <reputation_expression> "*"
                                     <reputation_expression>
```

```
<reputation_expression_divide> ::= <reputation_expression> "/"
                                   <reputation_expression>

<reputation_expression_paran> ::= "(" <reputation_expression> ")"

<reputation_expression_conditional> ::= <reputation_expression_conditional_equal>
                          | <reputation_expression_conditional_nonequal>
                            | <reputation_expression_conditional_greater>
                          | <reputation_expression_conditional_greater_equal>
                              | <reputation_expression_conditional_lower>
                        | <reputation_expression_conditional_lower_equal>
                              | <reputation_expression_conditional_and>
                                | <reputation_expression_conditional_or>
                              | <reputation_expression_conditional_paran>
                                | <reputation_expression_conditional_used>
                              | <reputation_expression_conditional_exists>

<reputation_expression_conditional_equal> ::= <reputation_expression> "=="
                                              <reputation_expression>

<reputation_expression_conditional_nonequal> ::= <reputation_expression> "!="
                                                 <reputation_expression>

<reputation_expression_conditional_greater> ::= <reputation_expression> ">"
                                                <reputation_expression>

<reputation_expression_conditional_greater_equal> ::= <reputation_expression> ">="
                                                      <reputation_expression>

<reputation_expression_conditional_lower> ::= <reputation_expression> "<"
                                              <reputation_expression>

<reputation_expression_conditional_lower_equal> ::= <reputation_expression> "<="
                                                    <reputation_expression>

<reputation_expression_conditional_and> ::= <reputation_expression_conditional>
                                    "&&" <reputation_expression_conditional>

<reputation_expression_conditional_or> ::= <reputation_expression_conditional>
                                    "||" <reputation_expression_conditional>

<reputation_expression_conditional_paran> ::=
                                    "(" reputation_expression_conditional> ")"

<reputation_expression_conditional_used> ::= "used" "(" <name> ")"

<reputation_expression_conditional_exists> ::= "exists" "(" <name> ")"


<metrics_module> ::= "metrics" "{" <metrics_configuration>
                    { <metrics_configuration> } <metrics_data> { <metrics_data> } "}"

<metrics_configuration> ::= "conf" "(" <name> ")" "{" <metrics_configuration_param>
                            { <metrics_configuration_param> } "}"

<metrics_configuration_param> ::= <name> "=" <metrics_param_value> ";"

<metrics_param_value> ::= { <text> | ":" | "." }
```

```
<metrics_data> ::= <metrics_data_simple> | <metrics_data_special>

<metrics_data_simple> ::= "data" "(" <qualified_name> ")" "{" <metrics_data_block>
                          { "#" <metrics_data_block> } "}"

<metrics_data_special> ::= "data" "+" | "*" "(" <name> ")" "{" <metrics_data_block>
                           { "#" <metrics_data_block> } "}"

<metrics_data_block> ::= <metrics_primitive_head> <metrics_primitive>
                         { <metrics_primitive> }

<metrics_primitive_head> ::= "primhead" <metrics_primitive_head_param>
                             { <metrics_primitive_head_param> }
                              <metrics_primitive_head_service_param>
                             { <metrics_primitive_head_service_param> } ";"

<metrics_primitive_head_param> ::= "[" <name> "]"

<metrics_primitive_head_service_param> ::= <metrics_service_param_size>
                                          | <metrics_service_param_energy>
                                          | <metrics_service_param_reputation>

<metrics_service_param_size> ::= "[" <metrics_service_param_size_with_unit>
                                | <metrics_service_param_size_without_unit> "]"

<metrics_service_param_size_with_unit> ::= "size" ":" "exact" | "block" "(" "B" ")"

<metrics_service_param_size_without_unit> ::= "size" ":" "ratio" | "sum_ratio" |
                                              "nested"

<metrics_service_param_energy> ::= "[" "current" ":" "exact" "(" "mA" ")" "]"

<metrics_service_param_reputation> ::= "[" "reputation" ":" "algorithm" "]"

<metrics_primitive> ::= "primitive" <metrics_primitive_argument>
                        { <metrics_primitive_argument> } ";"

<metrics_primitive_argument> ::= "[" <metrics_argument_value> "]"

<metrics_argument_value> ::= { <text> | ":" | "." }


<version_module> ::= "versions" "{" <version> { <version> } "}"

<version> ::= "version" <name> "{" <version_metrics_set> { <version_metrics_set> }
        <version_run_host> { <version_run_host> } [ <version_communication> ] "}"

<version_metrics_set> ::= "set" "host" <name> "(" <name> ")" ";"

<version_run_host> ::= "run" "host" <name> <version_channels>
                    [ <version_repetition> ] "{" { <version_run_process> } "}"

<version_channels> ::= "(" [ "*" | <comma_separated_names> ] ")"

<version_repetition> ::= "{" <valuei> "}"

<version_run_process> ::= <version_run_process_base> [ "->"
                          <version_run_process_follower> ]

<version_run_process_base> ::= "run" <name>
```

```
                             "(" [ "*" | <comma_separated_names> ] ")" <version_repetition>

<version_run_process_follower> ::= "run" <name> "(" [ "*"
                                   | <comma_separated_names> ] ")"

<version_communication> ::= "communication" "{" <version_medium>
                                 { <version_medium> } "}"

<version_medium> ::= "medium" "[" <name> "]" "{" <version_medium_elements> "}"

<version_medium_elements> ::= <medium_default_parameter> ";"
                                 { <medium_default_parameter> ";" }
                                 <version_medium_topology>

<version_medium_topology> ::= "topology" "{" <version_topology_rule>
                                 { <version_topology_rule> } "}"

<version_topology_rule> ::= <version_topology_rule_simple>
| <version_topology_rule_broadcast>

<version_topology_rule_simple> ::= <version_topology_rule_left_hosts>
                                     <topology_arrow> <version_topology_rule_right_hosts>
                                     [ ":" <topology_rule_simple_parameter>
                                     { "," <topology_rule_simple_parameter> } ] ";"

<version_topology_rule_broadcast> ::= <version_topology_rule_left_hosts> "->" "*" ":"
                                        <topology_rule_broadcast_parameter>
                                        { "," <topology_rule_broadcast_parameter> } ";"

<version_topology_rule_left_hosts> ::= <name> [ "[" <version_topology_indices> "]" ]

<version_topology_indices> ::= <version_topology_indices_one>
                                   | <version_topology_indices_two>
                                   | <version_topology_indices_left>
                                   | <version_topology_indices_right>

<version_topology_indices_one> ::= <valuei>

<version_topology_indices_two> ::= <valuei> ":" <valuei>

<version_topology_indices_left> ::= ":" <valuei>

<version_topology_indices_right> ::= <valuei> ":"

<version_topology_rule_right_hosts> ::= <version_topology_rule_left_hosts>
                                          | <version_topology_hosts_with_i_index>
                                          | "*"

<version_topology_hosts_with_i_index> ::= <name> "[" "i" [ "+" | "-" <valuei> ] "]"
```

A.2 Base QoP-ML algorithms

Table A.1: The parameters and variables for the QoP-ML processing algorithms.

SET	-	make a choice indication
READ	-	reading indication
DROP	-	operator dropping the communication operation
RETURN	-	processing functions will be ended
PASS	-	processing function will go on (used to show particular cases)
BREAK	-	processing loop will be interrupted
CALL	-	algorithm execution
num	-	the number of the **version** of the protocol
rep	-	the number of multiples hosts defined in the particular protocol
H	-	the number of high hierarchy processes (**host**) taking part in the specific version of the protocol (including host replication)
h	-	the index of current high hierarchy process
p	-	the index of current process in current host
o	-	the index of current operation in current process p and current host h
H_{max}	-	the number of all hosts
P_{max}	-	the number of all processes in current host **h**
H_{now}	-	temporary variable which holds the index of current host when checking FINISHED status
P_{now}	-	temporary variable which holds the index of current process when checking FINISHED status of hosts
$P[h]$	-	the process **P** of the host **h**
$O[h][P[h]]$	-	index of the operation **Op** for the host **h** and for the process **P** in the host **h**
$Op[h][p][o]$	-	the currently processed operation
$O_{\#}[h]$	-	the set of operations which were executed before **host** process starts - (# operator)
$CH[h]$	-	the set of possible communication channels for **host** process
$ALG[h]$	-	the schedule algorithm for **host** process
P_{last}	-	the index to the last process in current host **h**
o_{last}	-	the index to the last operationin current process **p** and current host **h**
$Status[h]$	-	the status for the host indexed by h; **RUNNING** - host **h** has operations to execute; **FINISH** - this status means that the host indexed byh have no more operation to execute

O^{loop}	-	the operation which refers to any loop type operator
O^{loop}_{do}	-	the operation which refers to **do** operator
O^{loop}_{while}	-	the operation which refers to **while** operator
O^{loop}_{break}	-	the operation which refers to **break** operator
$PUSH$	-	push the index to the stack
$STACK[h][p]$	-	the stack of indexes of the **loop** operations of process **p** in host **h**
POP	-	pop the operation index from the stack and return it
$CHECK$	-	check indication
o_{while}	-	the index of nearest **while** operator in current process **p** and host **h**
O^{comm}	-	the operation which refers to operator **in** or **out** (communication action)
O^{comm}_{out}	-	the operation which refers to **out** operator (communication action)
O^{comm}_{in}	-	the operation which refers to **in** operator (communication action)
$CH[h][p][o]$	-	the possible channel **CH** for specific communication operation indexed by **o** and process indexed **p** and host indexed by **h**
$CH[h][p][o][buf]$	-	the current size of the buffer **buf** of the specific **CH** for specific communication operation indexed by **o** and process indexed **p** and host indexed by **h**
$CH^{def}[h][p][o][buf]$	-	the defined size of the buffer **buf** of the specific **CH** for specific communication operation indexed by **o** and process indexed **p** and host indexed by **h**
$FIND$	-	operator seeking first operation connected to operation from argument; connected operation is an operation that has different communication action (in, out) and is connected with the same channel; if no linked operation is found, **False** is returned
$EXISTS$	-	operator checking if operation exists in table (has been added and not yet removed)
ADD	-	adds value to a table
$REMOVE$	-	removes value from a table
$Waiting^{in}[ch]$	-	the table of the operations which refer to the **in** communication action buffered on the channel **ch**
$Waiting^{out}[ch]$	-	the table of the operations which refer to the **out** communication action buffered on the channel **ch**

$LINK(Op[h_1][p_1][o_1], Op[h_2][p_2][o_2])$ - the communication connection is established between the operations of different communication action type and indexed by different triples (**h,p,o**); these operations must refer to the same channel; connection is bidirectional

$GETLINK(Op[h][p][o])$- returns the operation linked to operation from argument or **False** if no operation is linked

Op^{linked} -   variable containing the result of **FIND** and **GETLINK** operators

O^{qop} -   the operation which refers to any QOP operation

QOP^{label} -   the **qop label** for the current QOP operation

QOP^{fun} -   the **qop function** used in the current QOP operation

QOP^{opts} -   **qop options** used in the current QOP operation

$QOP^{metrics}[h][fun][opts][label]$ - metrics for function **fun** read from configuration of host **h** specified by options **opts** and label **label**

ω -   the parameter specifying multiple metrics used

$QOP^{metrics}[h][fun][opts][label](sec)(\omega)$ - the set of the security metrics for function **fun**, specified for the concrete security attribute **sec** and with multiplication parameter ω

$T^{global}[h]$ -   absolute execution time of the protocol measured relative to the host **h**

$HOST$ -   the operator returns index of the host of the operation from parameter

$\overline{T}$ -   the minimum value of the units of time set for a given protocol

$T^{global}_{in}[h]$ -   the absolute execution time of the protocol measured relative to the host **h**, which set the communication connection (**LINK**), containing **in** operation

$\Delta(T^{global}_{out,in})$ - the difference between the execution time of the protocol between the host which proceed operation **out** and host performing operation **in**

end -   the operator in QoP-ML which finish the protocol with success

T_{Total} -   the total execution time of the protocol

$max(T^{global}[h{=}1], ..., T^{global}[h{=}H])$ - the maximum of the $T^{global}[h]$ for all host taking part in the protocol

Algorithm A.1:
Init

Require: definition of: functions, equations, channels, security metrics; protocol modeled by QoP-ML; process instantiation.

1: **SET** *num*
2: **READ** *rep*
3: **SET** *H*
4:
5: **for** $h = 1$ to H **do**
6:    **READ** $O_\#[h]$
7:    **READ** $CH[h]$
8:    **READ** $ALG[h]$
9:    $h \leftarrow h + 1$
10: **end for**
11:
12: **for** $h = 1$ to H_{max} **do**
13:    P[h] $\leftarrow 1$
14:    Status[h] $\leftarrow$ RUNNING
15:    **for** $p = 1$ to P_{max} **do**
16:       O[h][p] $\leftarrow 1$
17:    **end for**
18: **end for**
19:
20: h $\leftarrow 1$
21: p $\leftarrow 1$
22: o $\leftarrow 1$
23: **CALL** Main

Algorithm A.2:
Main

1: **if** $Op[h][p][o] = Op^{comm}$ **then**
2:    **if** $GETLINK(Op[h][p][o])! = False$ **then**
3:       O[h][p] $\leftarrow$ O[h][p] + 1
4:    **else if** $Op[h][p][o] = Op_{in}^{comm}$ **then**
5:       **if** EXISTS $Op[h][p][o]$ in $Waiting^{in}[CH[h][p][o]]$ **then**
6:          **CALL** Next operation
7:          **CALL** Main
8:          RETURN
9:       **end if**
10:    **end if**
11: **end if**
12: **CALL** Check protocol state
13: **CALL** Execute operation

Algorithm A.3:
Check protocol state

```
 1:  H_now ← h
 2:  repeat
 3:      if Status[h] = RUNNING then
 4:          BREAK
 5:      end if
 6:      if h = H^max then
 7:          h ← 1
 8:      else
 9:          h ← h + 1
10:      end if
11:  until h = H_now
12:  if (Status[h] = FINISHED) && (h = H_now) then
13:      CALL Final QoP evaluation
14:      end
15:  end if
16:  p ← P[h]
17:  P_now ← p
18:  repeat
19:      if O[h][p] ≤ o_last then
20:          BREAK
21:      end if
22:      if p = P^max then
23:          p ← 1
24:      else
25:          p ← p + 1
26:      end if
27:  until p = P_now
28:  P[h] ← p
29:  h ← 1
30:  if (O[h][p] > o_last) && (p = P_now) then
31:      Status[h] = FINISHED
32:      if h = H^max then
33:          h ← 1
34:      else
35:          h ← h + 1
36:      end if
37:      CALL Main
38:      RETURN
39:  end if
40:  o ← O[h][p]
```

Algorithm A.4:
Execute operation

1:
2: **if** $Op[h][p][o] = O^{comm}$ **then**
3:     **CALL** Communication
4: **end if**
5:
6: **if** $Op[h][p][o] = O^{qop}$ **then**
7:     **for** each security attribute **do**
8:         **CALL** QoP evaluation
9:     **end for**
10: **end if**
11: **CALL** Next operation
12: **CALL** Main

Algorithm A.5:
Next operation

1: **if** $Op[h][p][o] = Op^{loop}$ **then**
2:     **CALL** Loop next operation
3: **else if** $Op[h][p][o] = Op^{comm}$ **then**
4:     **CALL** Communication next operation
5: **else**
6:     $o \leftarrow o + 1$
7: **end if**
8:
9: $O[h][p] \leftarrow o$
10: **if** $ALG[h] = $ RR **then**
11:     **if** $p < P_{max}$ **then**
12:         $p \leftarrow p + 1$
13:     **else**
14:         $p \leftarrow 1$
15:     **end if**
16: **else if** $ALG[h] = $ FIFO **then**
17:     PASS
18: **end if**
19: P[h] $\leftarrow$ p
20: **if** $h < H_{max}$ **then**
21:     $h \leftarrow h + 1$
22: **else**
23:     $h \leftarrow 1$
24: **end if**

Algorithm A.6:
Communication

1: **if** $CH[h][p][o] \not\subseteq CH[h]$ **then**
2:    **DROP** $Op[h][p][o]$
3:    **RETURN**
4: **end if**
5:
6: **CALL** Link

Algorithm A.7:
Link

1: **if** $Op[h][p][o] = O_{out}^{comm}$ **then**
2:    **if** $(CH[h][p][o][buf] = 0 \ \&\& \ CH^{def}[h][p][o][buf] > 0)$ **then**
3:       **DROP** $Op[h][p][o]$
4:       **RETURN**
5:    **end if**
6:    **if** $CH^{def}[h][p][o][buf] = 0$ **then**
7:       $Op^{linked} \leftarrow$ FIND for $Op[h][p][o]$ in $Waiting^{in}[CH[h][p][o]]$
8:       **if** $Op^{linked} =$ False **then**
9:          **DROP** $Op[h][p][o]$
10:       **else**
11:          REMOVE Op^{linked} from $Waiting^{in}[CH[h][p][o]]$
12:          LINK(Op[h][p][o], Op^{linked})
13:       **end if**
14:    **else**
15:       $Op^{linked} \leftarrow$ FIND for $Op[h][p][o]$ in $Waiting^{in}[CH[h][p][o]]$
16:       **if** $Op^{linked} =$ False **then**
17:          ADD $Op[h][p][o]$ to $Waiting^{out}[CH[h][p][o]]$
18:          $CH[h][p][o][buf] \leftarrow CH[h][p][o][buf] - 1$
19:       **else**
20:          REMOVE Op^{linked} from $Waiting^{in}[CH[h][p][o]]$
21:          LINK(Op[h][p][o], Op^{linked})
22:       **end if**
23:    **end if**
24: **else if** $Op[h][p][o] = O_{in}^{comm}$ **then**
25:    **if** $CH^{def}[h][p][o][buf] = 0$ **then**
26:       ADD $Op[h][p][o]$ to $Waiting^{in}[CH[h][p][o]]$
27:    **else**
28:       $Op^{linked} \leftarrow$ FIND for $Op[h][p][o]$ in $Waiting^{out}[CH[h][p][o]]$
29:       **if** $Op^{linked} =$ False **then**
30:          ADD $Op[h][p][o]$ to $Waiting^{in}[CH[h][p][o]]$
31:       **else**
32:          REMOVE Op^{linked} from $Waiting^{out}[CH[h][p][o]]$
33:          $CH[h][p][o][buf] \leftarrow CH[h][p][o][buf] + 1$
34:          $LINK(Op[h][p][o], Op^{linked})$
35:       **end if**
36:    **end if**
37: **end if**

Algorithm A.8:

QoP evaluation (availability)

1: $T^{global}[h] = T^{global}[h] + QOP^{metrics}[h][QOP^{fun}][QOP^{opts}][QOP^{label}]$
$(availability)(\omega)$

2:

3: $Op^{linked} = GETLINK(Op[h][p][o])$

4: **if** $(Op^{linked} \neq False) \&\& (Op[h][p][o] = O_{out}^{comm})$ **then**

5: $\quad \overline{T}_{in}^{global}[h] = \dfrac{T_{in}^{global}[HOST\ Op^{linked}]}{\overline{T}}$

6: $\quad \overline{T}_{out}^{global}[h][= \dfrac{T_{out}^{global}[h]}{\overline{T}}$

7: $\quad \Delta(T_{out,in}^{global}) = \overline{T}_{out}^{global}[h] - \overline{T}_{in}^{global}[HOST\ Op^{linked}]$

8:

9: $\quad$ **if** $\Delta(T_{out,in}^{global}) > 0$ **then**

10: $\qquad T^{global}[HOST\ Op^{linked}] = T_{in}^{global}[h] + \Delta(T_{out,in}^{global}) * \overline{T}$

11: $\quad$ **else if** $\Delta(T_{out,in}^{global}) < 0$ **then**

12: $\qquad T^{global}[h] = T_{out}^{global}[h] + |\Delta(T_{out,in}^{global})| * \overline{T}$

13: $\quad$ **else if** $\Delta(T_{out,in}^{global}) = 0$ **then**

14: $\qquad$ **PASS**

15: $\quad$ **end if**

16: **end if**

Algorithm A.9:

Final QoP evaluation (availability)

1: $T_{Total} = max(T^{global}[h = 1], ..., T^{global}[h = H])$

Algorithm A.10:
Loop next operation

1: **if** $Op[h][p][o] = O_{do}^{loop}$ **then**
2:    **PUSH** $o + 1$ to **STACK**[h][p]
3:    $o \leftarrow o + 1$
4: **end if**
5: **if** $Op[h][p][o] = O_{while}^{loop}$ **then**
6:    **if** $Op[h][p][o]$ = True **then**
7:       o $\leftarrow$ **POP STACK**[h][p]
8:       **PUSH** o to **STACK**[h][p]
9:    **else if** $Op[h][p][o]$ = False **then**
10:      **POP STACK**[h][p]
11:      $o \leftarrow o + 1$
12:   **end if**
13: **end if**
14: **if** $Op[h][p][o] = O_{break}^{loop}$ **then**
15:   **POP STACK**[h][p]
16:   $o \leftarrow o_{while} + 1$
17: **end if**

Algorithm A.11:
Communication next operation

1: **if** $Op[h][p][o] = O_{out}^{comm}$ **then**
2:    $o \leftarrow o + 1$
3: **end if**
4: **if** $Op[h][p][o] = O_{in}^{comm}$ **then**
5:    $Op^{linked} = GETLINK(Op[h][p][o])$
6:    **if** Op^{linked} != False **then**
7:       $o \leftarrow o + 1$
8:    **end if**
9: **end if**

A.3 The data for QoP evaluation of TLS protocol

A.3.1 The rules definition for TLS cryptographic protocol

The fact based rules:

$f_1(cipher) \vee f_2(cipher) \vee f_3(cipher) \rightarrow f(cipher)$

$f_1(bs) \vee f_2(bs) \rightarrow f(bs)$

$f_1(IV) \vee f_2(IV) \rightarrow f(IV)$

$f_1(key) \vee f_2(key) \vee f_3(key) \vee f_4(key) \rightarrow f(key)$

$f_1(mac) \vee f_2(mac) \vee f_3(mac) \vee f_4(mac) \rightarrow f(mac)$

$f_1(mac-len) \vee f_2(mac-len) \vee f_3(mac-len) \vee f_4(mac-len) \rightarrow f(mac-len)$

$f_1(k-len) \vee f_2(k-len) \vee f_3(k-len) \rightarrow f(k-len)$

$f_1(PK) \vee f_2(PK) \vee f_3(PK) \vee f_4(PK) \vee f_5(PK) \vee f_6(PK) \rightarrow f(PK)$

$\sim f(cipher) \rightarrow \neg f_1(key) \wedge \neg f_2(key) \wedge \neg f_3(key) \wedge \neg f_1(bs) \wedge \neg f_2(bs) \wedge \neg f_1(IV) \wedge \neg f_2(IV)$

$\sim f(mac) \rightarrow \neg f(mac-len) \wedge \neg f(k-len)$

$f_1(mac) \rightarrow f_1(mac-len) \wedge f_1(k-len)$

$f_2(mac) \rightarrow f_2(mac-len) \wedge f_2(k-len)$

$f_3(mac) \rightarrow f_3(mac-len) \wedge f_3(k-len)$

$f_4(mac) \rightarrow f_4(mac-len) \wedge f_3(k-len)$

$f_1(cipher) \rightarrow f_1(key) \wedge \neg f_1(IV) \wedge \neg f_2(IV) \wedge \neg f_1(bs) \wedge \neg f_2(bs)$

$f_2(cipher) \rightarrow f_4(key) \wedge f_1(IV) \wedge f_1(bs)$

$f_3(cipher) \rightarrow f_2(IV) \wedge f_2(bs)$

The rules which define the exclusive facts :

$f_1(cipher) \rightarrow \neg f_2(cipher) \wedge \neg f_3(cipher)$

$f_2(cipher) \rightarrow \neg f_1(cipher) \wedge \neg f_3(cipher)$

$f_3(cipher) \rightarrow \neg f_2(cipher) \wedge \neg f_1(cipher)$

$f_1(bs) \rightarrow \neg f_2(bs)$

$f_2(bs) \rightarrow \neg f_1(bs)$

$f_1(IV) \rightarrow \neg f_2(IV)$

$f_2(IV) \rightarrow \neg f_1(IV)$

$f_1(key) \rightarrow \neg f_2(key) \wedge \neg f_3(key) \wedge \neg f_4(key)$

$f_2(key) \rightarrow \neg f_1(key) \wedge \neg f_3(key) \wedge \neg f_4(key)$

$f_3(key) \rightarrow \neg f_2(key) \wedge \neg f_1(key) \wedge \neg f_4(key)$

$f_4(key) \rightarrow \neg f_2(key) \wedge \neg f_3(key) \wedge \neg f_1(key)$

$f_1(mac) \rightarrow \neg f_2(mac) \wedge \neg f_3(mac) \neg f_4(mac)$

$f_2(mac) \rightarrow \neg f_1(mac) \wedge \neg f_3(mac) \neg f_4(mac)$

$f_3(mac) \rightarrow \neg f_2(mac) \wedge \neg f_1(mac) \neg f_4(mac)$

$f_4(mac) \rightarrow \neg f_1(mac) \wedge \neg f_2(mac) \neg f_3(mac)$

$f_1(mac-len) \rightarrow \neg f_2(mac-len) \wedge \neg f_3(mac-len) \neg f_4(mac-len)$

$f_2(mac-len) \rightarrow \neg f_1(mac-len) \wedge \neg f_3(mac-len) \neg f_4(mac-len)$

$f_3(mac-len) \rightarrow \neg f_2(mac-len) \wedge \neg f_1(mac-len) \neg f_4(mac-len)$

$f_4(mac-len) \rightarrow \neg f_1(mac-len) \wedge \neg f_2(mac-len) \neg f_3(mac-len)$

$f_1(k-len) \rightarrow \neg f_2(k-len) \wedge \neg f_3(k-len)$

$f_2(k-len) \rightarrow \neg f_1(k-len) \wedge \neg f_3(k-len)$

$$f_3(k-len) \rightarrow \neg f_2(k-len) \wedge \neg f_1(k-len)$$
$$f_1(PK) \rightarrow \neg f_2(PK) \wedge \neg f_3(PK) \wedge \neg f_4(PK) \wedge \neg f_5(PK) \wedge \neg f_6(PK)$$
$$f_2(PK) \rightarrow \neg f_1(PK) \wedge \neg f_3(PK) \wedge \neg f_4(PK) \wedge \neg f_5(PK) \wedge \neg f_6(PK)$$
$$f_3(PK) \rightarrow \neg f_2(PK) \wedge \neg f_1(PK) \wedge \neg f_4(PK) \wedge \neg f_5(PK) \wedge \neg f_6(PK)$$
$$f_4(PK) \rightarrow \neg f_2(PK) \wedge \neg f_3(PK) \wedge \neg f_1(PK) \wedge \neg f_5(PK) \wedge \neg f_6(PK)$$
$$f_5(PK) \rightarrow \neg f_2(PK) \wedge \neg f_3(PK) \wedge \neg f_4(PK) \wedge \neg f_1(PK) \wedge \neg f_6(PK)$$
$$f_6(PK) \rightarrow \neg f_2(PK) \wedge \neg f_3(PK) \wedge \neg f_4(PK) \wedge \neg f_5(PK) \wedge \neg f_1(PK)$$
$$f_1(key-a) \rightarrow \neg f_2(key-a) \wedge \neg f_3(key-a)$$
$$f_2(key-a) \rightarrow \neg f_1(key-a) \wedge \neg f_3(key-a)$$
$$f_3(key-a) \rightarrow \neg f_2(key-a) \wedge \neg f_1(key-a)$$

A.3.2 The facts order definition for the TLS cryptographic protocol

Orders between facts:
$$f_3(cipher) >_C f_2(cipher) >_C f_1(cipher)$$
$$f_1(cipher) >_A f_2(cipher) >_A f_3(cipher)$$
$$f_2(bs) >_C f_1(bs)$$
$$f_2(IV) >_C f_1(IV)$$
$$f_3(key) >_C f_2(key) >_C f_1(key)$$
$$f_1(key) >_A f_2(key) >_A f_3(key)$$
$$f_3(mac) >_I f_2(mac) >_I f_1(mac)$$
$$f_1(mac) >_A f_2(mac) >_A f_3(mac)$$
$$f_4(mac-len) >_I f_3(mac-len) >_I f_2(mac-len) >_I f_1(mac-len)$$
$$f_1(mac-len) >_A f_2(mac-len) >_A f_3(mac-len) >_I f_4(mac-len)$$
$$f_3(k-len) >_I f_2(k-len) >_I f_1(k-len)$$
$$f_1(k-len) >_A f_2(k-len) >_A f_3(k-len)$$
$$f_2(PK) >_{AU} f_1(PK)$$
$$f_3(PK) >_{AU} f_1(PK)$$
$$f_4(PK) >_{AU} f_2(PK)$$
$$f_5(PK) >_{AU} f_2(PK)$$
$$f_4(PK) >_{AU} f_3(PK)$$
$$f_5(PK) >_{AU} f_3(PK)$$
$$f_1(PK) >_A f_2(PK)$$
$$f_1(PK) >_A f_3(PK)$$
$$f_2(PK) >_A f_4(PK)$$
$$f_2(PK) >_A f_5(PK)$$
$$f_3(PK) >_A f_4(PK)$$
$$f_3(PK) >_A f_5(PK)$$
$$f_3(key-a) >_C f_2(key-a) >_C f_1(key-a)$$
$$f_1(key-a) >_A f_2(key-a) >_A f_3(key-a)$$

A.3.3 The QoP evaluation rules definition for the TLS cryptographic protocol

The evaluation rules:

$f_1(cipher) \Rightarrow Inf^1(A)$
$f_2(cipher) \Rightarrow Inf^2(A)$
$f_3(cipher) \Rightarrow Inf^3(A)$
$f_1(cipher) \Rightarrow Inf^1(C)$
$f_2(cipher) \Rightarrow Inf^2(C)$
$f_3(cipher) \Rightarrow Inf^3(C)$
$f_1(bs) \Rightarrow Inf^1(C)$
$f_2(bs) \Rightarrow Inf^2(C)$
$f_1(IV) \Rightarrow Inf^1(C)$
$f_2(IV) \Rightarrow Inf^2(C)$
$f_1(key) \Rightarrow Inf^1(C)$
$f_2(key) \Rightarrow Inf^2(C)$
$f_3(key) \Rightarrow Inf^3(C)$
$f_1(key) \Rightarrow Inf^1(A)$
$f_2(key) \Rightarrow Inf^2(A)$
$f_3(key) \Rightarrow Inf^3(A)$
$f_1(mac) \Rightarrow Inf^1(I)$
$f_2(mac) \Rightarrow Inf^2(I)$
$f_3(mac) \Rightarrow Inf^3(I)$
$f_4(mac) \Rightarrow Inf^4(I)$
$f_1(mac) \Rightarrow Inf^1(A)$
$f_2(mac) \Rightarrow Inf^2(A)$
$f_3(mac) \Rightarrow Inf^3(A)$
$f_4(mac) \Rightarrow Inf^4(A)$
$f_1(mac - len) \Rightarrow Inf^1(I)$
$f_2(mac - len) \Rightarrow Inf^2(I)$
$f_3(mac - len) \Rightarrow Inf^3(I)$
$f_4(mac - len) \Rightarrow Inf^4(I)$
$f_1(mac - len) \Rightarrow Inf^1(A)$
$f_2(mac - len) \Rightarrow Inf^2(A)$
$f_3(mac - len) \Rightarrow Inf^3(A)$
$f_4(mac - len) \Rightarrow Inf^4(A)$
$f_1(k - len) \Rightarrow Inf^1(I)$
$f_2(k - len) \Rightarrow Inf^2(I)$
$f_3(k - len) \Rightarrow Inf^3(I)$
$f_1(k - len) \Rightarrow Inf^1(A)$
$f_2(k - len) \Rightarrow Inf^2(A)$
$f_3(k - len) \Rightarrow Inf^3(A)$
$f_1(key - a) \Rightarrow Inf^1(A)$
$f_2(key - a) \Rightarrow Inf^2(A)$
$f_3(key - a) \Rightarrow Inf^3(A)$
$f_1(COM) \Rightarrow Inf^4(A)$
$f_2(COM) \Rightarrow Inf^1(A)$
$f_1(cipher) \wedge f_3(key) \Rightarrow Inf^1(A)$

A.4   Algorithms for advanced communication

Algorithm A.12: Algorithm for **out** instruction.
Procedure: *SendMessage sender, channel, message, router* - Procedure sends *message* from *sender* through *channel*. Topology is defined by *router*.

1: **if** *sender* can use *channel* **then**
2:     *filteredRequests ← FilteredRequests(message, router)*
3:     **for** *request* in *filteredRequests* **do**
4:         *receiver ← get_receiver(request)*
5:         *buffer ← get_buffer(channel, receiver)*
6:         Add *message* to *buffer*.
7:     **end for**
8:     *BindMessagesWithReceivers(channel)*
9: **end if**

Algorithm A.13: Algorithm for **in** instruction
Procedure: *WaitForMessage channel, request* - Procedure processes **in** instruction and adds *request* to *channel*'s requests list.

1: **if** *request* exists in *channel*'s requests list **then**
2:     **if** *request* is not in waiting state **then**
3:         *request*'s state← *WAITING*
4:     **end if**
5: **else**
6:     Add *request* to *channel*'s requests list
7: **end if**
8: *BindMessagesWithReceivers(channel)*

Algorithm A.14: Algorithm of filtering requests
Procedure: *FilteredRequests message, router* - Procedure returns list of requests that can accept the message.

1: *filteredRequests* ← empty list
2: *sender* ← *get_sender(message)*
3: **for** *request* in all waiting requests **do**
4:     *receiver* ← *get_receiver(request)*
5:     **if** link between *sender* and *receiver* does not exist in *router* topology **then**
6:         Continue to the next loop
7:     **end if**
8:     **if** *message* cannot be accepted by *request* **then**
9:         Continue to the next loop
10:     **end if**
11:     *requestFilters* ← *get_filters(request)*
12:     **if** not *PassFilters(message, filters)* **then**
13:         Continue to the next loop
14:     **end if**
15:     Add *request* to *filteredRequests* list.
16: **end for**
17:
18: **return** *filteredRequests*

Algorithm A.15: Algorithm of binding sent messages with its receivers.
Procedure: *BindMessagesWithReceivers channel* - Procedure binds messages from the buffers with existing requests.

1: **for** *request* in all waiting requests **do**
2:      *receiver* ← *get_receiver*(*request*)
3:      *buffer* ← *get_buffer*(*channel*, *receiver*)
4:      **if** *request* is waiting for message **and** message has not been assigned yet **and** *buffer* is not empty **then**
5:          *filters* ← *get_filters*(*request*)
6:          **for** *message* in *buffer* **do**
7:              **if** *PassFilters*(*message*, *filters*) **then**
8:                  Assign *message* to *request*
9:                  Remove *message* from *buffer*
10:                 Break
11:             **end if**
12:         **end for**
13:     **end if**
        {*Request* was waiting for message and obtained it.}
14:     Set variable from *request* in *receiver* with value from *message*
15:     Move *receiver* to the next instruction
16:     **if** *channel* is synchronous **then**
17:         Remove *request* from *buffer*
18:     **else**
19:         Set *request*'s status← *NOTWAITING*
20:     **end if**
21: **end for**
22: **if** *channel* is synchronous **then**
23:     Clean all buffers.
24: **end if**

Algorithm A.16: Algorithm of checking if message is sent for the request by comparing its elements with request's filters.

Procedure: *PassFilters message, filters* - Procedure returns *True* if message passes the *filters* from request.

```
 1: if filters is empty then
 2:
 3:     return True
 4: else
 5:     expression ← get_expression(message)
 6:     if expression is not tuple or size of expression is smaller than filters size
        then
 7:
 8:         return False
 9:     else
10:         for filter in filters do
11:             if filter is star then
12:                 Continue to the next filter
13:             else
14:                 tupleElement ← get_next_element_from_expression(expression)
15:                 if tupleElement is not equal to filter then
16:
17:                     return False
18:                 end if
19:             end if
20:         end for
21:     end if
22:
23:     return True
24: end if
```

A.5 Validation algorithms for security metrics

Notation used:

{} stands for an empty array (set)

$X = \{x_0, x_1, ..., x_{N-1}\}$ is an array (set) of elements of size N

x_i is the *ith* element of the array (set)

Algorithm A.17:
Procedure: Calculate Q_{exp_1}. X is the set of collected measurement results and N is the size of the set.

1: $Q_{exp_1} \leftarrow 0.0$
2: **if** $N \geq 3$ **and** $N \leq 7$ **then**
3:     $Q_{exp_1} \leftarrow (x_1 - x_0)/(x_{N-1} - x_0)$
4: **else if** $N \geq 8$ **and** $N \leq 10$ **then**
5:     $Q_{exp_1} \leftarrow (x_1 - x_0)/(x_{N-2} - x_0)$
6: **else if** $N \geq 11$ **and** $N \leq 13$ **then**
7:     $Q_{exp_1} \leftarrow (x_2 - x_0)/(x_{N-2} - x_0)$
8: **else if** $N \geq 14$ **then**
9:     $Q_{exp_1} \leftarrow (x_2 - x_0)/(x_{N-3} - x_0)$
10: **end if**
11: **return** Q_{exp1}

Algorithm A.18:
Procedure: Calculate Q_{exp_N}. X is the set of collected measurement results and N is the size of the set.

1: $Q_{exp_N} \leftarrow 0.0$
2: **if** $N \geq 3$ **and** $N \leq 7$ **then**
3:     $Q_{exp_N} \leftarrow (x_{N-1} - x_{N-2})/(x_{N-1} - x_0)$
4: **else if** $N \geq 8$ **and** $N \leq 10$ **then**
5:     $Q_{exp_N} \leftarrow (x_{N-1} - x_{N-2})/(x_{N-1} - x_1)$
6: **else if** $N \geq 11$ **and** $N \leq 13$ **then**
7:     $Q_{exp_N} \leftarrow (x_{N-1} - x_{N-3})/(x_{N-1} - x_1)$
8: **else if** $N \geq 14$ **then**
9:     $Q_{exp_N} \leftarrow (x_{N-1} - x_{N-3})/(x_{N-1} - x_2)$
10: **end if**
11: **return** Q_{exp_N}

Algorithm A.19:

Procedure: Reject x_1 from the measurement results set (x_1 is an outlier). X is the set of collected measurement results and N is the size of the set.

1: $tmp \leftarrow \{\}$
2: **for** each i from 1 to N exclusive **do**
3:    $tmp_{i-1} \leftarrow x_i$
4: **end for**
5: $x \leftarrow tmp$
6: **return** $N - 1$

Algorithm A.20:

Procedure: Reject x_N from the measurement results set (x_N is an outlier). X is the set of collected measurement results and N is the size of the set.

1: $tmp \leftarrow \{\}$
2: **for** each i from 0 to $N - 1$ exclusive **do**
3:    $tmp_i \leftarrow x_i$
4: **end for**
5: $x \leftarrow tmp$
6: **return** $N - 1$

Algorithm A.21:

Procedure: Check the stationarity by calculating the *coefficient of variation*. X is the set of collected measurement results, N is the size of the set.

1: $stationary \leftarrow false$
2: $mean \leftarrow$ CALCULATEMEAN x, N
3: $stddev \leftarrow$ CALCULATESTDDEV x, N
4: $CV \leftarrow (stddev/mean) * 100\%$
5: **if** $CV \geq 10\%$ **then**
6:    $stationary \leftarrow false$
7: **else**
8:    $stationary \leftarrow true$
9: **end if**
10: **return** $stationary$

Algorithm A.22:
Procedure: Do the *Dixon's Q test*. X is the set of collected measurement results, CL is the confidence level and N is the size of the set.

  1: SORTASCENDING x, N
  2: $Q_{critic} \leftarrow$ GETQCRITIC CL, N
  3: $newSetSize \leftarrow N$
  4: $Q_{exp_1} \leftarrow$ CALCULATEQEXP1 $x, newSetSize$
  5: $Q_{exp_N} \leftarrow$ CALCULATEQEXPN $x, newSetSize$
  6: **if** $Q_{exp_1} > Q_{critic}$ **then**
  7:     $newSetSize \leftarrow$ REJECTX1 $x, newSetSize$
  8: **end if**
  9: **if** $Q_{exp_N} > Q_{critic}$ **then**
10:     $newSetSize \leftarrow$ REJECTXN $x, newSetSize$
11: **end if**
12: **return** $newSetSize$

Algorithm A.23:
Do the validation process. X is the set of collected measurement results, N is the size of the set.

  1: $stationary \leftarrow false$
  2: $stationary \leftarrow$ CHECKSTATIONARITY x, N
  3: **if** $stationary$ **then**
  4:     SORTASCENDING x, N
  5:     $N \leftarrow$ DIXONSQTEST x, CL, N
  6: **else**
  7:     MAKESTATIONARY x, N
  8:     SORTASCENDING x, N
  9:     $N \leftarrow$ DIXONSQTEST x, CL, N
10: **end if**

References

[1] Gartner blog network. `http://blogs.gartner.com/david\_cappuccio/2012/06/07/the-case-for-the-infinite-data-center/`.

[2] Greenhouse gas equivalencies calculator. `{http://www.epa.gov/cleanenergy/energy-resources/calculator.html}`.

[3] How many information security staff do we need? `http://infosecisland.com/blogview/8327-How-Many-Information-Security-Staff-Do-We-Need.html`.

[4] How much carbon dioxide is produced per kilowatthour when generating electricity with fossil fuels? `{http://www.eia.gov/tools/faqs/faq.cfm?id=74\&t=11}`.

[5] Power consumption of pc components in watts. `{http://www.buildcomputers.net/power-consumption-of-pc-components.html}`.

[6] Cc2420 data sheet. `http://inst.eecs.berkeley.edu`, 2004.

[7] The web page of the qop-ml project. `http://qopml.org/`, 2014.

[8] RFC 5246. The transport layer security (tls) protocol. `https://tools.ietf.org/html/rfc5246`, 2008.

[9] Jaquith A. *Security Metrics: Replacing Fear, Uncertainty, and Doubt.* Addison-Wesley, 2007.

[10] Martín Abadi and Cédric Fournet. Mobile values, new names, and secure communication. In *Proceedings of the 28th ACM SIGPLAN-SIGACT Symposium on Principles of Programming Languages*, POPL '01, pages 104–115, New York, NY, USA, 2001. ACM.

[11] Martin Abadi and Andrew D. Gordon. A calculus for cryptographic protocols: The spi calculus. *Information and Computation*, 148:36–47, 1999.

[12] Frédéric Adam. 20 years of decision making and decision support research published by the journal of decision systems. *Journal of Decision Systems*, 21(2):93–99, 2012.

[13] Avesh K. Agarwal and Wenye Wang. On the impact of quality of protection in wireless local area networks with ip mobility. *Mobile Networks and Applications*, 12(1):93–110, 2007.

[14] Sylvain Arlot and Alain Celisse. A survey of cross-validation procedures for model selection. *Statist. Surv.*, 4:40–79, 2010.

[15] A. Armando, D. Basin, Y. Boichut, Y. Chevalier, L. Compagna, J. Cuellar, P.Hankes Drielsma, P.C. Hem, O. Kouchnarenko, J. Mantovani, S. Mdersheim, D. von Oheimb, M. Rusinowitch, J. Santiago, M. Turuani, L. Vigan, and L. Vigneron. The avispa tool for the automated validation of internet security protocols and applications. In Kousha Etessami and SriramK. Rajamani, editors, *Computer Aided Verification*, volume 3576 of *Lecture Notes in Computer Science*, pages 281–285, Edinburgh, Scotland, UK, 2005. Springer Berlin Heidelberg.

[16] J. W. Backus. The syntax and semantics of the proposed international algebraic language of the Zurich ACM-GAMM Conference. In *Information Processing: Proceedings of the International Conference on Information Processing, Paris*, pages 125–132. UNESCO, June 1959.

[17] David Basin, Jürgen Doser, and Torsten Lodderstedt. Model driven security: From uml models to access control infrastructures. *ACM Trans. Softw. Eng. Methodol.*, 15(1):39–91, January 2006.

[18] B. Blanchet. Automatic proof of strong secrecy for security protocols. In *Security and Privacy, 2004. Proceedings. 2004 IEEE Symposium on*, pages 86–100, Berkeley, California, USA, May 2004.

[19] M. Burrows, M. Abadi, and R.M. Needham. A logic of authentication. In *Proceedings of the Royal Society of London, A 426*, 1989.

[20] A. J. Shah, C. D. Patel. Cost model for planning, development and operation of a data center. http://hpl.hp.com/, 2005.

[21] Hash J., Bartol N., Brown A., Chew E., Clay A. NIST Special Publication 800-80: Guide for Developing Performance Metrics for Information Security, 2006.

[22] Stine K., Bartol N., Brown A., Robinson W., Chew E., Swanson M. NIST Special Publication 800-55: Performance Measurement Guide for Information Security, 2008.

[23] Cas J. F. Cremers. The scyther tool: Verification, falsification, and analysis of security protocols. volume 5123 of *Lecture Notes in Computer Science*, pages 414–418. Springer, 2008.

[24] Crossbow. Imote2 data sheet. http://wsn.cse.wustl.edu, 2004.

[25] Crossbow. Micaz data sheet. http://wsn.cse.wustl.edu, 2004.

[26] Rohrabacher D. B. *Dixon's Q-Tables for Multiple Probability Levels*. Analytical Chemistry, 1991.

[27] Yvo Desmedt. Man-in-the-middle attack. In Henk C. A. van Tilborg and Sushil Jajodia, editors, *Encyclopedia of Cryptography and Security (2nd Ed.)*, page 759. Springer, 2011.

[28] Dunn Patric F. *Measurement and Data Analysis for Engineering and Science*. CRC Press, New York, 2005.

[29] S. Feuerstein and B. Pribly. *Oracle PL/SQL Programming*. O'Reilly Media Inc, 4th edition, 2005.

[30] Nicolas Fournel, Marine Minier, and Stphane Ubda. Survey and benchmark of stream ciphers for wireless sensor networks. In Damien Sauveron, Konstantinos Markantonakis, Angelos Bilas, and Jean-Jacques Quisquater, editors, *Information Security Theory and Practices. Smart Cards, Mobile and Ubiquitous Computing Systems*, volume 4462 of *Lecture Notes in Computer Science*, pages 202–214. Springer Berlin Heidelberg, 2007.

[31] Albert Greenberg, James Hamilton, David A. Maltz, and Parveen Patel. The cost of a cloud: Research problems in data center networks. *SIGCOMM Comput. Commun. Rev.*, 39(1):68–73, December 2008.

[32] N. Haller and C. Metz. A One-Time Password System, 1996.

[33] C. A. R. Hoare. *Communicating Sequential Processes*. Prentice Hall, New York, 1985.

[34] Intel. Intel core i7-2760qm processor data sheet. http://ark.intel.com.

[35] ISO/IEC 27001:2005. Information technology – security techniques – information security management systems – requirements, 2005.

[36] Jürjens J. *Secure System Development with UML*. Springer, 2007.

[37] Hage Jaap. *Studies in legal logic*. Springer, 2005.

[38] Jan Jürjens, Jrg Schreck, and Peter Bartmann. Model-based security analysis for mobile communications. In Wilhelm Schäfer, Matthew B. Dwyer, and Volker Gruhn, editors, *ICSE*, pages 683–692. ACM, 2008.

[39] Jan Jürjens and Pasha Shabalin. Tools for secure systems development with uml. *STTT*, 9(5-6):527–544, 2007.

[40] J. G. Koomey. Estimating total power consumption by servers in the U.S. and the world, phd thesis. http://www.koomey.com, 2007.

[41] Z. Kotulski. Optimization of sensors' location in a stochastic extrapolation problem. *Journal of Sound and Vibration*, 138(3):351 – 363, 1990.

[42] Bogdan Ksiezopolski. Qop-ml: Quality of protection modeling language for cryptographic protocols. *Computers & Security*, 31(4):569–596, 2012.

[43] Bogdan Ksiezopolski and Zbigniew Kotulski. Adaptable security mechanism for dynamic environments. *Computers & Security*, 26(3):246 – 255, 2007.

[44] Bogdan Ksiezopolski, Zbigniew Kotulski, and Pawel Szalachowski. Adaptive approach to network security. In Andrzej Kwiecien, Piotr Gaj, and Piotr Stera, editors, *CN*, volume 39 of *Communications in Computer and Information Science*, pages 233–241. Springer, 2009.

[45] Bogdan Ksiezopolski, Damian Rusinek, and Adam Wierzbicki. On the efficiency modeling of cryptographic protocols by means of the quality of protection modeling language (qop-ml). In Khabib Mustofa, Erich, J., Neuhold, A., Min Tjoa, Edgar Weippl, and Ilsun You, editors, *Information and Communication Technology*, volume 7804 of *Lecture Notes in Computer Science*, pages 261–270. Springer Berlin Heidelberg, 2013.

[46] Bogdan Ksiezopolski, Adam Wierzbicki, and Damian Rusinek. On the modeling of the computer security impact on the reputation systems. In Linawati, Made Sudiana Mahendra, Erich J. Neuhold, AMin Tjoa, and Ilsun You, editors, *Information and Communication Technology*, volume 8407 of *Lecture Notes in Computer Science*, pages 526–531. Springer Berlin Heidelberg, 2014.

[47] Bogdan Ksiezopolski, Tomasz Zurek, and Michail Mokkas. Quality of protection evaluation of security mechanisms. In *The Scientific World Journal*, volume 2014, pages 1–18, 2014.

[48] Szalachowski P. Ksiezopolski B, Kotulski Z. On qop method for ensuring availability of the goal of cryptographic protocols in the real-time systems. In *European Teletraffic Seminar*, pages 195–202. Jasart Studio, 2011.

[49] Ralf Küsters and Tomasz Truderung. Using proverif to analyze protocols with diffie-hellman exponentiation. In *CSF*, pages 157–171. IEEE Computer Society, 2009.

[50] Sachs L. *Applied Statistics. A Handbook of Techniques.* Springer, 1984.

[51] Costas Lambrinoudakis, Stefanos Gritzalis, Fredj Dridi, and Günther Pernul. Security requirements for e-government services: a methodological approach for developing a common pki-based security policy. *Computer Communications*, 26(16):1873–1883, 2003.

[52] Elizabeth LeMay, Willard Unkenholz, Donald Parks, Carol Muehrcke, Ken Keefe, and William H. Sanders. Adversary-driven state-based system security evaluation. In *Proceedings of the 6th International Workshop on Security Measurements and Metrics*, MetriSec '10, pages 5:1–5:9, New York, NY, USA, 2010. ACM.

[53] Leszczynski Leszek. *Issues of theory of application of law (Zagadnienia teorii stosowania prawa)*. Zakamycze, 2001.

[54] Stefan Lindskog, Stefan Lindskog, Stefan Lindskog, Chalmers Reproservice, and Stefan Lindskog. Modeling and tuning security from a quality of service perspective, 2005.

[55] An Liu and Peng Ning. Tinyecc: A configurable library for elliptic curve cryptography in wireless sensor networks. pages 245–256. IEEE Computer Society, 2008.

[56] Torsten Lodderstedt, David A. Basin, and Jürgen Doser. Secureuml: A uml-based modeling language for model-driven security. In Jcan-Marc Jzquel, Heinrich Humann, and Stephen Cook, editors, *UML*, volume 2460 of *Lecture Notes in Computer Science*, pages 426–441. Springer, 2002.

[57] An'an Luo, Chuang Lin, Kai Wang, Lei Lei, and Chanfang Liu. Quality of protection analysis and performance modeling in ip multimedia subsystem. *Computer Communications*, 32(11):1336–1345, 2009.

[58] Hawkins D. M. *Identification of Outliers*. Chapman and Hall, 1980.

[59] I. Mansour, G. Chalhoub, and M. Misson. *Security architecture for multi-hop wireless sensor networks*. CRC Press Book, 2014.

[60] Ismail Mansour, Damian Rusinek, Grard Chalhoub, Pascal Lafourcade, and Bogdan Ksiezopolski. Multihop node authentication mechanisms for wireless sensor networks. In Song Guo, Jaime Lloret, Pietro Manzoni, and Stefan Ruehrup, editors, *Ad-hoc, Mobile, and Wireless Networks*, volume 8487 of *Lecture Notes in Computer Science*, pages 402–418. Springer International Publishing, Benidorm, Spain, 2014.

[61] Raimundas Matulevicius, Henri Lakk, and Marion Lepmets. An approach to assess and compare quality of security models. *Comput. Sci. Inf. Syst.*, 8(2):447–476, 2011.

[62] Katarzyna Mazur and Bogdan Ksiezopolski. Comparison and assessment of security modeling approaches in terms of the qop-ml. In Zbigniew Kotulski, Bogdan Ksiezopolski, and Katarzyna Mazur, editors, *Cryptography and Security Systems*, volume 448 of *Communications in Computer and Information Science*, pages 178–192. Springer Berlin Heidelberg, 2014.

[63] Katarzyna Mazur, Bogdan Ksiezopolski, and Wierzbicki Adam. On the modelling of the influence of access control and management to the system security and performance. *7th International Conference on Enterprise Information Systems*, Barcelona, pages 346–354, 2015.

[64] Katarzyna Mazur, Bogdan Ksiezopolski, and Zbigniew Kotulski. The robust measurement method for security metrics generation. *Computer Journal*, (accepted paper).

[65] Robin Milner. *Communicating and Mobile Systems: The &Pgr;-calculus*. Cambridge University Press, New York, NY, USA, 1999.

[66] NIST. Descriptions of sha-256, sha-384, and sha-512. `csrc.nist.gov`.

[67] Chui Sian Ong, Klara Nahrstedt, and Wanghong Yuan. Quality of protection for mobile multimedia applications. In *ICME*, pages 137–140. IEEE, 2003.

[68] Szalachowski Pawel, Ksiezopolski Bogdan, and Kotulski Zbigniew. Optimization of the tls security protocol. *Annales UMCS Informatica*, 2:59–75, 2009.

[69] Dorina C. Petriu, C. Murray Woodside, Dorin Bogdan Petriu, Jing Xu, Toqeer Israr, Geri Georg, Robert B. France, James M. Bieman, Siv Hilde Houmb, and Jan Jürjens. Performance analysis of security aspects in uml models. In Vittorio Cortellessa, Sebastián Uchitel, and Daniel Yankelevich, editors, *WOSP*, pages 91–102. ACM, 2007.

[70] Daniel J. Power and Ramesh Sharda. Model-driven decision support systems: Concepts and research directions. *Decision Support Systems*, 43(3):1044–1061, 2007.

[71] H. Prakken and G. Vreeswijk. Logics for defeasible argumentation. In D. Gabbay and F. Guenthner, editors, *Handbook of Philosophical Logic, second edition, vol. 4*, pages 219–318. Dordrecht etc., 2002.

[72] Henry Prakken. An abstract framework for argumentation with structured arguments. *Argument & Computation*, 1(2):93–124, 2010.

[73] Henry Prakken and Giovanni Sartor. A dialectical model of assessing conflicting arguments in legal reasoning. *Artif. Intell. Law*, 4(3-4):331–368, 1996.

[74] Pavel Pribyl and David Barta. Knowledge based decision support system of its standards deployment. In Jerzy Mikulski, editor, *TST*, volume 239 of *Communications in Computer and Information Science*, pages 392–402. Springer, 2011.

[75] L. R. Rabiner. A tutorial on hidden Markov models and selected applications in speech recognition. In *Proceedings of IEEE*, volume 77, pages 257–286. IEEE, 1989.

[76] D.M. Ritchie and B.W. Kernighan. *The C programming language*. Bell Laboratories, 1988.

[77] Damian Rusinek, Bogdan Ksiezopolski, and Wierzbicki Adam. Security trade-off and energy efficiency analysis in wireless sensor networks. *International Journal of Distributed Sensor Networks*, 2015 (In press).

[78] Reijo Savola. A security metrics taxonomization model for software-intensive systems. *JIPS*, 5(4):197–206, 2009.

[79] Reijo M. Savola. Quality of security metrics and measurements. *Computers & Security*, 37:78–90, 2013.

[80] Phyllis A. Schneck and Karsten Schwan. Authenticast: An adaptive protocol for high-performance, secure network applications. Technical report, 1997.

[81] SECG. Standards for efficient cryptography group. `http://www.secg.org/`, 1998.

[82] ISO/IEC International Standard. ISO/IEC 27004 (2009) Information technology - Security techniques - Information security management - Measurement, 2009.

[83] Yan Sun and Anup Kumar. Quality-of-protection (qop): A quantitative methodology to grade security services. In *ICDCS Workshops*, pages 394–399. IEEE Computer Society, 2008.

[84] P. Szalachowski, B. Ksiezopolski, and Z. Kotulski. Cmac, ccm and gcm/gmac: Advanced modes of operation of symmetric block ciphers in wireless sensor networks. *Inf. Process. Lett.*, 110(7):247–251, March 2010.

[85] Kotulski Z. Szczepinski W. *Error Analysis with Applications in Engineering.* Springer, 2009.

[86] Leendert, W. N. van der Torre, and Yao-Hua Tan. The many faces of defeasibility in defeasible deontic logic. In Donald Nute, editor, *Defeasible Deontic Logic*, volume 263 of *Synthese Library*, pages 79–121. Springer Netherlands, 1997.

[87] Wamberto Weber Vasconcelos, Andrs Garca-Camino, Dorian Gaertner, Juan A. Rodrguez-Aguilar, and Pablo Noriega. Distributed norm management for multi-agent systems. *Expert Syst. Appl.*, 39(5):5990–5999, 2012.

[88] Luca Vigan. Automated security protocol analysis with the avispa tool. *Electr. Notes Theor. Comput. Sci.*, 155:61–86, 2006.

[89] G. A. W. Vreeswijk. Abstract argumentation systems. *Artificial Intelligence*, 90(1–2):225–279, 1997.

[90] Tomasz Zurek. Modeling of *a fortiori* reasoning. *Expert Systems with Applications*, 39(12):10772 – 10779, 2012.

[91] Schlosser, A., Voss, M., Brückner, L: On the simulation of global reputation systems. *Journal of Artificial Societies and Social Simulation*, 2006, 9(1).

Index